THE GENESIS DEBATE

THE GENESIS DEBATE

Persistent Questions About Creation and the Flood

RONALD YOUNGBLOOD, Editor

BAKER BOOK HOUSE

Grand Rapids, Michigan 49516

Scripture quotations in this publication appear from the following Bible versions:

The New English Bible. © The Delegates of the Oxford University Press and the Syndics of the Cambridge University Press 1961, 1970. Reprinted by permission.

Today's English Version Bible. Copyright © American Bible Society 1976. Used by permission.

The New American Standard Bible, © The Lockman Foundation 1960, 1962, 1963, 1968, 1971, 1972, 1973, 1975. Used by permission.

The Revised Standard Version of the Bible, copyrighted 1946, 1952, © 1971, 1973 by the Division of Christian Education of the National Council of the Churches of Christ in the U.S.A.

King James Version. Thomas Nelson Inc., Publishers.

Holy Bible: New International Version. Copyright © 1978 by the New York International Bible Society. Used by permission of Zondervan Bible Publishers.

The Jerusalem Bible. Copyright © 1966 by Darton, Longmann, and Todd, Ltd. and Doubleday and Co.

The New King James Version. © Thomas Nelson, Inc., Publishers 1979, 1980, 1982.

Library of Congress Cataloging in Publication Data

The Genesis debate: persistent questions about Creation and the
  Flood / edited by Ronald Youngblood. —Baker Book House ed.
    p. cm.
  Includes bibliographies.
  ISBN 0-8010-9896-3
    1. Bible. O.T. Genesis I-XI—Criticism, interpretation, etc. 2.
Creationism. 3. Deluge. I. Youngblood, Ronald F.
BS1235.2.G39   1990   90-45928
222'.11067—dc20   CIP

CONTENTS

INTRODUCTION

More than nineteen centuries ago, an Alexandrian Jew named Philo wrote a series of six slim volumes entitled *Questions and Answers on Genesis*. His original work covered most of Genesis 2:4-28:9, with volumes one and two including nearly two hundred questions on 2:4-10:9—a crucial section of Genesis and roughly the equivalent of *The Genesis Debate,* the book you are about to read.

Each question in Philo's series relates to a biblical verse or part of a verse, and to almost every question he gives two answers—one addressed to the literal meaning of the verse, the other to its supposed allegorical meaning. In Philo's terminology the allegorical answer inherent in the verse may include one or all of three subdivisions: (1) physical (that is, theological or cosmological); (2) ethical; (3) mystical. By contrast, the answers given by the authors of *The Genesis Debate* to the eleven questions posed in the book are addressed only to the literal (that is, ordinary or intended) meaning of the Biblical text. Theological and other considerations, however, will obviously play a part in fully explaining that literal meaning—although nothing of Philo's bizarre results finds its parallel in these pages.

As Philo's efforts (and many others that could be mentioned) indicate, even in ancient times readers of Genesis were already asking the book all sorts of questions. How did God accomplish his work of creation? Did Satan originate evil and bring it into the world, or was he a secondary sinner used by someone else? Where did Cain get his wife? The questions range from the most simplistic to the most discerning, and the responses given to them are incredibly numerous and varied.

Our attempt in this book is to ask a number of carefully focused questions that might be expected to plague the modern reader of Genesis. Our final choice of questions was by no means easy, since we wanted to give our authors the opportunity to answer them in a reasonably full way. We eventually settled on eleven topics, and we formulated questions concerning them in a manner that would enable a writer to answer either "Yes" or "No" and then give his reasons for doing so. Beginning with "Were the days of creation twenty-four hours long?" and ending with "Does Genesis 9 justify capital punishment?" we attempted to include the most significant questions covering matters of interest to the widest possible range of readers. The answers set forth in these pages have all been formulated by Christian scholars—exegetes, theologians, scientists—who are committed to the full inspiration and authority of Scripture and have therefore tried to give thoroughly biblical answers to the questions posed to them.

Many books of questions and answers on the Bible use the following format: They offer a question and then give only one answer to it—presumably the only possible valid answer. In such cases the answer can often be very brief indeed, and in fact usually is. One example from my own library is a 92-page volume entitled *5500 Questions and Answers on the Holy Bible!* Although such books may provide a useful function, the giving of expansive answers is not one of them—nor is that their intention. *The Genesis Debate,* as it turns out, deals with only two-tenths of one percent of the number of questions in the above-mentioned book, and it offers to its readers a "pro" and a "con" answer to each of them. The author arguing for the "pro" viewpoint on his particular question read the essay of the "con" viewpoint author, and vice versa. Each was then allowed to modify his essay if he wished to do so.

The Genesis Debate means to do exactly what its title implies: to stimulate friendly debate around each of its focused questions. We hope our readers will not only rejoice in the answers that they find familiar and comfortable but also wrestle with and seriously consider the answers that they have tended to reject. In so doing, each of us may well be encouraged to ask a few new questions: Will the biblical text really bear the interpretation that I have demanded of it up till now? Can I be absolutely certain that my understanding of this verse or subject is the only possible one? Is the Holy Spirit (through the efforts of one or more of these writers) trying to expand my horizons of biblical knowledge, or is he attempting to focus my perception a bit more specifically? How can a proper understanding of God's world (general revelation) and proper interpretation of God's Word (special revelation) supplement each other and help me arrive at truth?

In his question on Genesis 6:4, Philo assumes that the phrase "sons of God" in 6:1-2 means "angels." But in his answer to the question "Why were the giants born from angels and women?" he comments that Moses sometimes gives "to good and excellent men the name of 'sons of God'." Philo does not make it clear, in his extended discussion relating to this particular question and answer, whether he prefers "angels" or "human beings" in this specific context. Indeed, his method of interpretation would allow both.

Although we too might often like to have it both ways, students of Scripture today can afford no such luxury. "Sons of God" in Genesis 6:1-2 means either "angels" or "human beings," but not both. The first of the two authors responding to this issue in *The Genesis Debate* vigorously expounds one point of view while the second, with equal vigor, expounds the other. We invite you to carefully consider the sets of arguments on both sides of this fascinating question. And we further invite you to think along with the rest of our authors as they respond to ten other questions in our modest attempt to advance biblical understanding.

RONALD YOUNGBLOOD
Bethel Seminary West
San Diego, California

CONTRIBUTORS

AUSTIN, STEVEN A., associate professor of geology, Institute for Creation Research, Santee, California

BOARDMAN, DONALD C., late professor of geology emeritus, Wheaton College, Wheaton, Illinois

BORLAND, JAMES A., professor of biblical studies, Liberty Baptist Theological Seminary, Lynchburg, Virginia

CHRISTENSEN, DUANE L., professor of Old Testament languages and literature, American Baptist Seminary of the West, Berkeley, California

FRETHEIM, TERENCE E., professor of Old Testament, Luther Northwestern Theological Seminary, St. Paul, Minnesota

HAUSER, ALAN J., professor of philosophy and religion, Appalachian State University, Boone, North Carolina

HECK, JOEL D., assistant professor of religion, Concordia College Wisconsin, Mequon, Wisconsin

HENRY, CARL F. H., visiting professor in theology, Trinity Evangelical Divinity School, Deerfield, Illinois

HILLMER, MARK, professor of Old Testament, Luther Northwestern Theological Seminary, St. Paul, Minnesota

HOBBS, HERSCHEL H., pastor emeritus, First Baptist Church, Oklahoma City, Oklahoma

HUEY, F. B., JR., professor of Old Testament, Southwestern Baptist Theological Seminary, Fort Worth, Texas

KUFELDT, GEORGE, professor of Old Testament, School of Theology, Anderson College, Anderson, Indiana

MCCONE, R. CLYDE, professor of anthropology and linguistics, California State University, Long Beach, California

MERRILL, EUGENE H., professor of semitics and Old Testament studies, Dallas Theological Seminary, Dallas, Texas

MOORE, JOHN N., professor emeritus of natural science, Michigan State University, East Lansing, Michigan

NEWMAN, ROBERT C., professor of New Testament, Biblical Theological Seminary, Hatfield, Pennsylvania

REID, MALCOLM A., professor of philosophy, Gordon College, Wenham, Massachusetts

SCHRADER, STEPHEN R., associate professor of Hebrew and Old Testament, Liberty University, Lynchburg, Virginia

SEAFORD, H. WADE, JR., professor of anthropology, Dickinson College, Carlisle, Pennsylvania

THRONTVEIT, MARK A., assistant professor of Hebrew and Old Testament, Luther Northwestern Theological Seminary, St. Paul, Minnesota

WALTON, JOHN H., assistant professor of Bible, Moody Bible Institute, Chicago, Illinois

YOUNG, DAVIS A., professor of geology, Calvin College, Grand Rapids, Michigan

1   *Were the Days of Creation Twenty-Four Hours Long?*

YES: TERENCE E. FRETHEIM

This question has often been debated in the history of the Church. While recent scientific developments may have intensified the debate in many ways, the issue of the interpretation of the days of Genesis 1 is almost as old as the Church itself. The Genesis days were interpreted in an allegorical way by such figures as Origen and Augustine, while Martin Luther defended a literal interpretation of Genesis 1: "We assert that Moses spoke in the literal sense, not allegorically or figuratively, i.e., that the world, with all

NO: R. CLYDE McCONE

Many seemingly unresolvable controversies regarding the Bible are the result of attempting to find scriptural answers to questions that contain non-biblical assumptions. One such controversy focuses on questions concerning the date of "the beginning" (Gen. 1:1) and the length of the days of creation. Such questions carry the assumptions that (1) creation was an event that took place in time, that (2) the Genesis account describes a process in time that is scientifically explain-

its creatures, was created within six days, as the words read."[1] The understanding of days in terms of periods of time predates the Darwinian revolution.

In the nineteenth century, however, sharp differences in the interpretation of the days of Genesis 1 became even more commonplace. The reason for this development is clear: Emerging scientific theories about the age of the earth seemed to call into question the idea of a six-day creation. In the last one hundred years the books and articles devoted to this topic alone would constitute a substantial library. Even with all of the discussion, however, no consensus has emerged. Although very little in the way of new information has surfaced during this period, the same pieces of the puzzle can be rearranged in an amazing variety of ways.

One of the more striking things about the question is that scholars with widely different perspectives can agree on its answer, at least at one level. On the one hand, defenders

YES

NO

able, and that (3) Genesis was written to make known the original point in time as well as the subsequent process through time.

Origins of the Search for Origins

It is important that we ask the question, What is the source of these assumptions? Do they come from the Bible, or are they foreign to the Bible? Historically these questions come from the Greek foundations of western civilization. Among the Greek philosophers of the sixth and fifth centuries B.C. there developed scientific explanations of the order of nature as well as historical interpretations of the order of mankind. After the Christian evangelization of the Greek world, which began in the latter half of the first century A.D., questions about origins began to arise in the Greek mind. Explanations for origins were developed in the same manner as the explanations for the order of nature. By this time the Greek world was under the political dominance of the Roman Empire. When Constantine adopted Christianity as a religion of the state, the Bible was made to answer Greek questions concerning the "when" and "how" of creation.

The Bible, however, is quite explicit about its being a

of the literal interpretation can be found among the most liberal interpreters as well as the most conservative (e.g. Skinner; Young).² On the other hand, very conservative scholars and critical scholars alike will defend a position that understands the word "day" in more symbolic terms (e.g. the *Scofield Reference Bible;* Hyers).³ Significant differences do arise, however, once the implications of the exegetical decisions are drawn out, as we shall see. It is my opinion that those who defend the literal meaning of the word have the preponderance of the evidence on their side. I would agree with Gerhard von Rad: "The seven days are unquestionably to be understood as actual days and as a unique, unrepeatable lapse of time in the world."⁴ While not every point of view or piece of evidence can be rehearsed here, I trust that enough will be said to make that case.

One of the distressing aspects of this discussion is the extent to which efforts are made to harmonize these texts with

YES

modern science, and this on the part of representatives

NO

revelation rather than an explanation or an interpretation. In Hebrews 11:3 the writer makes clear that biblical faith is neither an historical interpretation of ideas nor a scientific explanation of a temporal process. This verse does not state that by faith we understand "how" or "when" the worlds were framed by the Word of God; rather, we understand "that" the worlds were framed by the Word of God. It is the opening statement in the great chapter of the Bible on faith, in which the object of faith is not an interpretation or an explanation of a temporal process but a revelation of the eternal Person who is the Creator. He is a Person who has spoken, and he is known only in a personal relationship, not by theoretical ideas about him or his works.

In what sense then is the question "Are the days of Genesis 1 twenty-four hours in length?" an issue in my relationship to the Creator? Does it really make any difference? On the other hand, is not believing "what" God has said distinctly related to "who" he is? Hence it is a factor in my relationship of confidence in him who has spoken to us in these last days by his Son, by whom he made the worlds (Heb. 1:2).

Our efforts to understand creation have always

from the entire spectrum of opinion. On the one hand, there are conservatives who insist that the biblical writer had to know as much about the origins and nature of the world as modern science knows—indeed, as much as science will ever know. No room at all is given to the possibility, long current in the Church, that there was a divine accommodation to the knowledge of the time in which the texts were written for the sake of maximal communication and understanding regarding creation.

On the other hand, there are critical scholars who deny a literal interpretation, insisting that the texts are symbolic in character with only a religious or theological intent. Ironically both perspectives commonly end up affirming the same conclusion: There is no incompatibility between Genesis 1 and modern science. I believe, however, that in more recent discussions insufficient attention has been

YES

NO

started from where we are in time and space and from our state of intellectual or cultural development. Using the understanding that we have at the point in time in which we live, we travel into the past in an attempt to understand the origins of ourselves and our universe. This was true in the mythological cultures of ancient civilization, and it is also true in the modern scientific age of western civilization. However, it is also true when the Bible is used to bring creation and the Creator into the temporal, theoretical explanations of our perspective. We shall see that when the days of creation are made to be twenty-four hours in length, mankind is transported back in time to the beginning where he is an observer of the Creator acting within a framework of time. From this position, God is reduced to the dimensions of our comprehension. Paul reminds us that man by wisdom does not know God (1 Cor. 12:1). In fact the fundamental error is not in one's intellectual theoretical explanation, or in one's interpretation of the account in Genesis 1-2, but in one's spiritual relationship with the Creator.

Knowing the Creator Versus Understanding Creation

It is a function of the created mind of mankind to comprehend and order the phenomena of nature. To

given to an intermediate interpretation such as that represented by von Rad: "Everything that is said here is to be
accepted exactly as it is written; nothing is to be interpreted
symbolically or metaphorically. The language is actually
scientific, though not in the modern sense of the word."[5]

On the basis of the evidence laid out below, this perspective more than any other seems to set the stage for the best
reading of the text. But it also means that one will have to
deal with incompatibilities between Genesis 1 and modern
science.

In any discussion of this matter it is important to say
something about the nature and purpose of the material.
For the sake of compactness of presentation, however, we
will seek to do that in the course of addressing ourselves to
various issues.

YES

NO

make the "days" of creation "days" of time is to bring
the Creator down into the framework of his creation so
that we can understand and explain creation rather
than know the Creator. That the problem is first of all
spiritual before it is intellectual is suggested by God's
challenge to Job: "Where were you when I laid the foundations of earth? Tell me if you have understanding.
Who determined its measurements? Surely you know!
Or who stretched the line upon it? To what were its
foundations fastened? Or who laid its cornerstone?"
(Job 38:4–5).[1]

The result of God's lengthy questioning of Job did not
result in a more scientific or historically accurate explanation of the process of creation. Rather, Job came to
know the Creator: "I have heard of you by the hearing of
the ear, but now my eye sees you. Therefore I abhor myself, and repent in dust and ashes" (42:5–6). If we attempt to understand creation from the perspective of a
creature in time, observing a process in time, we may
find it easier to understand. But all such attempts are
met by God's challenge to Job: "Were you there?"

The use of the Bible as a means to transport us as observers to the beginning of time has led to dating the
beginning and to regarding the six days of creation as
the first 144 hours of time. The effort to understand the
origins of nature in the same scientific manner as the
order of nature is a misapplication of the Greek founda-

The Evidence for Interpreting "Day" in Its Normal Sense

1. *The word "day" in the singular is probably never used in the Old Testament for a long period of time.* Given the more than 2200 references, this is striking. It is the plural form "days" that is sometimes used with reference to a period of time, such as one's life (e.g. Gen. 26:1). The singular is used, as in English, for a twenty-four-hour period, or for the time of daylight (both uses are present in Gen. 1:5). It can also be used indefinitely for a point in time, particularly in the future (such as in the phrase "day of the Lord"). Its use in the phrase "in the day that" (e.g. Gen. 2:4) is as a part of an adverbial construction, meaning "when" or "after" or "at the time of," and as such the noun carries no special meaning. Its use in Psalm 90:4 is as part of an analogy: One day (or part of a day—"a watch in the night") is like a thousand years to God (see TEV), given God's eternality. A day is not said to equal a thousand years.

Generally, to suggest that the word "day" in Genesis has reference to a special divine "day" (and hence also a spe-

YES

NO

tions of science. The climax of this error, when addressed to biblical origins, was reached when Lightfoot of Cambridge University calculated that creation occurred on October 23, 4004 B.C., at nine o'clock in the morning.

We may facetiously protest: "Did not the biblical days begin in the evening? And was this date the beginning of the first day when light was created, or is it the later part of the sixth day when man was created?" More crucial is the irrationality of any attempt to date creation. This becomes obvious when we ask Lightfoot, "Nine o'clock where?" If we make it Greenwich mean time this would locate the Creator in space as well as time and would make England the location from which the creation of mankind, if not also the heavens and the earth, took place. This historical interpretation would make Genesis in many ways similar to the creation myths of Babylon and Egypt.

While few take Lightfoot's dates seriously today, still it is an example of trying to comprehend creation by establishing a point in time as the beginning of time—and of attempting to use the Bible to do so.

cial divine evening and morning) is to give the word an eso-
teric meaning that it has nowhere else in the Old
Testament. Time references with respect to God in the Old
Testament are used in a normal way. For example, the reference to God's "years" in Psalm 102:24, 27 makes its
point only if the years are understood in the everyday
sense.[6]

2. *When the word "day" is used with a specific number, it
always has reference to a normal day* (cf. Gen. 8:14;
17:12). In Zechariah 14:7, the one seeming exception, the
usual Hebrew word for "one" is not used as a number, and
the word "day" refers to daylight, not the full day or any
other definite or indefinite period of time. Here the phrase,
sometimes translated "one day," does not function in the
normal way (no other number but "one" could be so used)
and would be better translated "only daylight" (cf. TEV). It is
a reference to the fact that there will only be daylight in the
new heaven and earth, and evening and morning will be
no more. If the phrase were used in this way in Genesis 1,

YES

NO **Creation from Human or Divine Perspective**

The first chapter of Genesis does not begin with
where mankind is in time or space, nor with his current
understanding of the heavens and the earth. Bernard
Ramm correctly and lucidly states that "the language
of the Bible is phenomenal" and that "there is no theory
of matter in the Bible." He goes on to say: "Genesis 1
does not defend Aristotle or Ptolemy or Copernicus, or
Newton, or Einstein or Milne . . . . The Bible is singu-
larly lacking in any definite *theorizing* about astronomy, ecology, physics, chemistry, zoology, and
botany."[2]

The first verse of Genesis takes mankind from where
he is in time, and from his knowledge of temporal
things, to the beginning and introduces him to the One
whom he does not know as the Creator of the heavens
and the earth. These are the heavens and the earth that
all mankind since creation have gazed upon, have been
dependent upon, and have sought to comprehend.

In verse 2 we are taken away from those heavens and
earth of space and time that both ancient and modern
people have used in an attempt to explain origins. Here
theorists with a human perspective have introduced

then evening-and-morning language would be inappropriate, as would reference to subsequent days.

3. *In the entire Old Testament, when the word "day" is used in a numbered series, it always has reference to a normal day* (cf. Num. 29). It should be noted that the use of the phrase "one day" instead of "first day" is the normal way of enumeration in the Old Testament (cf. Gen. 2:11), as in the Semitic languages generally.

4. *The reference to "evening and morning" for each of the six days of creation entails the normal daily interchange of light and darkness.* If "day" is not understood in its normal sense, then "evening and morning" cannot be either (which is never otherwise the case in the Old Testament, even in the sometimes cited Psalm 90:5-6, where an analogy is at work).

5. *The references to the days of creation in Exodus 20:11 and 31:17 in connection with the Sabbath law make sense only if understood in terms of a normal seven-day week.* It should be noted that the references to creation in

YES

NO

temporal processes in time. One attempt, known as the gap theory, holds that the original heavens and earth of verse 1 were reduced to a chaotic condition by divine judgment on disobedient spiritual beings. In contradistinction to the temporal explanation of the gap theory, God takes mankind, in the only rational manner possible, to the beginning and hence to himself. The earth, or our theories about it, is not to be used in an explanation of its origins.

The earth was "without form." Form is the medium of perception and conception by mankind—God is speaking to mankind. Thus the earth was without material existence. But it was also "void." Isaiah says of the Lord who created the heavens and the earth that "he did not create it to be empty, but formed it to be inhabited" (Isa. 45:18). All life is included. The earth was without conceivable material existence and without life. The heavens also were nonexistent, for verse 2 adds that "darkness was over the surface of the deep." Darkness is the absence of light. The deep is the absence of the expanse or firmament.

Light was the creation of the first day, while the expanse or space was the creation of the second day.

Exodus are not used as an analogy—that is, your rest on the seventh day ought to be like God's rest in creation. It is, rather, stated in terms of the imitation of God or a divine precedent that is to be followed: God worked for six days and rested on the seventh, and therefore you should do the same. Unless there is an exactitude of reference, the argument of Exodus does not work. From a critical perspective all of these passages are said to belong to the "Priestly" writing, in which case we would have to do essentially with cross-referencing within a few pages.

To suggest that the seventh day is an indeterminate period of time because evening and morning are not mentioned flies in the face of clear evidence to the contrary. In Genesis 2:3 God blesses and hallows that day, clearly indicating that it is a specified day that is set aside as a special holy day. Then in Exodus 20:11 that blessed and hallowed day is identified with the normal Sabbath day. Generally, to argue from the absence of something in the text is treacherous; there is not an absolute exactness of repetition in the first six days either ("and it was so" is missing from the fifth day, for example). The occasional appeal to Hebrews 4 cannot be sustained, not least because the language is eschatological. That text simply does not address the ques-

YES

NO

Since the waters were prior to all of the creative acts of God, they were not created waters. In Hebrews 11:3 we read that "the things which are seen were not made of things which are visible." In the "waters" of verse 2 God is calling "things which do not exist as though they did" (Rom. 4:17). We are also told that God uses "the things which are not, to bring to nothing the things which are" (1 Cor. 1:28). In creation the things that are not were used to bring into existence the things that are.

Ramm reads Gen. 1:2 in a similar manner as presented here: "We believe Genesis 1:2 is not referring to ruin and destruction but to *vacancy awaiting informing*."[3] In this second verse there is nothing but an active Creator—the Spirit of God.

Since by divine revelation we are taken to the beginning and the Creator, we are then taken forward from God's perspective in eternity, not backward in time from human perspective. The days of Genesis 1, by the

tions of the length of the seventh day of creation (though it might be noted that "day" is used in the normal way in verses 7-8) or how the seventh day is related to God's eternal rest.

It might here be noted that this connection with the Sabbath week should prohibit any numerological speculation regarding the number seven, however important its symbolical usage elsewhere. The use of the number seven has to do with what the seventh day is, and not the number seven in itself.[7] Also the seven-day week was a common time period in the ancient Near East, though without a Sabbath connection.

6. *The Exodus references are important in assessing whether or not we have here an ancient Near Eastern literary convention where the use of six days, climaxing in the seventh day, is used in an indefinite way.*[8] Its use in Ugaritic literature (and in the Gilgamesh epic) suggests such a literary device. In the Old Testament this usage could be present in Exodus 24:16; Joshua 6; Judges 14:17-18 (cf. 1 Kgs. 18:43-44; 20:29; Esth. 1:10). It is difficult to tell whether these passages have reference to an indefinite period of time in the interests of stressing a climactic event or have a literal reference. But even if the former is commonly

YES

NO

most literal reading, are days of creation and not days of time. God begins with himself, with a Person in eternity, not with a point in time or with a process in time.

Problems of the Twenty-Four-Hour Day

The twenty-four-hour day is the product of a finished creation with an earth turning on its axis in relationship to the sun. In the creation account the earth was created on the third day, while the heavenly bodies, including the sun and the moon, were created on the fourth day. We have observed the irrationality of attempting to explain creation by confining the Creator to the "time" of the twenty-four-hour days of his creation. Doing so leads to many problems that challenge the rational revelation of the Creator. These problems are compounded by an associated error.

The twenty-four-hour days are an integral part of the completed material universe and therefore could not be

the case, Genesis 1 also has to be interpreted in light of its own context. The evening-and-morning sequence is not a part of any of these other instances. Moreover in the Genesis account each of the days in and of itself has a fullness of important content that is not true of any of the other seven-day examples. It would be difficult to maintain that the interest of the account is finally only in what happens on the seventh day. The chronological whole is also important. It is even problematic to suggest that what happens on the seventh day is the climax of the account. Moreover the Exodus references to Genesis 1, as noted, depend upon a literal reference to the seven-day sequence.

There are no known references in other ancient Near Eastern literature to a seven-day creation.[9] The seven tablets of the Babylonian creation account (Enuma elish) are of no known significance here.

7. The reference to the creation account as "generations" (2:4) is directly paralleled by the use of this language elsewhere in Genesis (see 5:1; 6:9; 10:1, 32). The translation "generations" might suggest that the days are comparable to the length of time from one individual to the next in the

YES

NO

rationally conceived of as existing "in the beginning." To thus materialistically conceive of creation in time leads to problems that have been variously wrestled with by theorists. First, there is the creation of light before the creation of the source of light. Second, there is the creation of the earth on the third day before the solar system of which it is an integral part. Then there is also on the third day the creation of plant life with its growth, including trees that have annual rings. The necessary source of chlorophyll in light from the sun is not created until the fourth day.

In the heavens there is the problem of the vast distances of stars being millions of light-years apart. That it took God twenty-four hours to create the almost infinite time-space system is at best void of meaning.

Finally, there is the problem of the sixth day. Gleason Archer points out that the twenty-four-hour-day theory of creation brings the first chapter of Genesis into conflict with chapter 2 and hence calls into question the inerrancy of the Bible. He notes that the "crucial passage

genealogies and hence understood as a period of time.
The Hebrew word, however, only refers to a genealogy, or
succession of related names or families, and not to the duration of time involved. At the same time the use of the
word for the successive creative acts of God suggests that
the days may be understood in as literal a way as the ages of
individuals in the genealogies.

8. *There is no reason to think that the content of any of
the days would be inappropriate to a literal reference.* The
creation of "light" before the creation of the heavenly
"lights" (plural) does not constitute a problem, for it is likely
that the Hebrews believed that the ultimate source of light
was other than the heavenly bodies (cf. Isa. 60:19-20; Ps.
104:2; Job 38:19; Rev. 22:5) and that the luminaries
functioned as signs and "rulers" (Gen. 1:16, 18) over an
already existing situation, and perhaps also as a light supplement.[10] In any case, one ought not to second-guess
what was believed possible for God in the early moments of
creation. It may have been thought that God himself had
the power to create the light and to separate the light from

YES

NO

in Genesis 1:27 tells us very clearly that Eve was created as well as Adam during the sixth creative day . . . .
Since man is not mentioned in the list of sixth-day creations until all of the other terrestrial animals had been
produced (vv. 24-25), it is fair to assume that no more
than an hour or two would have been left toward the
close of the sixth day for the introduction of Eve upon
the scene."[4]

Obviously Archer perceives the days of creation in
terms of time, but he senses that twenty-four hours is
not long enough. This is essentially the crux of the dis-
agreement among those who regard the creation in
Genesis as a process in time to be observed and explained from a human perspective.

Problems of the first day of creation become most
crucial when a day of the material earth with its evening
and morning is used as a temporal measurement of a
day of creation. The scriptural relationship of the material to the spiritual is illustrated when we remember
that in both the Hebrew and Greek languages the same
word is used for "wind" and "spirit." It by no means fol-

the darkness initially (so 1:4) and that this function was later given to the luminaries. (One wonders about comparable origins for the two English words "sunlight" and "daylight.")

As regards the sixth day, much depends on how one views the relationship between the first and second chapters. If one believes that all of the events of the second chapter had to happen on the sixth day, then there could conceivably be a problem (though not necessarily, if one holds a high view of the power of God for such acts as are reported in 2:9, 19). In any case, there is certainly not enough here to turn the linguistic evidence around. If on the other hand one understands the second chapter to be a parallel account (whether the product of the same author or of someone else), functioning perhaps as a retelling of certain aspects of the story of Genesis 1 and in different terms without a concern for chronological matters, then there is no issue. The general temporal reference in 2:4b (see above), with its reference to the creation of the "earth and the heavens," as well as the sequential creation of

YES

NO

lows that wind, though unseen, is spirit. Yet material forms are necessarily used to denote spiritual objects and truths. Jesus frequently made use of this principle in his parables.

The days of creation are the work of the Spirit of God. It is God who moved, and it is God who spoke. Are his workings then to be measured by the movements of the material solar system? And did all of his works result in material reality? The materialistic error is at the crux of the problems of the first day of creation. What was the light of the first day if the sources of light were not created until the fourth day? Most answers are found in speculative explanations that either have the sources of light hidden or suggest that the light was a form of cosmic radiation. But the cosmos itself is viewed as not yet created.

If we turn completely from the influence of a materialistic explanation, we will observe that there is a considerable number of biblical references to indicate that the light of the first day was spiritual and that its source was God. The reference in 2 Corinthians 4:6 is quite clearly

plants (1:11-12; 2:5) and people (1:26; 2:7), suggests the latter interpretation.

Generally speaking, any difficulties in relating the creative acts to one another (e.g. creation of plants twenty-four hours or less before the sun) are beside the point. We are dealing with the understanding of the world of the biblical author, who in any case would certainly have believed that God could have accomplished what he pleased in creating.

Options for Interpretation

1. *One could conclude that the days are sequential but not consecutive.* They were intermittent, so that much of the creation actually occurred between the days and hence over a much longer period of time. But there is no evidence in the text itself that there were breaks between the days, and this makes problematic the understanding of the seventh day in terms of the Sabbath. This point of view seems to be motivated primarily by a concern to reconcile the Bible with the findings of modern science.

2. *One could conclude that the days are symbolic, that* **YES**

NO

to creation: "For it is the God who commanded light to shine out of darkness who has shone in our heart to give the light of the knowledge of the glory of God in the face of Jesus Christ." The subsequent separation of light from darkness is not the distinction between evening and morning. Rather, it is an absolute and permanent separation between spiritual light and spiritual darkness. Here is to be the moral-spiritual space in which people are to live and move and have their being.

Paul in writing to Timothy speaks of Jesus Christ as the King of kings and Lord of lords, "who alone has immortality, dwelling in unapproachable light, whom no man has seen or can see" (1 Tim. 6:16). If we can neither dwell in nor approach the uncreated light of God, then it was necessary for God to create the realm of light for our moral-spiritual dwelling place. Walking in light and walking in darkness is referred to frequently in the Bible, including 1 John 1:6-7: "If we say we have fellowship with him and walk in darkness, we lie and do not practice the truth. But if we walk in the light as he is

they are used in the interests of a schematic arrangement, the parts of which serve to connote a swift, complete and orderly divine creative activity. The days then are normal days but their significance is symbolic, concerned not with a chronology of creation but with the swiftness and orderliness of it. To this might be added the observation regarding the parallel arrangement of the first three days and second three days (e.g. light on the first day; luminaries on the fourth). This could suggest that one does not have to be concerned about the relationship of one day to another. The arrangement may well be topical and the days not sequential.

Such a perspective cannot finally be refuted, but it does not seem likely. The key question is this: What is there in the text itself that suggests a symbolic significance for the word "days"? If one were to tie chapter 1 closely to chapter 2, with its special trees and other such matters, then a symbolic interpretation could perhaps more easily be defended. But the section 1:1—2:4a as a discrete unit seems to be informed by language that is quite straightforward. The language of the chapter is simple, compact, precise.

YES

NO

in the light [as he walked in the flesh in this world], we have fellowship with one another and the blood of Jesus Christ cleanses us from all sin." Jesus said, "He who follows me shall not walk in darkness but have the light of life."

The process of the work of creation is spiritual, and its days are divisions of distinct creative acts. The connection between these days is not one of temporal development. The product of this work is both material and spiritual, in which there are days of time.

Explanatory Theories About Creation

Ramm lists four patterns of thought about the origin of the universe: (1) fiat creationism; (2) progressive creationism; (3) theistic evolution; (4) naturalistic evolution.[5] Fiat creationism is usually associated with the young-earth and twenty-four-hour-day theory of creation. As Ramm states, it is sometimes supported by Psalm 33:9: "For he spake and it was done; he com-

The chapter is carefully structured, but so are many other prose narratives, and this does not prejudice the case one way or another on the meaning of "day." A topical and schematic correlation of the six days is quite compatible with a notion of sequential days, particularly when a natural progression to the creative acts can be discerned. "Everything that is said here is to be accepted exactly as it is written; nothing is to be interpreted symbolically."[11]

Trees are trees, animals are animals, water is water, and days are days. In fact, the connection with the Sabbath suggests that the significance of the days depends upon their literal reference. The burden of proof lies on those who would claim a meaning of "day" other than the literal one, especially in view of the uses of words elsewhere in the chapter.

It might be noted here that the language of "literalness" is often used in unhelpful ways—for example, as a code word for designating an overly conservative interpretation of these texts. This is ironic, for one of the concerns of Reformation biblical scholarship—and indeed of critical

YES

NO

manded and it stood fast" (KJV). Ramm correctly observes: "This verse asserts nothing about *time* in creation, but it does assert the *certainty* with which Nature obeys the divine will."[6] Ramm by presenting his progressive creationism does so as "the only way out of the impasse" in which "conservative Christianity is caught between the embarrassments of simple fiat creationism, which is indigestible to modern science, and evolutionism, which is indigestible to much of fundamentalism."[7]

Ramm's progressive creationism seeks apparently to avoid the problem of time, not just the amount of time. He states: "The author sternly resists any effort to dogmatize about time involved in creation, and any effort of fiat creationists to reduce progressive creationism to evolution."[8]

H. Blocher presents four rival theories of interpretation regarding the six days of creation, three of which regard creation as days of time.[9] The first is called the literal interpretation theory,[10] which is similar to Ramm's twenty-four-hour-day creation by fiat. In the

scholarship—was that the interpretation of the text be freed from a variety of nonliteral approaches. The text should be interpreted literally unless there is good reason in the text itself for moving in other directions. To interpret a text literally, of course, does not mean that the contexts in which the words are used do not have deep levels of significance.[12]

3. *One could conclude that the language is liturgical.* It is probable that the material in this chapter had its origins in a liturgical celebration of the creation. But if so, these materials have now been freed from that cultic setting and made a part of a larger narrative in which it now functions as "the beginning of a series of events."[13] The days now function in terms of that larger context. While the Sabbath indicates a liturgical interest on the part of the author, the Sabbath rest is not simply a liturgical matter. It concerns the temporal order of the creation.

4. *One could conclude that the days are actual days.* With respect to the days, it seems clear that the text is less concerned with individual days, or with a succession of

YES days, than with the seven-day pattern as a whole, the

NO face of the objections of scientists, miracles are used to support this position, which would have the earth revolving on its axis for twenty-four hours before the solar system was created. Yet we must not forget that our speculation about what God could do cannot take the place of what God is doing, and what he is doing here is bringing the laws and order of the material universe into existence.

The reconstruction theory holds that Genesis 1:2 is an event in time in which the heavens and earth of verse 1 were destroyed.[11] In these first two verses can be located all the events of geologic time. The six days are days of reconstruction in time and are not days of the original creation.

The concordist theory is one that regards the days of time as geological ages even though these ages are not equal in length.[12]

Blocher then lists a classification of theories that he calls literary,[13] and these he prefers. These theories, of which he lists Ramm as one adherent, are not con-

workweek plus the Sabbath. This rhythm of work and rest is built into the very structure of the creation. It, too, is a part of the created order of things and not just that which was created on the individual days. That is why it is stated in 2:2 that it was only on the seventh day that God "finished the work that he had done." Creation thus has to do not simply with spatial order but also with temporal order—indeed, a specific temporal order. Creation was completed only when the seven-day rhythm had been built into the very structure of the world order. The references in Exodus to this (see above) indicate that the observance of the seven-day rhythm in the human community was a way for people to be "in tune with the creation as God intended it to be."[14]

Israel's observance of the Sabbath was a sign indicating that there was one small spot in the midst of a disordered world where God's created temporal order was being actualized. When all the world rests on the Sabbath day, that created temporal order will once again be complete, as intended from the beginning. Hence there is a universal validity to the Sabbath observance. The creation of the

YES

NO

cerned about explaining creation as events in time but rather are concerned only with how the account of creation was written. Some "take the form of the week attributed to the work of creation to be an artistic arrangement . . . not to be taken literally. It is possible that the logical order [the author] has chosen coincides broadly with the actual sequence of the facts of cosmogony; but that does not interest him. He wishes to bring out certain themes and provide a theology of the sabbath."[14]

The literary theory is a shift from an explanatory theory about how God created the earth in six twenty-four-hour days to an explanation regarding how it was written. It seems that literary theories only shift the questions to problems of inspiration and present little substantive revelation of God. There is no doubt that God used the personality characteristics with which he endowed each of the writers of Scripture. Still the revelation is of God, not of the writers.

What is more significant about the analysis of kinds

luminaries for the purpose of signification and governance (1:14-18) was in the interests of showing forth and maintaining this temporal created order. The interest in the account, then, is not basically chronological or calendrical but the very temporal structures of creation. In this sense the material is regarded as historical.

In this connection I can agree with Westermann[15] that the account is concerned not just with seven times twenty-four hours but with the temporal whole. The temporal whole, however, is a week culminating in the Sabbath. Its significance is more than numerical, but that further importance is dependent upon the significance of the specific temporal limits of the seven-day rhythm of work and rest.

Matters of Scientific Interest

These great declarations of faith are made in the form of, and in closest connection with, the "natural science" available at that time, as von Rad has demonstrated.[16] The importance of this is considerable and is not often enough

YES

NO

of explanations of creation by Ramm and Blocher is that they both recognize and turn from these theories that use time—evolutionary or twenty-four-hour-day— in a theoretical explanation of the days of creation. In spite of this, Blocher closes with statements that do not appear to be consistent. "If God creates time, he creates *with* time, as Augustine stresses, and even *in* time, as Luther and Karl Barth dare to assert. The presentation of the seven days at least suggests so."[15] We find the opposite to be true.

The Sabbath

The six days of completed creation are followed by the cessation of creative work on the day called the Sabbath. If we were to hold that each of the six days was twenty-four hours in length because they are a model for our six days of labor, then to be consistent we should regard God's Sabbath also as twenty-four hours in length. In doing so we are reversing the order and making our temporal-physical week a model for God's creative-spiritual week. Should we not then expect him to go out after the first twenty-four-hour Sabbath to go

recognized by critical scholars in the interest of refuting certain conservative claims.

Theological and "scientific" knowledge are herein combined. There is a variety of matters in the account that point to the concern for the latter. The chapters are prescientific in the sense that they predate modern science, but not in the sense of having no interest in those types of questions. For example, there is the mediation of the earth and the waters in the creation of certain things (1:11-12, 20); the ordering of created things from the lowest to the highest; the classification of plants into three distinct kinds that reproduce themselves according to their kinds, and a comparable interest in the animal world. We know that Israel had such an interest from a variety of other Old Testament passages (1 Kgs. 4:29; wisdom literature).

Genesis 1 certainly depicts things as they appeared to ordinary observation, but it is more than surface observation. It is observation that betrays a concerted effort to come to some understanding about the nature of the world in which they lived.

Israel's theology was able to take the science of its time

YES

NO

through another workweek of creation—and hence continue on in this pattern forever since he is eternal?

In the Sabbath day we are indeed presented with time because creation is complete and mankind is present. In him the physical and the spiritual are joined; the temporal and the eternal are related in the human self. In the first Sabbath, however, people were not called to rest from their labors but were invited to enter into God's rest. God's rest was from the completion of his creative labors for mankind.

Throughout the creative week God saw that what he had done was good. Good for what or whom? Not for himself, for God had no need. It was good for mankind, who could enter into what the Creator God had done for him by accepting his Creator as God, knowing what was good and what was not good for him. In the temptation mankind failed to enter into the rest of God's provisions by choosing to violate the Creator's position as God and trying to take his place and become as gods, knowing good and evil. It was then that God broke his

and use it as an instrument to speak about creation. One can speak of this matter from both scientific and theological perspectives, and in the interests of truth about the nature of the world they need one another. Otherwise theology gets bracketed out from other spheres of life or becomes presumptuous in thinking that it has the answers to every question.[17]

Genesis 1 is a beautiful example of how to keep these matters integrated in a search for the truth about the world. The chapter does have a fundamentally religious purpose, but in its statement of this it betrays a significant interest in related matters. While the central concern is in questions of "why," Israel is also interested in questions of "how" the world came into being, and herein the ancient author integrates them into one holistic statement of the truth about the world. In effect, we are asked to do the same in every age.

If in fact one holds that the text speaks of the world as created in six twenty-four-hour days, then one is confronted with the hermeneutical issue of deciding how to reconcile such an understanding with current evidence

YES

NO

own rest by instituting his plan and work of human redemption. He promised through the seed of the woman to destroy the serpent's work (Gen. 3:15) and to restore man to fellowship with himself. This Sabbath day's work was provisionally complete when Jesus on the cross cried, "It is finished." It will be prophetically complete when, as Paul wrote, "the last enemy that will be destroyed is death" (1 Cor. 15:26).

In God's work of redemption he entered into time through the birth, crucifixion, resurrection, and ascension of his Son. That God broke his Sabbath by his work of human redemption is clearly expressed by Jesus when he was accused of breaking the Jewish Sabbath regulations. His response: "My Father has been working until now, and I have been working" (John 5:17). It is obvious that God's Sabbath day was not a twenty-four-hour day. Even though redemption is a work that takes place in time, it is beyond temporal theoretical explanation. But through it God draws all people to himself. As Jesus said: "And I, if I am lifted up

that the world came into being over a much longer period of time. The author used those understandings of the world available at that time. If one has a view of the Bible that insists that all information in it, of whatever sort, has to correspond with reality, then one is in some difficulty. I would encourage such persons to move to an "accommodationist" view—namely, that God, in working with the author, accommodated the telling of the story of creation to the knowledge of the times.

This does not mean that we are called to separate the theological material from the "scientific" material and rewrite the chapter from our own scientific perspective (however much that does have to be done for other purposes). The Genesis text remains forever—not simply as an indispensable theological resource but also as an important paradigm on how to integrate theological and scientific realities in a search for the truth.

YES

---

from the earth, will draw all peoples to myself" (John 12:32).

NO

Paul wrote to the Ephesians that grace had been given to him to "preach among the Gentiles the unsearchable riches of Christ" (Eph. 3:8). To the Corinthians he wrote: "Thanks be to God for his indescribable gift" (2 Cor. 9:15). So here in the Sabbath day's work of redemption we do not have a theoretical explanation or interpretation of a temporal process. As in the creation account, we are introduced to the Creator who became our Savior.

Theoretical knowledge makes us the intellectual masters of things in nature. Revelational knowledge brings us to know the God who knows us and is our Lord. It is this kind of knowledge that comes from the revelation of the Creator in the first two chapters of Genesis.

ENDNOTES

YES

1. M. Luther, *Lectures on Genesis: Chapters 1–5, Luther's Works* (Saint Louis: Concordia, 1958), 1, 5.

2. J. Skinner, *Genesis* (Edinburgh: T. and T. Clark, 1910); E. Young, *Studies in Genesis One* (Philadelphia: Presbyterian and Reformed, 1964).

3. C. Hyers, *The Meaning of Creation: Genesis and Modern Science* (Atlanta: John Knox, 1984) 73–92.

4. G. von Rad, *Genesis: A Commentary* (Philadelphia: Westminster, 1962) 65.

5. G. von Rad, "The Biblical Story of Creation," in *God at Work in Israel* (Nashville: Abingdon, 1980) 99.

6. See T. Fretheim, *The Suffering of God: An Old Testament Perspective* (Philadelphia: Fortress, 1984) 39–44. Job 10:5 has reference to the content of God's days and years, not their duration.

7. See C. Westermann, *Genesis 1–11* (Minneapolis: Augsburg, 1984) 89.

8. See F. McCurley, Jr., "'And After Six Days' (Mark 9:2): A Semitic Literary Device," *Journal of Biblical Literature* 93 (1974) 67–81.

9. See Westermann, *Genesis,* 89.

10. See S. Aalen, " 'ôr," in *The Theological Dictionary of the Old Testament* (ed. G. Botterweck and H. Ringgren; Grand Rapids: Eerdmans, 1974), 1, 151–56.

11. Von Rad, "Biblical Story," 99.

12. Words in and of themselves do not carry theological meaning; sentences do.

13. Westermann, *Genesis,* 93.

14. T. Fretheim, *Creation, Fall, and Flood* (Minneapolis: Augsburg, 1969) 27.

15. Westermann, *Genesis,* 90.

16. Von Rad, "Biblical Story."

17. Cf. Westermann, *Genesis,* 176.

NO

1. All Scripture quotations are from the *New King James Version* except where otherwise indicated.

2. B. Ramm, *The Christian View of Science and Scripture* (Grand Rapids: Eerdmans, 1954) 67–69.

3. Ibid., 116.

4. G. L. Archer, Jr., "A Response to the Trustworthiness of Scripture in Areas Relating to Natural Science," in *Hermeneutics, Inerrancy and the Bible* (ed. E. D. Radmacher and R. D. Preus; Grand Rapids: Zondervan, 1984) 325.

5. Ramm, *Christian View,* 113.

6. Ibid., 114.

7. Ibid., 117.

8. Ibid., 114.

9. H. Blocher, *In the Beginning* (Leicester, England: InterVarsity, 1984) 41–42.

10. Ibid., 46–49.

11. Ibid., 41–43.

12. Ibid., 43–46.

13. Ibid., 49–52.
14. Ibid., 50.
15. Ibid., 58.

2   *Are the Events in the*

Genesis Creation Account Set Forth in Chronological Order?

YES: ROBERT C. NEWMAN

Evidence for Chronological Order

The first chapter of Genesis certainly gives the impression that it is to be understood as a chronological account of God's activity in creation. Genesis 1:1—2:3 is primarily structured by a device consisting of a sequence of days numbered one through seven. Interspersed among these days are God's creation commands and the events fulfilling the commands.

NO: MARK A. THRONTVEIT

This study will focus upon the ordering of the events set forth in Genesis 1, discuss the major attempts to justify a nonchronological ordering of those events, and suggest an approach that sees the creative week as the basic unit of time in the creation account.

The Nature of the Problem

At first glance, one's immediate response to the question in the title is: "Of course they are! One has only to

The account uses a number of chronological terms. It starts with a "beginning" (1:1), which is followed by the sequence of "days" mentioned above (1:5, 8, 13, 19, 23, 31; 2:2-3). Except for the seventh day (2:2-3) each member of this sequence of days also includes a reference to an "evening and morning" constituting that particular day. All of this is very chronological. Other chronological terms occur in the passage, although these are not so directly relevant to the question we are considering. Thus the pair "day" and "night" occurs three times (1:5, 14, 16); references to "seasons" and "years" occur in 1:14. It is generally agreed that these other chronological terms refer to literal days, nights, seasons, and years. Though they do not prove that the sequence of days in Genesis 1 must be chronological, they certainly indicate that chronology is not a concept foreign to the author.

More important is the numerical sequence itself. In Hebrew, as in English, there are two sets of numbers: (1) car-

YES

NO

read the text to see that the events of day two follow upon those of day one, just as those of day three follow upon day two and so on until that final, seventh day of culmination." But as one reads the creation account a number of items cloud the issue and render the question ambiguous. For example:

If the events are chronologically ordered, how does one explain the existence of evening and morning, which technically have reference to the setting and rising of the sun, before God "makes" the sun on day four (Gen. 1:16)?

In a similar way, how can the text speak of "days" at all before the sun is appointed to separate day from night and serve as a sign of seasons, days, and years (verse 14)?

Furthermore, plant life is dependent upon the sun for the process of photosynthesis. Yet our "chronologically" ordered text places vegetation, plants yielding seed and fruit trees bearing fruit on day three (verses 11–13)—once again, prior to God's making of the sun.

All of these items share a common problem: How can events (evening and morning) or things (plant life) that are somehow dependent upon the sun for their existence be spoken of prior to the "making" of the sun in a

dinal numbers, indicating quantity (one, two, three, four, etc.); (2) ordinal numbers, indicating sequence (first, second, third, fourth, etc.). The days in Genesis 1 are numbered with the standard ordinal numbers used in Hebrew sequences, though the first one is ambiguous and could be either cardinal or ordinal. Literally, we have "one day" or "a first day" (1:5); "a second day" (1:8); "a third day" (1:13); "a fourth day" (1:19); "a fifth day" (1:23); "the sixth day" (1:31); and, finally, "the seventh day" (2:2-3). Note also the presence of the definite article "the" with the last two days.

As mentioned above, the number used in 1:5, 'eḥåd, is ambiguous; it could be either cardinal ("one") or ordinal ("first"). Its usage overlaps with ri'šôn, "first." Either may indicate first days; for some reason, ri'šôn is used for first months and 'eḥåd for first years. The words for "second," "third," "fourth," "fifth," "sixth," and "seventh," however, are simply the usual ordinals; all are used now and then for

YES days, months, and years. A sequence of numbered days

NO chronologically ordered sequence? In response to this problem the suggestion has been made that verse 16 should not be translated "and God made the two great lights," as in the RSV and most other translations, but rather "Now God had made the two great lights." Syntactically speaking, this pluperfect rendering of the verb is entirely possible. The difficulty with this solution is that it overlooks verses 14-15: "And God said, 'Let there be lights in the firmament of the heavens to separate the day from the night, and let them be for signs and for seasons and for days and for years, and let them be lights in the firmament of the heavens to give light upon the earth.'" Even if one were to concede the translation "had made" in verse 16, the jussives of verses 14-15 ("let there be," "let them be") cannot be translated in a way that would allow the existence of the sun before day four.

Another suggestion takes seriously the parallel statements in verses 4 and 18 concerning the separation of the light from the darkness. In verse 4 we read that "God separated the light from the darkness." In verse 18 "the two great lights" (verse 16) are said "to separate

that is clearly chronological is the set of twelve days on which the tribal leaders in turn presented their dedicatory offerings to the tabernacle (Num. 7:10-83).

Naturally, ordinal numbers do not have to be used with chronological words. In Genesis, for example, we have the four rivers of Eden (2:10-14) and the three floors of the ark (6:16). In such cases the use of ordinals indicates an ordering scheme in the mind of the author. For the four rivers of Eden, it is not clear what this scheme was—perhaps a circuit around the compass points, or the sequence in which these rivers diverge from their source river as one goes downstream.[1] The context gives no clue, and we do not know enough about the geography of Eden to be sure. In the case of the ark, however, the use of "lower" in the context indicates that the floors are numbered upward from the bottom.

But even when used with nonchronological words, ordinal numbers often indicate a chronological order. The birth of the six sons of Leah is narrated in Genesis 29:31-35 and

YES

NO

the light from the darkness." These two statements might indicate that the events of the first and the fourth days are coterminous, that the means by which God separates light from darkness on day one are the separations afforded by "the greater light and the lesser light" of day four. That there is a relationship between days one and four is obvious and will be addressed later. Whether that relationship implies a coterminous existence of days one and four is less clear, though a coterminous existence would seem to militate against a chronological ordering of those events in that one then has to resolve the incongruity of coterminous events taking place on clearly differentiated days.

At this point it should be stated that a cardinal rule in the interpretation of any biblical text prohibits asking the text questions it does not address. Any attempts to harmonize the creation account with the findings of modern science should be avoided. Whether one's position is informed by a perspective of creation science or of evolutionary theory, it is extremely important to realize that the text of Genesis 1 addresses neither explanation. There is not a bit of text, not a single silent *shewa*, between God's command, "Let there be light!" and the

30:17-20. The first four sons are not numbered, but the last two are labeled "fifth" and "sixth." Clearly the ordering principle is chronological by time of birth. This is so even though the definite article is not used (paralleling days one to five of Genesis 1)—that is, Leah gives birth to "a fifth son" and "a sixth son." Since the genealogical term "generations" is used to structure the whole book of Genesis, a chronological ordering of Genesis 1 would fit in nicely with this pattern.

Ordinal numbers often occur with "day," "month," or "year" even when no explicit sequence is given. In each of these cases the day, month or year is the nth in some implied sequence, usually named in the context, such as the nth day of the week or month, the nth day since some event, the nth month of the year, or the nth year of a king's reign. I know of no cases where ordinal numbers are used with chronological terms when the sequence of ordering is not chronological. Consequently it seems that the burden

YES

NO

report of the fulfillment of God's command, "And there was light" (verse 3). This gap in the text is the proper arena for the debate between creationism and evolution, the "how" of God's creation. The appropriateness of the various scientific theories will need to be decided in the court of scientific investigation abiding by the canons of that discipline. Genesis 1 has other concerns—namely, the theological questions of "who" and "why."

Proposed Solutions

The scholarly community, cognizant of the difficulties involved in maintaining a chronological interpretation of the six-day sequence in Genesis 1, noticed early on that the number of creative works stands in some tension with the number of creative days. Eight works have been compressed into the space of six days, with two creative works each assigned to days three and six. The consensus today is that the framework of the six days has been imposed upon the earlier account of eight creative works. Several suggestions have been made in an attempt to account for this six-day structure. Three representative approaches follow:

of proof is upon those who wish to claim that Genesis 1 is nonchronological.

Of course, this need not indicate that all events mentioned in Genesis 1 fall within this sequence. A narrative will often depart from chronological order to carry some strand through to a conclusion and then return to its chronological sequence. This is commonly done for a character who is about to enter or leave the narrative (Gen. 31:55; Mark 5:20). Nether does evidence of chronological ordering require that the days of Genesis be twenty-four-hour days or that they succeed one another immediately or without overlap. Some of these possibilities will be discussed below, and others are treated elsewhere in this book.

Objections to Chronological Order

A number of objections have been raised against interpreting Genesis 1 as a chronological account of creation.[2] We will here try to respond to the main ones, moving from **YES**

NO

1. *Liturgical.* S. H. Hooke suggested that Israel's priests introduced the six-day scheme (plus the addition of the seventh day in 2:1–3) to shape the creation account as a "liturgy of creation" for use in the cult, specifically for a seven-day New Year festival modeled upon the Babylonian *akitu* festival.[1] While few scholars have accepted Hooke's proposal of the New Year festival, many have adopted his liturgical explanation for the addition of the six/seven-day framework.

2. *Catechetical.* A second position is represented by P. J. Wiseman who, after a curious exegesis of Exodus 20:11, maintains that the six days were six days of instruction given to Moses on Mount Sinai rather than a description of the six days of creation.[2] As in the case of Hooke, this catechetical or instructional approach has received more support than Wiseman's specific application.

3. *Polemical.* A third way of accounting for the discrepancies in a chronological ordering of the creation events is to recognize the polemical motivation present in the text. This approach explains the creation of the sun after the creation of light as either an utter denunci-

more scientific objections to more exegetical ones.

Some have rejected a chronological interpretation of Genesis 1 as inconsistent with the findings of modern science.[3] There are, in fact, tensions between some scientific theories and some chronological interpretations of Genesis 1. Such tensions, however, do not apply equally to all chronological interpretations.

Some of these tensions involve the time of creation: whether it began thousands of years ago or billions of years ago, whether it lasted one week or billions of years. For those who believe that science is mistaken about the age of the earth, there is no reason to reject the idea that Genesis 1 is to be interpreted chronologically. For those who believe science is right about the age of the earth (as I do), there are yet a number of interpretive schemes that harmonize Genesis 1 and science without rejecting a chronological interpretation of the Genesis account. An old earth with **YES** a long period of God's creative activity does not itself rule out chronological order from Genesis 1.

NO ation of every form of sun-worship or a desacralization of nature.[3]

Various critiques have been made against these representative attempts to understand the six-day sequence of Genesis 1 in a nonchronological way. It is not my intention to disparage these views or depreciate those who hold them. From an exegetical point of view, however, these are not the only possibilities. All three share the common presupposition that the creation account is comprised of a series of day-long units. But what if the basic unit of time described in Genesis 1:1 — 2:3 is in fact the creation week itself? Evidence for such a reconceptualization can be gathered from a spectrum of expositors that ranges from the conservative writings of Benno Jacob and Umberto Cassuto to the critical writings of Claus Westermann.

The English translation of Benno Jacob's Genesis commentary begins: "The story of creation leads up to man, the subject of all history. The earth is prepared for him so that he may live, work and rest upon it. All this is placed into the frame of 'six days', not to write a historical account in the sequence of time, but to construct before our eyes the universe as a meaningful cosmos."[4]

Nor does it matter whether evolution has or has not occurred if one argues for chronology in Genesis 1. One who
believes that mankind arose gradually as a whole population from common ancestors with the ape will indeed find
some tensions in Genesis 2, with the details about the origin of Adam and (especially) Eve, and in Genesis 3, with
the fall.[4] But the chronological order of Genesis 1 is not itself a problem.

Several objections revolve around determining the origin of the sun. For instance, how is one to understand the
terms "day," "evening," and "morning" mentioned as early
as day one (1:5) if the sun was not created until day four
(1:16)? Young-earth creationists respond by postulating
that day one involved the creation of a light with intensity
and directionality like that of the sun, while the earth was
rotating on its axis with a period of rotation like that today.[5]
Thus we have day, evening, and morning of the usual
length, and we have adequate light levels without a sun.

As an old-earth creationist I find this rather strained. On **YES**

NO

After examining relevant Akkadian and Ugaritic materials, Umberto Cassuto claims that "a series of *seven
consecutive days* was considered a perfect *period* (unit
of time) in which to develop an important work, the
action lasting six days and reaching its conclusion and
outcome on the seventh day."[5]

Already in the 1930s and 1940s Jacob and Cassuto
were drawing our attention to the one act of creation in
their references to "a perfect period (unit of time)" to develop "an important work," and "a meaningful cosmos," rather than "a historical account in the sequence
of time."

Claus Westermann refutes W. H. Schmidt's suggestion that Genesis presents a six-day succession of
events by pointing out that "P does not present 'a succession of six days ending with the Sabbath'; he
presents a whole, an articulated chronological unity,
which is a whole because of its goal. It is not a question
of seven times 24 hours, but of the chronological unity
which is the basis of all else and which is itself articulated in the same way."[6] Nearly one hundred pages later
Westermann returns to this point with the following

the basis of scientific evidence and Job 38:8–11, I believe that the earth was covered with a heavy cloud layer early in its history (when the oceans were born, approximately Gen. 1:6). As a result the source of daylight could not be observed from the earth's surface (which appears to be the standpoint of the Genesis 1 narrative) until day four, when the cloud cover cleared.[6]

What about the survival of plant life without a sun? Young-earth creationists have their sun-like light illuminating the plants for a day or so, just as we sometimes grow plants with artificial light today; old-earth creationists have sunshine diffusing through the clouds with sufficient intensity for photosynthesis.[7] In fact, for old-earth creationists it is this photosynthesis that oxygenates the earth's atmosphere, not only to prepare breathable air for the animals that God is soon to create but also to convert the atmosphere from one that acts as a strong greenhouse and supports a heavy cloud cover to one that as a weak greenhouse will only support a partial cloud cover, thus

YES

NO

programmatic statement: "We must take as our starting point that when P arranged the works of creation in a seven-day pattern he was not concerned merely with a succession of seven days, but with a whole, with a basic unit of time, which becomes a whole in the climax of the seventh day."[7]

These observations that the creation account is best described as "a chronological unity," "a whole," "a basic unit of time" free the six-day schema from interpretations that emphasize the chronological ordering of the events of Genesis 1 and invite a more formal investigation of its structure to determine as precisely as possible what it is that God says through that structure. The remaining pages of this essay will be concerned with such an investigation.

Form and Function of the Creative Week

B. W. Anderson persuasively argues that the creation account in Genesis is a unity that runs from 1:1 through 2:3. He recognizes that the epilogue in 2:1–3 echoes the superscription of 1:1–2 and thus forms a frame that relates the end of the account to its begin-

leading to the appearance of the sun, moon, and stars on day four.[8]

According to this latter scenario the sun, moon, and stars were really made earlier in God's creative activity (the sun, for instance, when God said, "Let there be light"). They are only made visible at the earth's surface on day four. Thus the command "Let there be lights in the expanse of the sky" (NIV) is qualified by the functions of these lights: "to separate the day from the night," "to mark seasons, days, and years," to be "lights in the sky," and to dominate day and night.

Does this view square with the Hebrew verb form of "made" in Genesis 1:16 (God "made" two great lights)? Can it be translated as a pluperfect ("had made") instead of simple past ("made"), or is this just special pleading? There certainly are cases in Hebrew where such verb forms must refer to an event preceding events just narrated.[9] When Laban enters Rachel's tent to search for the stolen idols, this

YES

NO

ning and encloses the main body of the creation story in 1:3–31.[8] Robert Alter reaches a similar conclusion:

> And God completed on the seventh day His work which He had made.
> And He ceased on the seventh day from all His work which He had made.
> And God blessed the seventh day and He hallowed it.
> For on it He had ceased from all His work which God created to make.
>
> We have here not only incremental repetition but, as I have tried to show through this rather literal translation, a tightly symmetrical envelope structure, the end returning to the beginning: the first line of the passage ends with God's making or doing, as does the last, while the end of the last line, by also introducing the seemingly redundant phrase "God created," takes us all the way back to the opening of the creation story, "When God began to create." In P's magisterial formulation, everything is ordered, set in its appointed place, and contained within a symmetrical form.[9]

The repetition of the salient parts of 1:1 in 2:1–3 serves to emphasize the unity of God's creative act, "his work" (singular). Within this unifying framework the six–day schema unfolds not to order the events of creation chronologically but, again, to emphasize other aspects of God's one creative event. To clarify what these aspects are we must turn to the structure of 1:3–31.

construction is used to note that she "had hidden" them under a camel saddle (Gen. 31:34). In fact, evangelical interpreters do the same in Genesis 2:8, 19 (see the NIV rendering "had planted," "had formed") to avoid having the trees and animals created after man; otherwise there would be a different order of creation in Genesis 2 than in Genesis 1. A pluperfect translation is neither required nor forbidden by Hebrew grammar, so the choice will depend on the interpreter's model of what is happening. In fact, we are frequently faced with interpretive decisions that we will solve one way if we believe the Bible is a revelation from God and another if we believe it is merely an ancient human work.

YES

NO

For the last one hundred years expositors have noticed the symmetrical arrangement of verses 3–31. The six days of creation are divided into two panels of three days and four creative acts each. Each panel displays the same structure with a first day containing a single creative act, a second day consisting of one creative act with two aspects and, finally, a third day with two separate creations. Further adding to the symmetry of these versions is the chiastic reversal of the products of the middle days. The whole structure is graphically represented in this chart:

PANEL ONE	PANEL TWO
Day 1 — light (1:3–5)	lights (1:14–19) — Day 4
2 — firmament (1:6–8): sky / seas	inhabitants (1:20–23): fish / birds — 5
3 — dry land (1:9–10) vegetation (1:11–13)	land animals (1:24–26) human beings (1:27–31) — 6

In Genesis 1 a correlation is often proposed between days one and four, two and five, and three and six.[10] That is, day one speaks of the creation of light, day four of lights; day two of water, day five of water animals; day three of land, day six of land animals. This scheme is seen as an important structuring for the whole account. The earth is initially "without form and empty." Then the days proceed first to "form" (days one to three) and then to "fill" (days four to six) the realms of sky, air/sea, and land respectively. This structure is used to argue for Genesis 1 having a logical rather than a chronological order.

Some correlation of this sort really does appear to be present in the account. But it is not an argument against chronological order as well, since both structures occur in Genesis 1. No one would disagree that air, water, and land must exist (days two to three) before one can have air, water, and land animals (days five to six). The same must be true for land and land vegetation (both on day three). There is good scientific evidence for the sun beginning to

YES

NO

The tight formal correspondence evidenced by the chart is matched by a close relationship in the content of the paired days (day one with day four, day two with day five, day three with day six). Various categories have been suggested to describe the correlation between the two panels of God's activity, with "separation and adornment" and "preparation and accomplishment" being the most frequently encountered. When one remembers, however, that God's creative action essentially involves bringing order out of chaos it is instructive to see these panels as an orderly description of that whole process. As D. Kidner says: "Indeed the six days now to be described can be viewed as the positive counterpart of the twin negatives 'without form and void,' matching them with form and fullness."[10]

In panel one God separates from the formless chaos of verse 2 three spheres, three areas that will eventually house and shelter life. In panel two God fills those creatively ordered spheres with corresponding inhabitants (lights for light, fish for the sea and birds for the sky, land animals and human beings for the dry land). Regardless of the images chosen, the pronounced pan-

glow (early day one: "Let there be light") before the planet earth forms (late day one: "light" = "day," "dark" = "night," "evening and morning"), and for the oceans and atmosphere subsequently being outgassed from the formed planet (day two: "firmament in the midst of the waters"). Also the one peculiar feature that seems to be out of order in the Genesis account is vegetation, the first living thing, which is mentioned before sun, moon, and stars, the last nonliving things; otherwise the order is nonliving first, living afterward. But this really fits the scientific scenario of vegetation clearing the atmosphere and preparing it for animal life.[11] Why not see God as giving an account with both a scientifically accurate chronological order and an easily remembered structure?

Other interpreters have argued that the purpose of Genesis 1 is polemic rather than scientific.[12] The account is designed to parallel and rebut pagan cosmogonies with their chaos/order theme and their multiplicity of gods giving birth to and warring against one another. The Genesis

YES

NO

eling of the account offers another explanation for the placing of the sun after the creation of light that was so problematic in a chronological ordering of these events. In addition, it also strengthens the impression that the creation week rather than day is the basic unit of time in our text.

As satisfying as this structure is, resonating with the orderliness and purposefulness of creation, there is another structure that binds verses 3–31 together. Westermann has discerned a fivefold pattern that repeats in each of the six days:

1.	Introduction	And God said
2.	Command	Let there be/Let them be gathered, etc.
3.	Completion	And it was so
4.	Judgment	And God saw that it was good
5.	Time frame	It was evening and it was morning, day x

Westermann's point is that each creative act is "essentially the same event,"[11] but while he is surely right in

account, on this model, uses the chaos/order motif but re-places the multiple gods by the one God; it removes the warfare motif for unknown reasons; and it explicitly desig-nates the light, earth, sky, sun, moon, animals, and man as created beings rather than as gods.

I see no objection to thinking that such a scheme was in the mind of the author of Genesis 1. There would be no argument over the matter if such were explicitly stated in the passage—somewhat like the challenges God lays be-fore the idols in the prophetic books (see e.g. Isa. 41:21-24)—but it is not. In any case, there is no reason why the presence of such a theme should rule out either scientific or chronological value in the Genesis account, particularly since chronology is explicit and this is not. Certainly if God is the ultimate author of Genesis 1 he could easily select such events of creation as would be valuable for refuting polytheism without destroying the chapter's scientific value. A poet does not have to abandon facts to use imag-ery or rhyme.

YES

NO

this regard much more can be inferred from the pat-tern. It is also important to notice that the events of each successive day are presented in a slightly fuller way. Day one contains only the bare outline of the pat-tern, whereas day two expands upon section 3, the re-port of the completion or fulfillment of God's command, with a description of God's creating. This same pro-gression can be visualized simply by counting the lines of text devoted to each day in Snaith's edition of the He-brew Bible. Not only do the descriptions of the days be-come increasingly longer (with the exception of day five), but day six has twice as much space devoted to its proclamation than any other day.[12] Is it unreasonable to suggest that the six-day structure with its snowballing progression serves to direct the reader's attention to the sixth day?

Further evidence for this interpretation emerges from a closer examination of Westermann's fivefold pattern. Without gainsaying his conclusion—that the pattern serves to reinforce the impression that each day was es-sentially the same creative event—it is striking that while the pattern remains methodically the same

Some have argued that the days of Genesis 1 are a chronology of God's revelation of the creation account to Moses on Sinai rather than a chronology of the creation itself.[13] Thus during the forty days Moses was on the mountain, God told him about creation in the course of some seven days. On the first day he told Moses about the creation of light, on the second about creation of the firmament, and so on. The major problem with this suggestion is that it does not fit what the account says: There is nothing here about showing, and only God is described as seeing. The account is all about creating. Exodus 20:11 agrees with this: "For in six days the Lord made the heavens and the earth, the sea, and all that is in them, but he rested on the seventh day" (NIV). There is no good reason to assume that the chronology of Genesis 1 is other than that of the creation events.

YES

NO

through day five, day six systematically alters the pattern at every point except the introduction:

1. Command: Days one through five regularly employ jussives ("let there be," "let them be gathered," etc.) in this section. Day six breaks this established pattern by using the cohortative form, "Let us make."

2. Completion: In addition to the formulaic "and it was so" found in days one through five, much of the massive expansion found in day six can be attributed to the filling out of this report of completion or fulfillment. Furthermore, verse 27 employs poetry rather than prose in the report of the creation of humankind (cf. especially the format found in the *Jerusalem Bible*) as well as three of the six occurrences of the verb "create" found in this passage.

3. Judgment: Days one through five had been judged "good."[13] Day six, on the other hand, receives the verdict "very good" (verse 31).

4. Time frame: The Hebrew text scrupulously avoids attaching the definite article to the number of the particular day in days one through five, regularly following the pattern "it was evening and it was morning, day x."[14] The sixth day, however, does have the article, a nuance only recognized by the NASB and the New Jewish Version of English Bibles that I consulted. The omission of

Others have suggested that the days of Genesis 1 were chosen as a device for structuring the creation account not because they have anything to do with what actually happened at creation but merely because the Jews had a week of six workdays and one day of rest. "If the Hebrews had had a five-day or seven-day workweek, the account would have read differently."[14] But the Bible, on the contrary, suggests that the Hebrews' seven-day week was designed to commemorate creation, not vice versa (Exod. 20:8–11).

Conclusions

We have examined the evidence that Genesis 1 is a narrative in chronological order of the events of creation. We have suggested that its chronological terminology and its use of ordinal numbers with a sequence of days to structure the whole account point strongly in this direction. The fact that the first five days are designated without the definite article (e.g. "a third day") might allow for the days being a selection from a larger number and not immediately adja-

YES

NO

the definite article in days one through five may also show that a chronological ordering of the events is not the text's primary concern. Numbers 29, in which the ordering of the eight days of the Feast of Tabernacles is clearly the issue, employs ordinal numbers (as does Genesis 1) but always in conjunction with the definite article (verses, 17, 20, 23, 26, 29, 32, 35). That the definite article is regularly present in such chronological contexts can be seen from Numbers 6:9, 10; 7:12, 18, 24, 30, 36, 42, 48, 54, 60, 66, 72, 78; 19:12, 19; 31:19; Nehemiah 8:13, 18.

When the six-day schema is viewed as a whole, as a comprehensive picture of the creation divided into two panels representing God's bringing order out of the "formless void" of chaos, the unity of the whole process is emphasized. When the six-day schema is seen in terms of the regular repetition of recurring elements, the unity of the whole process is again emphasized. But when it is recognized that the sixth day regularly breaks that pattern at every point, in subtle but unmistakable ways, then the structure compels us to focus upon the sixth day. Theologically, this means that the

cent, but it gives no support to the idea that they are out of chronological order.

Objections to the Genesis chronology from science amount mostly to objections to a young earth. I suggest that the words of Genesis 1 are consistent with an old earth even though they have traditionally been interpreted in terms of a more recent creation.

The biggest stumbling block to a chronological interpretation from an old-earth perspective is undoubtedly the question of the creation of the sun. I suggest that this is no problem if its actual creation is seen as taking place when God says, "Let there be light." Its appearance to an earthbound observer does not occur until day four with the oxygenation and clearing of the atmosphere.

The question of the time of origin of seed-bearing plants relative to animals is the sort of problem most easily handled by having either overlapping "age-days" or successive

YES

NO

text is more concerned with relationship than with the theory of relativity, with our place as human beings in God's world than with "big bangs" or expanding universes.

But what of the seventh day? Anderson and Alter have shown how the repetitions in 2:1–3 bring us back to verse 1 and emphasize the creative week as the unit of time that underlies our text. Westermann continues along this line of approach:

> It is only then in the seven-day week as a whole and with the seventh day as the goal, that the importance of the seventh day is properly appreciated. This means that when he arranged the works of creation in the seven-day pattern, P intended to structure a unit of time which consists of two parts: it would not be a whole without the seventh day, which is something different from the six days . . . . When God sanctifies the seventh day (i.e., declares it holy), he sets it aside as something special. The sanctification of the seventh day determines the time which begins with creation as structured time, and within which one day is not just the same as another.[15]

With the sanctification of the seventh day (which also has the definite article), God completes the creative act and institutes time as a structured, orderly part of the created order. In a very real sense, any talk of chronology before this establishment of time is prema-

literal days with overlapping creative periods. Neither suggestion is unreasonable when we recall that a genealogical scheme organizes the whole book of Genesis and that genealogies involve sequential but overlapping lifespans.

The questions of a literary structure correlating the creative days by pairs and of a polemic against polytheism merit further study but seem to be reasonable suggestions. They should not be allowed to explain away the chronological structure of Genesis 1. Proper methodology demands a model that fits all the evidence, not one that uses some evidence to dismiss the rest.

YES

NO

ture. "Scripture has not taught anything regarding the sequential order" (Rashi).

This examination of the ordering of events in Genesis 1 has shown that difficulties arise upon a chronological reading of the text that are not easily explained. On the other hand, a close reading of the text suggests that the creation week is the chronological unit of time. This insight frees the ordering of events in Genesis 1 from a chronological interpretation and allows the strong structuring of the passage to have its say: God brings order and fullness out of the formless void and directs our attention to the importance of the sixth day.

ENDNOTES

YES

1. E. A. Speiser, *Genesis* (Garden City: Doubleday, 1964) 16–17, sees the four rivers as tributaries to one river; M. G. Kline, *Kingdom Prologue* (South Hamilton, 1981), 1, 68, sees them as distributaries from one river, in parallel with the eschatological picture in Ezekiel 47 and Revelation 22.
2. B. Ramm, *The Christian View of Science and Scripture* (Grand Rapids: Eerdmans, 1954) 217–23; H. Blocher, *In the Beginning* (Downers Grove: InterVarsity, 1984) 49–59; C. Hyers, *The Meaning of Creation* (Atlanta: John Knox, 1984) especially chapters 3 and 4.
3. Ramm, *Christian View,* 217–18.
4. J. O. Buswell, Jr., *A Systematic Theology of the Christian Religion* (Grand Rapids: Zondervan, 1962), 1, 159–62, 321–24; J. Murray, *Collected Writings* (Edinburgh: Banner of Truth, 1977), 2, chapters 1 and 7; F. A. Schaeffer, *No Final Conflict* (Downers Grove: InterVarsity,

1975) 33–34; C. F. H. Henry, *God, Revelation and Authority* (Waco: Word, 1976–83), 6, 206, 240–50.

5. H. M. Morris, *The Genesis Record* (Grand Rapids: Baker, 1976) 55, 65.

6. See R. C. Newman and H. J. Eckelmann, Jr., *Genesis One and the Origin of the Earth* (2d ed.; Grand Rapids: Baker, 1981) 51–52, 75–76, 80–81; see also Buswell, *Systematic Theology*, 1, 146–54; J. L. Wiester, *The Genesis Connection* (Nashville: Nelson, 1983) chapter 7.

7. Wiester, *Genesis Connection*, chapter 7.

8. Ibid.; Newman and Eckelmann, *Genesis One*, 51–52, 80–81, 84–85.

9. The verb *wayya'aś* is in the imperfect tense with the *waw* consecutive "and." It is often interchangeable with the perfect tense without *waw* (see E. Kautzsch, *Gesenius' Hebrew Grammar* [2d ed.; Oxford: Clarendon, 1910], section 111c)—thus imperfect with *waw*, "and he made"; perfect, "he made." Both can sometimes be translated as pluperfects (e.g., "had made" instead of "made"). Most occurrences of Hebrew verbs having a pluperfect (rather than simple past) force employ the perfect tense, as they are usually joined to the sentence by some construction such as "the place where," "the person who," etc., where the *waw* ("and") is not appropriate. Some cases of perfect verbs with pluperfect force in Genesis (according to the NIV) are "had been" (13:3), "had made" (13:4), "had been subject" (14:4), "had been taken captive" (14:14), "had stood" (19:27), "had lived" (19:29), "had closed" (20:18), "had said" (21:1), "had promised" (21:1). Some cases of imperfect with *waw* consecutive with such force (also NIV) are "had finished" (2:2), "had planted" (2:8), "had formed" (2:19), "had been closed" (8:2), "had stopped falling" (8:2), "had gone down" (8:3).

10. F. Filby, *Creation Revealed* (Westwood: Revell, 1964) 17–20, 89; Blocher, *Beginning*, 51; R. Youngblood, *How It All Began* (Ventura: GL/Regal, 1980) 25–27; Hyers, *Meaning*, 67–71; Kline, *Kingdom*, 1, 59 ff.

11. V. R. Eshelman, "The Atmospheres of Mars and Venus," in *Frontiers of Astronomy* (ed. O. Gingerich; San Francisco: Freeman, 1970) 48, 58; W. K. Hartmann, *Moons and Planets* (Belmont: Wadsworth, 1972) 336.

12. N. M. Sarna, "Understanding Creation in Genesis," in *Is God a Creationist?* (ed. R. M. Frye; New York: Scribners, 1983) 155–75; Hyers, *Meaning*, 28, 42–56, 61.

13. Cf. Ramm, *Christian View*, 218–29; P. J.Wiseman, *Creation Revealed in Six Days* (London: Marshall, Morgan, and Scott, 1948; revised, 1977).

14. Hyers, *Meaning*, 75.

NO

1. S. H. Hooke, *In the Beginning* (Oxford: Clarendon, 1947) 36.

2. P. J. Wiseman, *Creation Revealed in Six Days*, 33–34.

3. E.g. K. Barth, *Church Dogmatics*, 3, 1, 120–21. For an approach that combines all three see W. Brueggemann, *Genesis* (Atlanta: John Knox, 1982) 22–39.

4. B. Jacob, *The First Book of the Bible: Genesis* (ed. E. I. and W. Jacob; New York: Ktav, 1974) 1.

5. U. Cassuto, *A Commentary on the Book of Genesis* (Jerusalem: Magnes, 1961) 12–13. For an overview of six-day-plus-one-day literary patterns in Akkadian and Ugaritic literature see F. McCurley, " 'And After Six Days' (Mark 9:2): A Semitic Literary Device," *Journal of Biblical Literature* 93 (1974) 67–82, and the bibliography cited there.

6. C. Westermann, *Genesis 1–11: A Commentary* (Minneapolis: Augsburg, 1984) 90. "P" refers to the so-called "Priestly" document, one of the sources behind Genesis as posited by some critical scholars.

7. Ibid., 171.

8. B. W. Anderson, "A Stylistic Study of the Priestly Creation Story," in *Canon and Authority: Essays on the Theology and Religion of the Old Testament* (ed. G. W. Coats and B. O. Long; Philadelphia: Fortress, 1977) 159–60.

9. R. Alter, *The Art of Biblical Narrative* (New York: Basic, 1981) 143.

10. D. Kidner, *Genesis: An Introduction and Commentary* (London: Tyndale, 1967) 45–46. Cf. W. H. Griffith Thomas, *Through the Pentateuch Chapter by Chapter* (Grand Rapids: Eerdmans, 1957) 31.

11. Westermann, *Genesis*, 84.

12. Day one, 3 lines; day two, 4 lines; day three, 7 lines; day four, 8 lines; day five, 6 lines; day six, 16 lines.

13. The judgment "And God saw that it was good" must be supplied from the Septuagint in verse 6.

14. For similar observations see M. Fishbane, *Text and Texture: Close Readings of Selected Biblical Texts* (New York: Schocken, 1979) 8–9.

15. Westermann, *Genesis*, 171.

3   *Was the Earth Created*

a Few Thousand Years Ago?

YES: STEPHEN R. SCHRADER

The age of the earth has engendered a great deal of dialogue over the past decade.[1] Unfortunately the dialogue has reached a point where F. Howe has been prompted to make an appeal—in light of the heated nature of the debate—"that the kind of argumentation which is really harsh criticism or judgment of motives cease."[2] It must be noted at the outset that "there has been a rather long history of conflict between science and Christianity."[3] The tension has surfaced at various points historically. Initially,

NO: DAVIS A. YOUNG

Scripture clearly teaches that the heavens and the earth had a beginning, but it does not say when that beginning was. If, then, we would learn the age of the earth, we must turn to geology. A diverse and massive array of geological evidence indicates that the earth has experienced a long, complex and dynamic history that began about 4.5 billion years ago.

The contrary view that the earth is no more than a few thousand years old is based on (1) a literalistic in-

astronomy provided the first real encounter with the Copernican revolution, challenging the then-current prevailing geocentric conception. In time the conflict moved from astronomy to geology (the age of the earth) to biology (the issue of evolution) and then to anthropology (the origin of mankind). And today the conflict has focused especially on the behavioral sciences, involving such issues as freedom versus determinism and the essential goodness or depravity of human beings.[4]

The age of the earth has always intrigued mankind, and it is one point where there is conflict between science and the Bible. "With the advent of Darwinian evolution and a macroevolutionary framework of the earth has come the demand for a scientific construct or model in cosmogony that posits millions and millions of years for earth history."[5] Yet within the last twenty-five years there has been a re-emphasis on a young-earth model or framework by those

YES

NO

terpretation of Genesis 1, in which the six days of creation are regarded as the first six ordinary days of cosmic history; (2) a literalistic interpretation of the genealogies of Genesis 5 and 11, which allows for no gaps between names. The young-earth view has also been advanced by appeal to allegedly scientific arguments.[1] This view, however, cannot be sustained on either biblical or scientific grounds.

Insistence on the sole validity of literalistic interpretations of the relevant biblical texts is unwarranted. A century ago evangelical scholar W. H. Green demonstrated that biblical genealogies commonly omit several names and therefore cannot legitimately be used to construct rigorous chronologies.[2] Furthermore, biblical scholars have pointed out a variety of exegetical difficulties with the literalistic interpretation of Genesis 1. Although alternative exegeses such as the gap, day-age, and revelation-day interpretations have enjoyed wide acceptance among evangelicals and are compatible with an old earth,[3] none of these is fully satisfactory either. The gap theory collapses because it is based on a weak translation of Genesis 1:2: "The earth became formless and empty." The revelation-day theory completely violates the rationale given for the fourth com-

who support the efforts of creation science.[6] Davis Young describes the latter movement as follows:

> What is astonishing about the twentieth century evangelical scene is a remarkable resurgence of belief among many Christian scientists in the crucial geological role of the Flood and in the idea that the Earth is extremely young. A host of biologists, physicists, chemists, geographers, and engineers (extremely few geologists and astronomers) have recently been insisting on a return to a belief in creation in six twenty-four-hour days only a few thousand years ago, *an abandonment of all theories of harmonization, and wholehearted acceptance of a global deluge that accounted for the stratigraphic and paleontological record.*[7]

Scientific Evidence for an Old-Earth Model

Who is right, given such difference of opinion? It is important to address the question of whether scientific evidence better supports an early-earth or a late-earth theory. For what reasons do some evangelical scholars postulate long eons of time for earth history? What reasons lead other evangelical scholars to advocate a relatively recent creation and thus a young age for the earth?

YES Newman,[8] Pun,[9] Wonderly[10] and Young,[11] all evangelical scientists, are convinced that an old earth is a scientifi-

---

NO mandment as expressed in Exodus 20:11. The day-age interpretation, while better, inevitably runs aground on attempts to achieve a correspondence between geological-astronomical reconstructions of cosmic history and the creation of heavenly bodies on the fourth day.

The most acceptable view of Genesis 1 does not regard it as a chronicle of successive events during the first seven days (however long) of cosmic history. Rather, Genesis 1 should be regarded as a highly structured theological cosmology that extensively employs a royal-political metaphor because of the great importance of kingship in the world of ancient Israel. In contrast to the pagan, polytheistic myths of the cultures that surrounded the infant nation of Israel, Genesis 1 portrays God as the sovereign King who effortlessly creates and establishes his realm and who calls into existence by his royal decrees those creatures that the nations sinfully worshiped and the myths deified. The

cally verifiable fact. The following outline form is presented for ease of reference and study.[12]

I. Astronomical evidence

   A. Light-travel time
      Within specific assumptions, the time needed for light to reach the earth is computed. Presently the figuring is based on quasar-light source. Estimated age of the universe: 10 billion years.

   B. Expanding universe observations
      Complex calculations involving evidence of red-shift (Doppler effect) observations work back to the assumption of an original "big bang." Estimated age of the universe and this galaxy: 15 to 20 billion years.

   C. Stars: structure and energy sources
      Complex computations of star composition (hydrogen-helium ratios) are converted into time estimates. Estimated age of the sun and solar system: 5 to 10 billion years.

II. Selected radiometric evidence

   A. Meteorites: 4.5 billion years

   B. Earth rocks: 3.6 billion years or younger

   C. Moon rocks: 4.6 billion years

YES

NO

days are part of the literary portrayal of the royal council of divine creation and may be employed analogously to a temporal succession of decrees by an earthly king. The days are days in the sphere of divine action, a sphere that transcends time, not the first seven days of cosmic history.

Genesis 1 is therefore a theological statement and should not be used to answer scientific questions about the age and historical unfolding of the cosmos that would have been alien to the Israelites.[4] Genesis 1 tells us that God is Creator, but it does not tell us when or how he created.

If, then, Scripture gives no unequivocal information about the age of the earth, it is altogether appropriate for Christians to seek clues to the earth's age through scientific investigation. Certainly the biblical teaching about the interrelationships among God, man, and the world legitimizes scientific activity. God not only gave us minds that are curious and can have fruitful interac-

III. Selected nonradiometric evidence (Here no dates are listed for each item, but the evidence all points to the age of the earth as vastly greater than 6,000 to 10,000 years.)

    A. Carbonate deposits: The Great Bahama Bank, off the coast of Florida, has multiple layers over 14,500 feet thick.

    B. Ooids (small spheroidal bodies): Formation for adding many layers of mineral deposits involves massive time elements.

    C. Dolomite formation: Replacement of calcium carbonate particles in lime sediment or lime rock gives strong evidence of vast amounts of time required.

    D. Evaporites: The Castile Formation of West Texas has thin layers of anhydrite and calcium carbonate.

    E. Coral reefs, ancient and modern (example: Eniwetok atoll, 4,610 feet of coral deposit): The formation of coral reefs gives strong evidence of slow deposition.

    F. Organic banks (example: the Capitan Reef of West Texas, 2,000 feet thick in places, with fossilized remains of organisms): This translates into a demand for long time periods for formation, even hundreds of thousands of years.[13]

Responses to the Evidence for an Old-Earth View

YES

Only a few selected areas can be discussed in a brief es-

NO

tion with a divinely ordered world. He also blessed the human race in its God-given ruling and subduing task (Gen. 1:26–28), thus guaranteeing that we could progress in understanding and making sense of the earth he created. Given that blessing, we ought to expect that a patient study of God's creation would gradually yield answers to our questions about its structure, composition, behavior, and age. Christians have not hesitated to accept all sorts of scientific conclusions and to make use of the fruits of scientific and technological research. Why then should we be reluctant to accept scientific conclusions about the antiquity and history of our planet in view of the absence of any clear-cut information in Scripture about such matters?

Geological Evidence: Young Earth

What does scientific evidence suggest about the age of the earth? Surprisingly, many Christians think that scientific evidence favors the conclusion that the earth

say. Howe makes an interesting observation from an impartial perspective:

> It is vital to note that concerning the main lines of evidence for an old earth, advocates of the young-earth model, with equally impressive credentials and research in various science disciplines, respond with equally feasible lines of evidence for a young earth. In the opinion of this writer, the approach presented by the young-earth advocates *is not obscurantism or blind devotion to archaic concepts*. For example, ever since the late 1950s evangelical Christians who are scientists have raised a consistent voice of careful response to the appeal for an old earth from the radiometric data.[14]

1. *Radiometric dating techniques evaluated*. This is certainly one of the key areas to be addressed. Bradley,[15] Newman[16] and Young[17] all present the materials from a positive perspective for establishing the antiquity of the earth. Yet the young-earth advocates set forth the presuppositions demanded for any radiometric time clock to work accurately, and then they try to demonstrate that the various time clocks are inadequate at one level or another. Kofahl and Segraves suggest that the following tenets are necessary to read "time" into a ratio of chemicals in a rock specimen:

> 1. The time units must be meaningful and readable.
> 2. The timer must be sensitive enough to measure the interval in question. The same time would not be used for a hundred yard dash and the return of Halley's comet.
> 3. *We must know when the time was started*. True, some clocks have

YES

NO

is only a few thousand years old. Among the main "evidences" cited are the decay of the earth's magnetic field, the thickness of moon dust, and the stratigraphic column. Measurements made during the past one hundred fifty years indicate that the earth's magnetic dipole moment has been diminishing in strength. If the current rate of decay were extrapolated backward in time, the dipole moment would have had an astronomically high value only a few thousand years ago. Magnetic field decay would lead to such intense heating of the earth that life would be impossible. Hence young-earth adherents have argued that the earth cannot be more than a few thousand years old. However, such a contention totally ignores the abundant evidence from archaeological sites and rocks that indicates that the

a calendar, but a clock does not tell how many times its hands have gone around.

4. We must not only know when the timer was started, *but what the reading was on the timer scale when it started.* Was the stop watch at zero when the race began? Or was it on thirty seconds?

5. *The timer must run at a uniform rate; if it does not, we must know what the irregularities are in order to have a meaningful timer.*

6. *The timer must not have been disturbed in any way or reset since it was started.*[18]

They conclude with the following after their study of the geochronological time clocks (all of the shortcomings of this type of method certainly allow for the concept of "appearance of age," which all uniformitarians reject):

Generally speaking, the evidence as it has been presented indicates that the radiometric and non-radiometric clocks being used by scientists to time earth events fall short in one or more of the requirements for the ideal clock which we studied earlier . . . . In particular, the *last four of the requirements . . . are normally not met by the usual methods for measuring.*

There is no way to determine whether or not the "timer" was set at zero when it was started. As a matter of fact, if the world was created, we would expect it to display an appearance of age from the very beginning. Attempts to date it, then, would generally be expected to make it appear older than it really is.

Similarly, the requirements that the timer ran at a uniform rate and that it not be disturbed in any way *are not subject to experimental verification.* We cannot prove that these requirements have been met over the years since the earth came into existence. We know, however, of several kinds of events which could have disturbed the timer or the rate at which it has run. *The development of the industrial age, great storms on the sun, and variations in cosmic radiation are examples of such disturbances.*[19]

YES

NO   dipole moment has not diminished from an astronomically high value but has increased and decreased in strength cyclically through time.[5]

Prior to the manned lunar landings, scientists had predicted that a great thickness of lunar soil (regolith) would be found at the surface because of continued meteorite bombardment over millions of years. Because astronaut footprints showed that the loose surface soil is very thin (generally less than three inches), young-earth advocates have suggested that the moon has been bombarded for only a brief time. The earth-moon system must therefore be very young. However, this claim completely ignores the fact that lunar regolith is

E. C. Myers has dealt extensively with this issue too.[20]

R. Gentry in the late 1960s and early 1970s studied discolorations in certain minerals and came to the following conclusions with reference to the age of the earth:

> One isotope of polonium has a half life of only about three-and-a-half minutes. This means that the rock has to be solidified before or within seconds of the time the polonium isotope gets into it, or there will be no halo in the rock.
>
> In some instances, this isotope of polonium can be given by the decay of uranium, of which the polonium isotope is one by-product. However, sometimes polonium decay haloes are found in rocks without any possible uranium source for the polonium. This, Gentry explained, means the polonium had to be present in the rocks at the moment they solidified.
>
> This in turn, Gentry said, means the rocks had to solidify extremely rapidly, under conditions unknown to science today. This indicates the likelihood of a creation of the earth and its primordial rocks and elements by a supernatural creator, and cannot be explained on the basis of evolutionary assumptions . . . . Gentry said his research calls into serious doubt the traditional scientific idea that the earth must be 4.5 billion years old.[21]

Howe comments: "Interestingly, to this writer's knowledge, no advocate of an old-earth model has ever to the present time (1985) attempted to interact with the hard scientific

YES

NO

not all loose but is for the most part very highly compacted. Beneath the thin veneer of loose surface material, the average thickness of regolith on the lunar maria ("seas" or plains) is about five meters and in the highlands about ten meters. Thicknesses as great as 36.9 meters (well over one hundred feet) have been found locally.[6] Such great thicknesses of regolith are consistent with the moon's antiquity.

Those who believe that the earth is very young also claim that the vast bulk of earth's fossiliferous, stratified rocks were deposited by a global catastrophic flood of a year's duration (Noah's flood) rather than over long periods of time. Such was also the belief commonly held by many naturalists of the eighteenth century. But during the past three hundred years the wealth of geological data gradually accumulated by hundreds of careful students of the earth, Christian as well as non-Christian, rendered that conclusion untenable. Indeed, by the early nineteenth century that belief had been abandoned by virtually all knowledgeable geologists.[7]

data and the interpretation of the data that Gentry offers."[22] It was noted that his work has been well documented in journals for serious and scholarly evaluation, yet Davis Young only has the following comment:

> The work by Gentry . . . is indeed problematic for current theories of radiometric dating and decay constants of radioactive nuclides. But creationists should concentrate their energies in trying to solve such problems with the help of modern research rather than continuing to propagate the same fallacious arguments.[23]

Not only has Young failed to explain the research work of Gentry, who has challenged the assumed slow cooling of igneous earth materials and has suggested an instantaneous creation of the earth's crust, but he has failed to mention the canopy theory and its effects on a pre-flood environment and the changes wrought by a universal flood and the removal of the canopy.[24] Nor does Young mention the work of Clark, who indicates that the earth's vast sedimentary layers may have been deposited in just one year of universal flooding.[25] All of these topics certainly relate to the assumptions of radiometric dating and provide a viable option: that of a recent creation.

YES

J. Klotz made the following observation about the accu-

NO

There is currently within the geological community a virtual consensus that the earth has experienced an extremely long, complex, and dynamic history that has involved repeated interchanges of land and sea, repeated uplift and erosion of numerous mountain systems, migration and collision of continents, progressive development of life, and so on. The geological evidence for the earth's antiquity is overwhelming and can be summarized only briefly.

Geological Evidence: Old Earth

1. *Evidence from sedimentary rocks.* Vast portions of the earth's surface are underlain by thick accumulations of layered, sedimentary rocks such as sandstone, limestone, conglomerate, shale, coal, gypsum, and rock salt. These rocks commonly contain fossil remains of plants and animals. As examples, the Valley and Ridge province of the Appalachian mountains in the eastern United States consists of a complexly folded

racy and reliability of radiometric methods of dating.

> At the same time we must recognize that radiometric methods are not as accurate and as reliable as they appear at first glance to be. All too often, these determinations are pointed to as a *final proof that the earth is of great age*. But at the present time it can hardly be maintained that the uranium time clock possesses the reliability and accuracy we should like to find in science . . . . It might also be pointed out *that processes once thought to take long periods of time — millions and millions of years —* are now known to occur in much shorter periods of time. *It is generally assumed, for instance, that oil is formed only after the original complex organic matter is covered by several thousands of feet of overburden and after a lapse of several millions of years.* Yet Smith has found hydrocarbons (oil is a mixture of hydrocarbons) in sediments dated as "Recent." A composite sample of hydrocarbons taken from the Gulf of Mexico and dated by the C^{14} method gave an age of $12,300 \pm 1,200$ years — *a far cry from the millions of years previously thought necessary for their formation.*[26]

H. Morris gives a detailed analysis of the radiometric dating assumptions: (1) a constant half-life; (2) an isolated system; (3) known boundary conditions. He says that "none of these assumptions can be proved correct, or even tested, since they involve conditions during vast aeons when no observers were present to test their validity."[27] He suggests that with the precipitation of the prediluvian water canopy and all sorts of other physical convulsions taking place (for that world was "deluged and destroyed" according to 2 Pet. 3:6 NIV), radioactive decay processes might have been sharply accelerated. Even other global catastro-

YES

NO

and eroded stack of sedimentary rock layers as much as forty thousand feet thick. The Colorado plateau of the southwestern United States is underlain by about ten to twenty thousand feet of spectacularly eroded, nearly horizontal sedimentary rocks.[8] Such rock sequences characteristically contain a host of features that, considered cumulatively, indicate that the entire sequence has experienced a long history that had nothing to do with Noah's flood. Some examples of such features:

Rocks with fossil mudcracks. Modern mudcracks are typically, though not exclusively, formed on dry lake bottoms. As a lake evaporates and the shoreline recedes, the lake bottom is gradually exposed to air and sun. The soft wet muds slowly dry out and contract, and

phes that the uniformitarians have postulated (e.g. swarms of asteriods at the close of the Mesozoic era) might have had a similar effect. F. Jueneman (who is not a creationist) has noted this possibility:

> The age of our globe is presently thought to be some 4.5 billion years, based on radio-decay rates of uranium and thorium. Such "confirmation" may be shortlived, as nature is not to be discovered quite so easily. There has been in recent years the horrible realization that radio-decay rates are not as constant as previously thought, nor are they immune to environmental influences. *And this could mean that the atomic clocks are reset during some global disaster, and events which brought the Mesozoic to a close may . . . be . . . within the age and memory of man.*[28]

2. *Light-travel time as a method of dating.* Newman calculates the age of the earth using these specific assumptions:

> (1) Light has traveled at this speed everywhere in space throughout the history of the universe; (2) the light we observe actually came from the stars and other astronomical objects that it pictures; and (3) our distance measurements for these objects are sufficiently accurate.[29]

Howe mentioned that a creationist publication in Australia, *Ex Nihilo*, has placed experimental information before readers "replete with the results of sophisticated computerized research, to suggest that the date of the uni-

YES

NO

polygonal shrinkage cracks develop on the exposed lake bed. The plates of mud pull apart, curl up, and become hard and brittle during an extended period of drying.

Sedimentary rock layers, too, contain fossil mudcracks and curled mudplates. The presence of fossil mudcracks strongly indicates that the layer of sediment, prior to being solidified into rock, must have experienced at least one episode of wetting and extended drying before being buried under a new layer of sediment. Sequences of sedimentary rock commonly contain hundreds of mudcracked layers and must have formed during an extended period involving several distinct episodes of alternate wetting and thorough drying of the sediments. Such episodes are incompatible with the notion of a global flood.

Pebbles. Layers of conglomerate are extremely abundant in sedimentary rock sequences. Conglomerates

verse based on the calculations involving light years may be open to question."[30] The implications of these new studies (July 1983) are conveyed by Niessen:

> There are three "secular" or non-biblical possibilities to the problem of harmonizing a young universe with the allegedly great distances of the outer galaxies: (1) the distances may not be that great after all; (2) light may take a "short-cut" as it travels through deep space; (3) the speed of light may have been considerably faster in the past. These three are not mutually exclusive, and may in fact be used in conjunction with each other. The fourth solution, which may be used independently or in conjunction with the above three, *is that God created the light beams as well as the stars so that they could be — as indeed they were — seen on the fourth day of the creation week.*[31]

There is nothing unreasonable either philosophically or scientifically in this, although it does contradict the uniformitarian assumption. Certainly the universe could have been created as a functioning entity, complete with an "appearance of age" at the moment of creation.

3. *Expanding universe observations and stellar structure methods of dating.* These are discussed well by Newman. He notes that proponents of a young earth claim that the expansion did not start from the big bang "but rather from

YES

NO

contain pebbles and cobbles embedded in a finegrained sandy to clayey matrix. If the pebbles in a given layer of conglomerate were derived from the layer immediately below, then the layer below first had to be deposited as soft sediment, then cemented into hard rock, then uplifted and exposed at the surface of the earth, and then extensively weathered and eroded, most likely by running water, in order to form and transport the cobbles and pebbles that would be incorporated into a new deposit of sediment. The presence of hundreds of conglomerate layers in a typical thick sedimentary pile indicates that during accumulation of the total pile there must have been several distinct episodes of deposition, cementation, uplift, weathering, and erosion.

Further supporting such inferences is the fact that conglomerate layers covering areas of hundreds to thousands of square miles commonly overlie very irregular, undulating surfaces called unconformities and considered to be buried erosional surfaces. Some unconformities display such striking relief that some very

some more expanded configuration only a few thousand years ago."[32]

As far as the stellar structure's being a useful tool in dating, Newman acknowledges the difficulty in testing the assumptions. In relation to the third assumption he notes that it cannot be checked directly and that "those who believe that the Genesis account requires a universe only a few thousand years old will naturally assume that the stars were created instantaneously at various stages in their life cycles. This resurrects the problem of 'creation with apparent age.'"[33]

4. *Coral reefs and evaporites as methods of dating.* H. Morris notes that Young ignores the evidence of Nevins that the El Capitan Permian "reef complex" in west Texas was not a true reef but largely an "allochthonous (transported into place from elsewhere) deposit of fossilbearing lithified lime mud."[34] H. Blatt, G. Middleton, and R. Murray note the following in relation to carbonate reefs:

> Closer inspection of many of these ancient carbonate "reefs" reveals that they are composed largely of carbonate mud with the larger skeletal particles "floating" within the mud matrix. Conclusive evidence for a rigid organic framework does not exist in most of the ancient carbonate mounds. In this sense, they are remarkably different from modern coral reefs.[35]

YES MacNeil in 1954 indicated that much of the morphology of modern reefs is explicable in terms of growth of corals on

---

NO rugged and hilly terrain must have been buried and preserved under the conglomerate.[9] The bedrock beneath some unconformities is thoroughly weathered, suggesting that a soil zone had developed before burial under the conglomerate. Both the soil zone and erosional surface indicate that the rocks beneath the unconformity were uplifted and exposed at the earth's surface in order to undergo such extensive weathering and erosion that hills, valleys, stream channels, and soils could develop.

Virtually everything known about the cementation, weathering, soil formation, sculpting of hills and valleys, and erosion of ordinary sedimentary materials indicates that these are all relatively slow processes. If several such episodes occurred during the history of a

a pre-existing base, the shape of which was largely responsible for the form that the reef later took.[36] Thus "it is obvious that long ages are certainly not necessary for the construction of so-called coral reefs, either living reefs or fossil reefs."[37]

Morris confidently asserts that "evaporites are even more clearly the result of rapid processes, in spite of their very misleading name."[38] From the testimony of various scholars it seems most likely that the origin of salt deposits is not only catastrophic in nature but completely consistent with the flood model of geology. The standard uniformitarian explanation, voiced by Young,[39] is that these great thicknesses of salt beds, gypsum beds, etc., have been formed by slow and cyclically repeated evaporation from inland lakes or relict seas. But notice the testimony of Russian geologist V. I. Sozansky:

> The absence of remains of marine organisms in ancient salts indicates that the formation of the salt-bearing sections was not related to the evaporation of marine water in epicontinental seas. Other geologic data, such as the great thickness of salt deposits, the rapid rate of for-

YES

NO

given rock pile (and rock sequences generally do contain several unconformities), then the total history must be rather lengthy. These features would not develop in a global flood.

Beneath some erosional surfaces, layered rock sequences thousands of feet thick are severely tilted.[10] In such situations the sediments beneath the unconformity first had to be deposited, then cemented into solid rock, then tilted before being uplifted and eroded at the surface, and finally buried under the material above the unconformity. Folded, bent, or tilted rock layers are commonly found in mountain systems around the world. For example, along highways through the Appalachian Valley and Ridge province of Pennsylvania one can plainly see tilted and folded rocks. Like erosion and cementation, folding of solid rock layers is a process that does not occur quickly. Experimental and theoretical studies of layered rocks indicate that the times required to produce the observed fold patterns are on the order of thousands to hundreds of thousands of years.[11]

Varves. Some sedimentary rock accumulations contain varves—that is, pairs of extremely thin (one mil-

mation of salt-bearing sections, the presence of ore minerals in salts and in the caprocks of salt domes do not conform with the bar hypothesis.[40]

The analysis of recent geologic data, including data on the diapirs found in ocean deeps, permits the conclusion that these salts are of a juvenile origin—that they emerged from great depths along faults during tectonic movements. This process is often accompanied by the discharge of basin magmas.[41]

Sozansky comes to the conclusion that basins of salt accumulation were in active tectonic relation to depressions of block structure in which volcanic eruptions were common. He surmises that salt is not an evaporitic formation or a derivative from volcanic rock but a product of degasification of the earth's interior. "The salt precipitated from juvenile hot water which emerged along deep faults into a basin as a result of change in thermodynamic conditions."[42]

5. *Lakes, glaciers and deserts as a means of indicating age.* According to many the so-called lacustrine deposits, especially those containing varves or cyclic annual deposits, formed seasonally along the beds of large lakes. A noted one is the famous Green River old-shale formation in Wyoming and adjacent states. Yet the fact that "'abundant' fossil fish and 'enormous concentrations' of fossil birds are found in the Green River formation surely ought

YES

NO

limeter or less) laminations that have contrasting chemical and mineralogical compositions. In a typical pair one layer is thicker, coarser-grained, and rich in calcium carbonate, while the other layer is thinner, finer-grained, and rich in organic material. Modern varves form on lake bottoms in response to seasonally controlled variations in the composition and amount of sediment introduced and/or precipitated. Normally one varve pair represents an annual deposit formed during two major episodes of sedimentation.

The Green River Formation of Utah, Colorado and Wyoming contains a succession of a few million varves. Hence it is probable that the Green River Formation was deposited in ancient lakes over a period of a few million years. Several other features in the Green River Formation—including tracks of fossil shorebirds, skeletons of flamingo-like wading birds, skeletons of freshwater fish, mudcracks, deposits of algae, and accumulations of minerals that develop during severe

to satisfy anyone that this is not a varved lake-bed formation at all, but a site of intense catastrophism and rapid burial."[43]

The problem with glacial deposits is not in relation to the Pleistocene glacial deposits, which are accepted by both creationists and evolutionists, but with the "much more equivocal evidences of earlier ice ages."[44] Young mentions striated bedrock and conglomerates as glaciation indicators, but such phenomena can be produced by other causes than just glaciers. There is much evidence of catastrophism in conglomerates. For example:

> 55 billion cubic meters of coarse sedimentary rock in Australia, formerly interpreted as a "tillite," originally deposited in an ancient glacial period, were more recently shown to have been formed by subaquaeous mudflows.[45]

The desert formations, especially the sandstones of the Colorado plateau, are objects of considerable controversy among orthodox geologists. It has been noted that many are convinced they are water-laid rather than wind-laid formations.[46] The "sharp cross-bedding noted in some of these can be produced by violent water action."[47] It is also a

YES

NO

evaporation of lake water — are indicative of the lake environment suggested by the varves.[12] In addition the Green River Formation lies above several thousand feet of other layers that contain many conglomerates, soil zones, unconformities, and mudcracks.

Also of extreme importance is the fact that most sedimentary formations contain features that permit reconstruction of the depositional environment. By comparing sets of features in rocks with similar features in well-understood modern environments, it has been possible to argue compellingly that sedimentary rocks were formed as lake, river delta, river valley-floodplain, glacial margin, ocean bottom, coral reef, alluvial fan, saline evaporite basin, beach, desert dune, or other deposits.[13] The lake origin of the Green River Formation is one example. Another example is provided by the Navajo Sandstone of Utah, the Coconino Sandstone of Arizona, the Entrada Sandstone of Utah, and the De Chelly Sandstone of Monument Valley on the Arizona-Utah border.

fact that these sandstones contain interbedded mudstones and siltstones "with some of the best known fossil dinosaur graveyards in North America, and it is extremely unlikely that dinosaurs could have lived in a desert environment or that the fossil beds could have been formed in any way except by flooding."[48] It is very unlikely that there are wind-formed deposits in the geological column anywhere, except in Pleistocene and recent deposits. Even the great deserts in the modern world (e.g. Mojave, Sahara) were under great water in the very recent past, geologically speaking. It is a fact that sand is formed by water erosion and transport.[49]

Creationists recognize that there is much research yet needed (as well as reinterpretation of already available research) to provide a full explanation of the formations in every geological column in terms of the biblical model. But much has been done, and it is very apparent that in each of the five areas considered above the recent creationist is able to interpret the data to fit his particular model very well. The arguments used to support an old-earth stance are not as airtight and intimidating as its proponents would

YES

NO

That all of these thick sandstones represent desert sand dune deposits is generally recognized by geologists on the basis of their spectacular cross-stratification, tracks of quadruped reptiles, and the frosting and pitting of the quartz sand grain surfaces that are so typical of wind-blown sand in modern desert dunes. In addition, the Navajo Sandstone achieves a thickness of two thousand feet at Zion National Park. Without question, it takes a long time for a desert to accumulate as much as two thousand feet of pure quartz sand, which in turn must have been very thoroughly weathered and eroded out of previously existing rocks.

Still further, these desert dune deposits are interlayered with hundreds of feet of shallow marine, river, and desert lake deposits. The transition from one environment alone to another is a lengthy process.

2. *Evidence from igneous rocks.* Igneous rocks form as extremely hot molten rock material (magma) cools and solidifies. These form on the earth's surface as extrusive rocks where magma is erupted from volcanoes

like to imagine and in each case are open to serious challenges based upon the given data in light of a biblical model.

Final Considerations

Several points need to be made when considering the age of the earth within the framework of modern scientific theory. From the hypothesis of evolution, which is assumed to be a very slow process, there is a demand for an old earth. But by contrast the believer in special creation can function with either an old earth or a young earth, as far as theoretical speculation is concerned.[50] P. Zimmerman noted:

> Thus the evolutionist needs a very old earth. His theory is utterly without hope if the earth is young. . . . On the other hand the creationist can operate with a young earth or a very ancient one. . . . The creationist does not need millions of years to make his theory workable. For the believer in creation the question is a different one: (1) What does the Bible say about the date of creation? (2) Is this information at variance with the facts brought to light by scientific research? These questions the creationist seeks to answer. . . . *Actually neither the scientist nor the*

YES

NO

in the form of ash or lava. They also form far underground as intrusive rocks where magma congeals in fractures into which it has been injected. The Cascade range of Oregon and Washington consists of an accumulation of extrusive lava flows and ash deposits that is thousands of feet thick. The Sierra Nevada mountains of California consist largely of granite that was solidified miles below, and subsequently uplifted to, the surface. Igneous rocks also occur in some of the world's great sedimentary basins. Shiprock, in northwestern New Mexico, is an old eroded volcano that penetrates through the sedimentary layers of the Colorado plateau.

Just as it takes time for a Thanksgiving turkey to cool once removed from the oven, so it takes time for hot magma to lose enough heat to solidify and even more time to cool to the temperature of its surroundings. If it takes a 350°-F turkey a lot longer to cool when placed in a 200°-F oven than when placed on the table at room temperature, we might expect that intrusive rocks will require far more time to solidify than volcanic rocks be-

creationist can fix the date of the beginning. The Bible permits certain general conclusions, but it does not give the age of the earth. The scientist in turn can make certain interesting calculations, but his computations are often interlarded with slippery assumptions, and the results are beclouded by serious questions that rise in the research.[51]

D. Young, an adherent of the old-earth model, is quick to denounce the doctrine of evolution as unscriptural and contends that it should be opposed.[52] He believes that the modern view that the earth is extremely old was developed by Christian men who believed wholeheartedly in creation and the flood and who were opposed to evolution. He says they came to their view not because of a preconceived evolutionary philosophy but because of their intimate knowledge of rocks gained over many years of thorough field study.[53] He observes the following:

Christians should not, however, attempt to disprove evolutionary theory by discrediting the antiquity of the Earth. Evolution and the antiquity of the Earth are two separate matters and while evolution falls if the antiquity of the Earth falls, it does not necessarily stand if the antiquity of the Earth stands.[54]

YES With this in mind it is interesting to note that almost all of the early Christian expositors believed in a young earth, a

---

NO cause the surroundings underground are much warmer than at the surface. Similarly, if a ten-pound turkey cools off a lot faster than a twenty-pound turkey, we might expect larger volumes of magma to take far more time to solidify than smaller volumes. Thus if observation of small lava lakes at the surface in Hawaii indicates that a few years are required for complete solidification, then we would expect that large underground intrusions would require much more time to cool.

Direct observation of such underground intrusions is not possible, but it is possible to make reasonable estimates of the amount of time that it takes for such intrusions to cool and solidify on the basis of theoretically derived equations of heat conduction. These equations require knowledge of size and shape of the igneous body and of the thermal properties of the magma and its surroundings. All the relevant thermal properties of both magma and the cooler rocks into which it is in-

fact attested to by Young himself.[55] This view was held on the basis of biblical exegesis alone, since "the prevailing view among the Greeks, the Egyptians, the Babylonians and other advanced nations of the world at the time, was that the world was very old, probably eternal."[56] Young also shows that the Church writings of the medieval and Reformation periods likewise adhered to a young earth, literal creation days, and a worldwide flood. This was especially true of Martin Luther and John Calvin. Thus historically, when the writings of Scripture were taken at face value, they have been understood as teaching recent creation and a global flood.[57]

The traditional view of Genesis 1:1-3, which has the support of the majority of Jewish and Christian interpreters, is as follows: Genesis 1:1 is a declaration that God created the original mass called heaven and earth out of nothing, and verse 2 is a clarification that when it came from the Creator's hand the mass was unformed and unfilled. From a grammatical perspective, verse 1 is taken as an independent clause and verse 2 contains three circum-

YES

NO

jected may be readily determined by laboratory experiment or calculated from knowledge of their chemical compositions. The size and shape of the igneous body can be determined from field studies.

Some examples of calculations of solidification times include the Palisade Sill in New Jersey (about 700 years), the Stillwater Igneous Complex of Montana (about 50,000 years), the Skaergaard Intrusion of Greenland (about 130,000 years), the Bushveld Complex of South Africa (about 200,000 years), and the Southern California Batholith (about one million years).[14] Given that many mountainous regions consist of thick deformed piles of sedimentary rock that have been injected by several large volumes of magma in sequence at several different times, it becomes clear that earth history cannot be restricted to less than ten thousand years.

3. *Evidence from metamorphic rocks.* Many of the rocks presently exposed at the earth's surface contain sets of minerals that form in solid rocks only at very high temperatures and, in some cases, high pressures.

stantial clauses describing the condition of the earth when it first came into existence.[58] J. Calvin wrote: "For Moses simply intends to assert that the world was not perfected at its commencement, in the manner in which it is now seen, but that it was created an empty chaos of heaven and earth."[59]

This view affirms that God existed before all, and then he created matter with its potential for life. It presents a strictly monotheistic view of the universe. Luther wrote the following:

> The plain and simple meaning of what Moses (here) says is that all things that exist were created by God and that at the beginning of the first day, God put into it the light so that the light of day was shining and the shapeless heaven and earth could be seen. This was not unlike *a shapeless, crude seed from which things can be generated and produced.*[60]

Both of the finite verbs in verses 1 and 2 are traditionally identified as perfects but might more accurately be termed suffixed conjugation verbs. The suffixed conjugation merely states the fact of the action or state and is thus tenseless.[61] These verses provide statements of fact and very

YES helpful background information for the main body of the

NO These so-called metamorphic rocks must have been far below the surface in order to experience the indicated pressures and temperatures. But other evidence (e.g., the presence of fossils or distinctive chemical composition) indicates that many of these metamorphic rocks must have originated as surficial sediments such as shale or sandstone before being deeply buried. Clearly the rock also had to be uplifted back to the surface where it is presently exposed.

Metamorphism of rocks, too, demands a lot of time. First, the originally sedimentary rocks must be buried several miles below the surface. As one example, mineralogical evidence from metamorphic rocks in the Coast Ranges of California indicates that the pressures on the rocks at the time of metamorphism were so great that the depths of burial must have been as much as twenty miles. Thus metamorphism requires the very time-consuming process of burying surficial rock to such great depths and then bringing it back up to the

text (1:3-31), which is begun with a *wayyiqṭōl* form of the verb normally employed to indicate progress or sequence.[62] Of course the amount of time between the creation in verse 1 and God's command in verse 3 cannot be determined. The structure used here, employing suffixed conjugation verbs as the basis for the following narrative introduced by the *wayyiqṭōl* form, is common throughout Genesis (e.g. chapters 37 and 39). The information contained in verses 1 and 2 is logically and sequentially prior to the events of verses 3 and following. Even if the verb in verse 2 would be translated "became," this would not necessarily imply something negative—which could only be determined from other considerations, such as the meaning of the terms "formless" and "empty."

One last consideration relates to the genealogies contained in Genesis 5 and 11. It must be acknowledged that there are gaps in these genealogies. W. H. Green has demonstrated that abridgment is the key to all biblical genealogies.[63] But this does not prove that the gaps in chapters 5 and 11 are elastic enough to allow for an early-earth stance with its attendant four or five billion years for which to ac-

YES

NO

surface. As the rock is being buried, however, it must also be heated in order to achieve the temperatures, as high as 750° C (1382° F), indicated by the minerals.

Once again the principles of heat conduction suggest that volumes of hundreds to thousands of cubic miles of metamorphic rock would require tens to hundreds of thousands of years to be heated to these high temperatures. Then, once having been heated, the rock must be cooled again to surface temperature as the material is uplifted from great depths to the surface.

4. *Radiometric evidence.* The cumulative weight of such lines of evidence in every geological terrain around the world has led to the consensus in the geological community that the planet has experienced a vast history. None of these evidences, however, permits precise dating of any geological event or the age of the earth. Thus although geologists during the past two centuries have recognized the great antiquity of the earth, they were able to make only crude estimates of

count. Certainly there are gaps in Matthew 1:1: "The book of the generation of Jesus Christ, the son of David, the son of Abraham." But the time is only approximately one thousand years for each gap.

It should be noted that evidence concerning man's occupation on the earth is very brief in light of the fact that writing and history begin at Sumer around 3400 B.C. Also, archeological evidence can really only be affirmed back to about 10,000 B.C. And with an understanding of a universal flood that would have destroyed all evidence of the previous world, the genealogy of Genesis 11 and its attendant gaps cannot be very substantial. It would only be speculation to pick the amount of time for the period from Adam to Noah and his sons in Genesis 5. It is interesting that there is a symmetry between the genealogies contained in chapters 5 and 11 in form and structure. Other gaps such as

YES

NO

its age until this century. The discovery of radioactivity in 1896 opened up the possibility of precise dating. A wide variety of radiometric methods for the dating of rocks and minerals has been developed throughout the twentieth century. While some methods were eventually abandoned because of various inadequacies, several methods—including the K-Ar, Rb-Sr, Sm-Nd, and U-Th-Pb methods—have become well established, thoroughly tested, internally and externally consistent, reliable methods that repeatedly yield meaningful results.[15]

The basic assumptions of the methods are well understood and pose no threat to their validity. Dozens of laboratories around the world routinely produce thousands of consistent mineral and rock dates that are tens to hundreds of millions and, in some cases, billions of years. Moreover the results are consistent with the relative ages of rocks as determined from field relationships.

Although there is no known means for any direct determination of the age of the earth by radiometric dating, it is possible to calculate the age of the earth from theoretical equations of radioactive decay.[16] Such cal-

those between Amram and Moses, and between Joram and Uzziah, were three hundred and fifty years, not thirty thousand and five thousand (cf. Exod. 6:20; Num. 3:17-19, 27-28; Matt. 1:8).

Considering the fact that mankind is the climax of God's creation, it is rather inconceivable that the earth is four or five billion years old but that man is only a recent fixture. Why would God take so long before he made man in his own image to have fellowship with him? Psalm 33:6 gives the impression that the world was made rather quickly. It seems clear to this writer that the simplest and most logical way to interpret Genesis 1 coincides with the recent creationist's viewpoint, for as Erickson comments about this approach: "The ideal-time theory is ingenious and in many ways irrefutable *both scientifically and exegetically*."[64]

R. L. Harris' appeal many years ago seems quite apropos:

> I am appalled at the freedom with which our Christian scientists are toying with the Biblical texts. I may soften that by adding that our theologians are doing so too and so the scientists naturally are taking it up. But the scientists should have a chance to hear the criticisms of various theologians rather than jumping to the first far out exegesis of Genesis that seems to meet the scientific need.[65]

YES

NO

culations yield about 4.55 billion years as the age of the earth. This result is consistent with direct determinations of the age of the oldest known terrestrial rocks (3.7–3.9 billion years). This result is also consistent with direct radiometric determinations of the age of several meteorites. Dating by the Rb-Sr method yields ages of 4.5–4.6 billion years. Similarly, the calculated age of the moon is about 4.6 billion years.[17] Available radiometric evidence indicates that the solar system formed a little more than 4.5 billion years ago.

Conclusion

Interpretation of Genesis 1 as a theological statement that does not address scientific questions leaves completely open the issue of the age of the earth. Geological evidence accumulated over the past three hundred years overwhelmingly indicates that the planet has experienced a dynamic history measurable in billions of years.

ENDNOTES

YES

1. Those who have written in favor of an old-earth view include G. L. Archer, "A Response to The Trustworthiness of Scripture in Areas Relating to Natural Science," in *Hermeneutics, Inerrancy, and the Bible* (ed. R. D. Preus and E. D. Radmacher; Grand Rapids: Zondervan, 1984) 321–34; W. L. Bradley and R. Olsen, "The Trustworthiness of Scripture in Areas Relating to Natural Science," in ibid., 285–317 (which has an excellent summary of the various views of the interpretation of *yôm* ["day"] in Genesis 1); R. C. Newman and H. J. Eckelmann, Jr., *Genesis One and the Origin of the Earth* (Downers Grove: InterVarsity, 1977; reprint Grand Rapids: Baker, 1981); P. P. T. Pun, *Evolution: Nature and Scripture in Conflict?* (Grand Rapids: Zondervan, 1982); D. E. Wonderly, *God's Time-Records in Ancient Sediments* (Flint: Crystal, 1977; see also his Appendix 1, "Nonradiometric Data Relevant to the Question of Age," in Newman and Eckelmann, *Genesis One*); D. A. Young, *Creation and the Flood* (Grand Rapids: Baker, 1977); *Christianity and the Age of the Earth* (Grand Rapids: Zondervan, 1982). Only a few recent works are cited in favor of a recent creation or young earth: D. B. DeYoung, "Christianity and the Age of the Earth: A Review Article," *Grace Theological Journal* 4/2 (Fall 1983) 297–301; R. V. Gentry, "Radiohalos in a Radiochronological and Cosmological Perspective," *Science* (April 5, 1974) 62–66; M. L. Lubenow, "Does a Proper Interpretation of Scripture Require a Recent Creation," *Impact* (November 1978); H. M. Morris, "A Response to The Trustworthiness of Scripture in Areas Relating to Natural Science," in *Hermeneutics* (ed. Preus and Radmacher) 337–48; *Science, Scripture and the Young Earth* (El Cajon: Institute for Creation Research, 1983); *The Scientific Case for Creation* (San Diego: Creation–Life, 1977); R. Niessen, "Starlight and the Age of the Universe," *Impact* (July 1983); B. Setterfield, "The Velocity of Light and the Age of the Universe," *Ex Nihilo* 1 (1982) 52–93; J. C. Whitcomb, "Creation and Science and the Physical Universe: A Review Article," in *Grace Theological Journal* 4/2 (Fall 1983) 289–96. An excellent article tracing the conflict between science and theology in the nineteenth century is J. D. Hannah, "*Bibliotheca Sacra* and Darwinism: An Analysis of the Nineteenth-Century Conflict Between Science and Theology," *Grace Theological Journal* 4/1 (Spring 1983) 37–58.

2. F. R. Howe, "The Age of the Earth: An Appraisal of Some Current Evangelical Positions, Part 2," *Bibliotheca Sacra* 142 (April-June 1985) 128.

3. M. J. Erickson, *Christian Theology* (Grand Rapids: Baker, 1983), 1, 378, citing A. D. White, *A History of the Warfare of Science with Theology in Christendom* (New York: Dover, 1960).

4. Ibid., 378.

5. F. R. Howe, "The Age of the Earth: An Appraisal of Some Current Evangelical Positions, Part 1," *Bibliotheca Sacra* 142 (January-March 1985) 23.

6. Ibid.

7. D. A. Young, *Christianity*, 64 (italics mine).

8. Newman and Eckelmann, *Genesis One*.

9. Pun, *Evolution*.

10. Wonderly, *God's Time-Records*.

11. Young, *Christianity*.

12. Howe, "Age, Part 1," 33–34.

13. See also Newman and Eckelmann, *Genesis One*, 9–53, and Appendix 1 ("Nonradiometric Data Relevant to the Question of Age" by D. E. Wonderly, 89–103).

14. Howe, "Age, Part 2," 115 (italics mine).

15. Bradley and Olsen, "Trustworthiness," 302–04.

16. Newman and Eckelmann, *Genesis One*, 30–34.

17. Young, *Christianity*, 93–116.

18. R. E. Kofahl and K. L. Segraves, *The Creation Explanation* (Wheaton: Harold Shaw, 1975) 183 (italics mine).

19. Ibid., 211–12 (italics mine).

20. E. C. Myers, *Constructing a Creationist Geology* (master's thesis, Dallas Theological Seminary, May 1984) 27–28. He concluded "that the reliability of quantitative chronological findings is tempered by environmental effects. It is also tempered by the susceptibility of the relevant chronometric system to actual physical alteration in the pre-observational past."

21. This is a summary by N. L. Geisler in *The Creator in the Courtroom: "Scopes II"* (Milford: Mott Media, 1982) 154. Gentry was said to have also noted that similar experiments on polonium haloes found in coalified wood led him to postulate that the wood had been buried during a huge deluge and had turned rapidly to coal rather than very slowly, as evolutionary assumptions would predict. Gentry gave several examples of geologists who responded to his research simply by saying it must be wrong because if it were right it would require them to rethink all their theories about the age of the earth and the formation of the earth's geology (p. 155).

22. Howe, "Age, Part 2," 125.

23. Young, *Christianity*, 151.

24. J. C. Dillow, *The Waters Above: Earth's Pre-Flood Vapor Canopy* (rev. ed.; Chicago: Moody, 1982) 221–66.

25. H. W. Clark, *Fossils, Flood, and Fire* (Escondido: Outdoor Pictures, 1968).

26. J. W. Klotz, *Genes, Genesis, and Evolution* (St. Louis: Concordia, 1970) 114 (italics mine). His n. 59 is a reference to P. V. Smith, Jr., "The Occurrence of Hydrocarbons in Recent Sediments from the Gulf of Mexico," *Science* 116 (1952) 437–39.

27. Morris, *Science, Scripture and the Young Earth*, 15.

28. F. B. Jueneman, "Secular Catastrophism," *Industrial Research and Development* (June 1982) 21 (italics mine).

29. Newman and Eckelmann, *Genesis One*, 16.

30. Howe, "Age, Part 2," 119.

31. Niessen, "Starlight," iv (italics mine).

32. Newman and Eckelmann, *Genesis One*, 21.

33. Ibid., 28.

34. Morris, *Science, Scripture and the Young Earth*, 8. Nevins' work is entitled "Is the Capitan Limestone a Fossil Reef?" in *Speak to the Earth* (ed. G. E. Howe; Philadelphia: Presbyterian and Reformed, 1975) 16–59. Other leading geologists who are not creationists have come to similar conclusions about this and other fossil reefs; cf. e.g. C. J. R. Braithwaite, "Reefs: Just a Problem of Semantics?", *Bulletin of the American Association of Petroleum Geologists* 57 (June 1973) 1105.

35. H. Blatt, G. Middleton, and R. Murray, *Origin of Sedimentary Rocks* (Englewood Cliffs: Prentice-Hall, 1972) 410. As far as present living reefs are concerned, these have been shown to consist of a more or less superficial veneer of true coral growing on the surface of a noncoral base.

36. Cited in Braithwaite, "Reefs," 1108.

37. Morris, *Science, Scripture and the Young Earth*, 10.

38. Ibid.

39. Young, *Christianity*, 86–88, 91, 146.

40. V. I. Sozansky, "Geological Notes: Origin of Salt Deposits in Deep-Water Basins of Atlantic Ocean," *Bulletin of the American Association of Petroleum Geologists* 57 (March 1973) 590.

41. Ibid.

42. V. B. Porfirev, *Bulletin of the American Association of Petroleum Geologists* 58 (December 1974) 2543.

43. Morris, *Science, Scripture and the Young Earth*, 12–13. It was noted that even in modern lakes the so-called varves may well be formed by catastrophic turbid water underflows, with many being actually formed annually; cf. A. Lambert and K. J. Hsu, "Non-Annual Cycles of Varve-like Sedimentation in Walensee, Switzerland," *Sedimentology* 26 (1979) 453–61.

44. Morris, *Science, Scripture and the Young Earth*, 13.

45. Ibid. The work by J. F. Lindsay, "Carboniferous Subaquaeous Mass-movement in the Manning-Macleay Basin, Kempsey, New South Wales," *Journal of Sedimentary Petrology* 36 (1966) 719–32, was cited.

46. W. E. Freeman and G. S. Visher, "Stratigraphic Analysis of the Navajo Sandstone," *Journal of Sedimentary Petrology* 45 (1975) 651–68.

47. L. Brand, "Field and Laboratory Studies on the Coconino Sandstone (Permian) Vertebrate Footprints and their Paleoecological Implications," *Paleogeography, Paleoclimatology, Paleoecology* 28 (1979) 25–38.

48. Morris, *Science, Scripture and the Young Earth*, 14.

49. Ibid.

50. Howe, "Age, Part 1," 27.

51. P. A. Zimmerman, "The Age of the Earth," in *Darwin, Evolution and Creation* (ed. P. A. Zimmerman; St. Louis: Concordia, 1959) 144–45.

52. Young, *Christianity*, 66.

53. Ibid., 66–67.

54. Ibid.

55. Ibid., 19–23.

56. Morris, *Science, Scripture and the Young Earth*, 5.

57. Ibid.

58. B. K. Waltke, "The Creation Account in Genesis 1:1–3. Part III:

The Initial Chaos Theory and the Precreation Chaos Theory," *Bibliotheca Sacra* 132 (July-September 1975) 216.

59. J. Calvin, *A Commentary on Genesis* (London: Banner of Truth, 1965) 69.

60. M. Luther, *Luther's Commentary on Genesis* (Grand Rapids: Zondervan, 1958) 9.

61. W. L. Moran, *A Syntactical Study of the Dialect of Byblos as Reflected in the Amarna Tablets* (Ann Arbor: University Microfilms, 1967) 39. He notes that the perfect was originally a nominal sentence with personal pronominal elements affixed to a stem *qatal/qatil/qatul*. A nominal sentence is tenseless, the tense deriving from the context in any given case. The essence of the perfect is thus to predicate of the pronominal afformative the state (usually *qatil/qatul*) or the action (*qatal*) expressed by the respective stem. The perfect does not say anything of present, past, or future. It does not say whether the action or state is completed or not completed. It merely states the fact of the occurrence of the action or the existence of the state (35–36).

62. T. J. Finley, "The WAW-Consecutive with 'Imperfect' in Biblical Hebrew: Theoretical Studies and Its Use in Amos," in *Tradition and Testament. Essays in Honor of Charles Lee Feinberg* (ed. J. S. and P. D. Feinberg; Chicago: Moody, 1981) 252.

63. W. H. Green, "Primeval Chronology," in *Classical Evangelical Essays in Old Testament Interpretation* (ed. W. C. Kaiser, Jr.; Grand Rapids: Baker, 1972) 13–28. The idea of the presence of gaps in biblical genealogies is an accepted fact in evangelical scholarship. J. J. Davis says the flood might have "occurred anywhere from 18,000 to 15,000 B.C., although it may have been slightly later, depending on the accuracy of the dates assigned to Mesolithic and Neolithic sites"; this may not be the 4004 B.C. date assigned by Ussher, but it is not the 100 million to 24 million years of the evolutionary geologists either (*Paradise to Prison* [Grand Rapids: Baker, 1975] 31). J. C. Whitcomb and H. Morris, *The Genesis Flood* (Philadelphia: Presbyterian and Reformed, 1968) 474–89, give some helpful guidelines for determining the nature of the gaps and the possible amount of time involved.

64. Erickson, *Christian Theology*, 1, 382 (italics mine).

65. R. L. Harris, "Letter to the Editor," *Journal of the American Scientific Affiliation* 16 (December 1964) 127.

NO

1. The literature of the "creation science" or "scientific creationism" movement is replete with fallacious arguments of a purported scientific character. Among the more widely used arguments are those based on magnetic dipole moment field decay, an alleged shrinking sun, alleged thin layer of lunar soil, or supposed flood origin of sedimentary rocks.

2. W. H. Green, "Primeval Chronology," *Bibliotheca Sacra* 47 (1890) 285–303.

3. The gap theory maintains that the original perfect creation described in Gen. 1:1 lasted an indefinite amount of time sufficient to accommodate the billions of years of geological history. This original creation fell into a state of ruin and desolation through some kind of

catastrophe, as suggested by the translation of Gen. 1:2 employing "became" rather than "was." The six days of Genesis 1 are days of re-creation and reconstruction of the earth rather than original creation days. The day-age theory claims that the days are periods of time of indeterminate length on the basis of the idea that the seventh day of God's rest is still continuing. Indefinitely long days allow for harmonization with the billions of years of geological history. The sequence of events in Genesis 1 is said to correspond in broad outline to the sequence of events discovered by geology. The revelation-day theory says that the days of Genesis 1 are ordinary twenty-four-hour days in the experience of a prophet or seer who received successive revelations from God about the creative events. The days have nothing to do with how long it took for creation to occur, and thus this view is compatible with an ancient earth.

4. See e.g. M. G. Kline, "Because It Had Not Rained," *Westminster Theological Journal* 20 (1958) 146–57; H. Blocher, *In the Beginning* (Downers Grove: InterVarsity, 1984); C. Hyers, *The Meaning of Creation* (Atlanta: John Knox, 1984) 1–114; G. F. Hasel, "The Polemic Nature of the Genesis Cosmology," *The Evangelical Quarterly* 46 (1974) 81–102; B. Waltke, "The Creation Account in Genesis 1:1–3," *Bibliotheca Sacra* 132 (1975) 327–42.

5. For an excellent rebuttal of the magnetic field argument used by scientific creationists, consult G. B. Dalrymple, "Can the Earth be Dated from Decay of its Magnetic Field?", *Journal of Geological Education* 31 (1983) 124–33.

6. S. R. Taylor, *Planetary Science: A Lunar Perspective* (Houston: Lunar and Planetary Institute, 1982) 118–19.

7. For more detail on the development of geological ideas about the antiquity of the earth the reader should consult C. C. Albritton, *The Abyss of Time* (San Francisco: Freeman, Cooper, 1980); S. Toulmin and J. Goodfield, *The Discovery of Time* (New York: Harper, 1965); D. A. Young, *Christianity and the Age of the Earth* (Grand Rapids: Zondervan, 1982) 13–54. The reader should be aware that very many of the "founding fathers" of modern "old-earth" geology were active Christians.

8. The thicknesses of layers are measured perpendicular to the layering. For a popular introduction to the geology of the Colorado plateau see D. L. Baars, *The Colorado Plateau* (Albuquerque: University of New Mexico, 1983).

9. Relief is the difference in elevation between the highest and lowest point in an area. An area with high relief is generally rugged, while one with low relief is rather gentle. As an example, a prominent unconformity displayed toward the bottom of the Grand Canyon has a relief as much as eight hundred feet.

10. As e.g. at the profound angular unconformity between the horizontal Tapeats Sandstone and underlying tilted Unkar/Chuar Groups toward the bottom of the Grand Canyon. This unconformity is plainly visible on the north wall of the canyon when viewed from Lipan Point or Desert View on the south rim.

11. See M. A. Biot, "Theory of Folding of Stratified Viscoelastic Media and Its Implications in Tectonics and Orogenesis," *Geological Society of America Bulletin* 72 (1961) 1595–1620.

12. For a brief popular discussion of some aspects of the Green River Formation see A. Feduccia, "*Presbyornis* and the Evolution of Ducks and Flamingos," *American Scientist* 66 (1978) 298–304. None of the nu-

merous geologists who have studied the details of the Green River Formation has ever been persuaded of anything other than long-lasting lake origin.

13. For more detailed discussions of reconstruction of sedimentary environments see e.g. H. E. Reineck and I. B. Singh, *Depositional Sedimentary Environments* (2d ed.; New York: Springer-Verlag, 1980); A. D. Miall, *Principles of Sedimentary Basin Analysis* (New York: Springer-Verlag, 1984) 133–212.

14. For references to those calculations see D. A. Young, *Creation and the Flood* (Grand Rapids: Baker, 1977); D. Norton and H. P. Taylor, "Quantitative Simulation of the Hydrothermal Systems of Crystallizing Magmas on the Basis of Transport Theory and Oxygen Isotope Data: An Analysis of the Skaergaard Intrusion," *Journal of Petrology* 20 (1979) 421–86.

15. See G. Faure, *Principles of Isotope Geology* (New York: John Wiley, 1977), for details of the various methods. Those who are conversant with the methods recognize that the criticisms of young-earth advocates are without substance.

16. See the discussion of Patterson's treatment of the Holmes-Houtermans model for calculating the age of the earth in Faure, *Principles,* 227–31.

17. For lunar data see Taylor, *Planetary,* 233–42. For a summary of some meteorite data see Faure, *Principles,* 107–11, 229–31.

4   *Was Evolution Involved*

in the Process of Creation?

YES: MARK HILLMER

The idea that evolution was indeed involved in creation
has escaped notice for centuries because the cosmos appears to be changeless. But change there is, hidden behind
a mask of permanence due to a mind-boggling slowness.
By faith I call this process creation. And it is more than
merely substituting the term *creation* for evolution. I stand
with those who believe that the process in the "great chain
of being" is meaningful and purposeful and that it has a direction.

NO: JOHN N. MOORE

Primary for any consideration of first-origin questions is forthright acknowledgment that the methods of
professional scientists are limited. Particularly, professional scientists are limited to application of their
methods and procedures to study of the present conditions of the physical environment during their lifetime.
Or, stated in another way, scientists utilize their proper,
orderly procedures of repeatable observation, experimentation, and explanation only with respect to natu-

How have I come to this conclusion? I am not an expert in any of the applicable natural sciences. My training is in Bible, and though I have been looking over the shoulders of some scientists, most of what I will have to say is on the nature of the biblical narrative and its implications.

There is only space to deal with the first chapter of Genesis in this short essay, although chapters 2 (the second creation account) and 6—9 (the flood story) are also involved in this question.

This passage is not a modern scientific treatise. Virtually all the furor over the debate between science and the Bible is due to an erroneous interpretation that says that these passages yield eternally valid facts about how things came to be.

This passage can be summed up in a few words: It is an-

YES

NO

rally occurring objects and/or events in the immediately present environment. They research only the natural environment.

Therefore qualified scientists do not discuss first-origin questions as professional scientists but as natural philosophers, expressing themselves on metaphysical topics. Such modern natural philosophers really concern themselves about the nature of essential or ultimate reality (even assuming implicitly or explicitly that matter is eternal). This is so because the origin of the universe, the origin of life on the earth, and the origin of human beings did not occur in the "present" of any professionally trained observer. Such first origins occurred in the distant past. Furthermore, those origins are not repeatable but are past singularities that remain forever beyond application of scientific methods and procedures.

The reader should also be helped to avoid any ambiguities with respect to the words "evolution," "creation," and "process."

Quite often one finds the term "evolution" associated with any unfolding or with a change from one state or condition to another. Such a broad meaning for "evolution" is not useful in discussions of questions about origin. Thus authors have the responsibility to help others discern specifically the magnitude of change meant

cient, confessional knowledge, largely expressed in metaphor.

Genesis 1 Is Ancient

Ancient literature may indeed express some things unforgettably well, but modern scientific thought is not among the things addressed. To take an example from another culture: For all that Plato and Aristotle contributed to philosophy and science, they can hardly be expected to have much to say to the modern scientist in the laboratory. An ancient document may be studied and revered. But to study and revere a text is one thing; to make all reality conform to it is another.

YES   An additional point follows from the antiquity of Genesis. If the first chapter of the Bible dates from several centu-

---

NO   anytime the word "evolution" is used relevant to stars, galaxies, animals, plants, or even human beings.

Authors should always make explicitly clear whether the magnitude of change intended is of limited range or of broad range. With regard to changes observed in living things (or changes presumed in fossils), the practical and necessary clarification gained by use of "macro-evolution" and/or "micro-evolution" will be treated in the next section.

However, further clarification about "creation" and "process" must be presented here. The latter term reasonably involves a time span. A process might be continuous and slow or sudden and rapid. It might be small and limited or complex and multifacted. Nevertheless in each variant magnitude of change some time span would be involved.

Thus each process has a "history," and to apply the term "process" to all changes that ever occurred in the universe is essentially meaningless. Based upon the prior-mentioned limitation of application of proper, orderly scientific procedures to the present natural environment, "history" most conveniently refers to activities and involvements of human beings who make observations and measurements and who conduct experiments (processes).

From this position follows the conclusion that first-origin questions entailing use of the words "evolution"

ries B.C., it is not fair to compare it to documents written in the twentieth century. For example, no country would want its generals to wage war on the pattern of fighting described in Homer's *Iliad*. Again, one would hardly go to a medical doctor if one discovered that the doctor was using methods described on Old Babylonian cuneiform texts. Then why do we expect Genesis 1 to give clear guidance in matters of geology, biology, and astronomy?

I suppose one might expect full and final information on all things in the Bible if one believed that the Bible were God's last word. But what if the Bible is God's first word?[1]

The proper understanding of a text is its own context, and the context of the Old Testament is not today's scientific laboratory but the ancient Near East.

Genesis 1 Is Confessional

It has been observed for some time in biblical study that the creation account in Genesis 1 is only a slightly more **YES**

---

and "creation" involve "prehistory." Consequently questions about human ancestry, the beginning of life on the earth, and the origin of the cosmos are identified as prehistorical. **NO**

To inquire about the origin of stars, of living substance, or of human beings necessarily focuses one's attention upon some time span prior to human observers. Therefore proper, orderly methods and procedures of professional scientists cannot be applied to prehistorical objects and/or events.

And what is meant by "creation"? To avoid unnecessary ambiguity the reader should be willing to agree that "creation" might pertain to a process and/or to an end product. So "creation process" may be ambiguous, and authors have the responsibility to make clear what is intended: process or product.

As process, "creation" can refer to application of artistic talents, imaginative writing, or creative acts of the Creator. Of course in the latter case finite, limited human beings are forever unable to study or know the "how" or "when" of the Creator's work. The ways of God, the Creator of all things, are past finding out.

In contrast, "creation" as finished, as end product, is quite possible to study. An after-the-fact application of

orderly praise to the God of creation than are several of the Psalms. When the author of Psalm 8 takes a "look at thy heavens, the work of thy fingers, the moon and the stars which thou hast established" and ends with "O LORD, our Lord, how majestic is thy name in all the earth!" he is obviously praising God for creation. It is in the same spirit that Genesis 1:16 should be read: "And God made the two great lights, the greater light to rule the day, and the lesser light to rule the night; he made the stars also." Like the author of Psalm 8, the author of Genesis 1 is first and foremost praising God.

Creation statements in Psalm 104 like "Thou didst set the earth on its foundations, so that it should never be shaken" are surrounded by summonses to praise like "Bless the LORD, O my soul." Genesis 1:1, "In the begin-

YES

NO

proper, orderly methods and procedures of repeated observation, experimentation, and explanation of naturally occurring objects and/or events is quite possible. Such is the work of professional scientists. But any inquiries about before-the-fact existence of present, natural conditions necessarily partakes of metaphysical formulations and should not be confused by the reader with proper scientific theories[1] about atoms, molecules, or genes.

Must One Distinguish Between Macro-evolution and Micro-evolution?

Yes. Because of real and imagined changes necessarily entailed in any use of the term "evolution," macro-evolution should be distinguished from micro-evolution. Several specific patterns of expressions involving these concepts will be helpful to the reader.

As previously mentioned, anytime the word "evolution" is employed so as to convey the meaning of some change, each author has the responsibility of helping others discern the actual magnitude of change intended. Again, authors should always make explicitly clear whether the magnitude of change intended is of limited range or of broad range. For purposes of the present discussion limited-range change may be conveniently designated "micro-evolution" whereas broad-

ning God created the heavens and the earth," is not preceded by "Bless the Lord." But it might as well have been, because Genesis 1 is intended as praise of Israel's God and not as a textbook on astronomy.

When the psalmist in Psalm 139 describes human origins with the words, "For thou didst form my inward parts, thou didst knit me together in my mother's womb" (verse 13), there is an immediate transition to praise: "I praise thee, for thou art fearful and wonderful. Wonderful are thy works!" (verse 14). There is no similar praise in Genesis 2:7: "Then the LORD God formed man of dust from the ground, and breathed into his nostrils the breath of life"— but these words were meant to be read or sung by the be-

YES

NO

range change is designated "macro-evolution."

Or, to express the matter another way, micro-evolution is the most precise term associated with the magnitude of horizontal change *within* a group of living things, while macro-evolution is the most precise term associated with some amount of supposed vertical change *between* living things from one level of complexity to another.

The word "supposed" is used deliberately in association with the concept of vertical change of macro-evolution since such a concept is totally imagined and unobservable, at least with respect to any change in living things from one level of complexity of flora and fauna to another level. In contrast, horizontal change of micro-evolution is repeatedly observable by any investigator of present living animals and plants.

To further clarify this terminology the following sets of contrasting specifications about "evolution" will be useful to the reader:

Micro-evolution magnitude of change (limited-range change) has been repeatedly detected within any separate group of easily recognizable animals or plants. For example, within the common groups of dogs, cats, swine, or cattle on the one hand, or of apples, roses, corn, or wheat on the other hand, breeding records are the basis for the statement that horizontal change (micro-evolution) is fully documented. Furthermore a definite time line of properly historical nature is identifi-

lieving congregation. They were not meant primarily as essays on anthropology.

There is science in these early chapters of Genesis, but science in its infancy.

Genesis 1 Contains Phenomenological Terminology

If one wants to be faithful to the words of Scripture, one is driven to accept as phenomenological language what may appear to be literal language. One has only to conjure up the name of Galileo to remind oneself that this early scientist was put under house arrest by the Church because his findings ("The earth moves, not the sun") flatly contradicted the plain sense of Scripture ("The sun stood still," Josh. 10:13). One can easily enough preserve the Joshua passage from ridicule by saying, "That is how it looked

YES

NO

able because of the long accumulations of generations and generations of observed changes in these living things. Therefore limited, horizontal, micro-evolution change is real.

However, macro-evolution magnitude of change (broad-range change) between separate groups of easily recognizable animals and plants has not been detected. No known cross-breeding has ever occurred between fully separate groups of organisms. For example, the proposed or supposed change from one-celled to multi-celled organization in living things has not been observed at all in breeding practices. Any vertical change (macro-evolution), such as mammals coming from amphibians or birds from reptiles or human beings from some anthropoid group, are fully unobservable in the present and thus must be acknowledged as deduced ideas about the prehistorical and are, consequently, concepts that are not at all testable or documented genetically. Therefore broad, vertical, macro-evolution change is imagined, or at best supported only by evidence of circumstantial similarities of unexplained origin.

Micro-evolution magnitude of change (limited-range change) that has been repeatedly observed is essentially that of genetic variation within limits of an easily

then." In point of fact we still refer to the sun's rising and setting. But this is due to our poetic recognition of what is apparent. We would not seriously expect the astronomer to use our phenomenological language as a scientific basis.

Before looking at Genesis 1 in detail, let me say what I take evolution to be. I understand evolution to be a far-ranging, scientific theory about the origin and nature of the world. The most general definition of evolution is as follows: "The current state of a system is the result of a more or less continual change from its original state."[2] It is far-ranging in that it covers so many disciplines that no one person can be competent in all the various branches of knowledge affected by it.

Evolution is scientific in that it is a child of the post-Enlightenment mind, which is not deterred by any tradition in its pursuit of truth. That also implies that it is self-critical,

YES

NO

recognized animal or plant group. For example, varieties of camillias, lilacs, horses, and sheep are repeatedly documented along the historical time line of multiple breeding records of practical breeding and domestication by human beings.

However, there is no repeatable breeding record to support the idea that macro-evolution magnitude of change (broad-range change) has ever occurred through a vertical, unlimited dimension in the distant past such that one easily recognized group was ancestral to another easily recognized group in a continuous or discontinuous manner. For example, no known genetic connection can be established between starfish and frogs, between salamanders and snakes, between reptiles and birds, or between any mammal and human beings. No genetic connection can be documented between separate, easily recognizable groups of animals and plants. Again, unobservable macro-evolution change is prehistorical and at best supported only by evidence of circumstantial similarities of unexplained origin.

From all of the above, therefore, a broad generalization can be drawn that all easily recognizable animals and plants, whether living or dead, are distinct and discrete. Absolutely no so-called "transitional" forms exist

not even allowing its own tradition to stand in the way of knowledge. As soon as the pursuit of the notion of evolution refuses to be critical of itself it becomes evolutionism.

Evolution is a theory. A theory is a hypothesis that has been repeatedly verified by experiment. A fact is that which can be reproduced in the laboratory. Since much of evolution is a reading of ancient fossils and an examination of distant stars, evolution cannot be called a fact. (It is hard to reproduce ancient fossils or create a star in the laboratory.) But it is far more than "just a theory." It is the best explanation of the origin and structure of the cosmos and of planet earth that there is. If a better one comes along, someone will find it. Meanwhile it is one of the most widely accepted theories in science.[3]

YES   The old battle fought over evolution in the 1930s is being warmed up again by people who call themselves creation-

---

NO   according to carefully accumulated genetic data. There are basic, genetically unbridgeable gaps between all easily recognized different animals and plants. There is no scientific validity to the attractive, age-old concept of a "great chain of being."

Any proposal that *Archaeopteryx* or the duck-billed platypus are such transitional organisms is special pleading. They are only organisms with detectable characteristics of more than one classification group. Each, however, is a distinct organism, and the platypus is assuredly discretely separated genetically from any other living organism. Only a platypus comes from the mating of platypus pairs—that is, horizontal, micro-evolution-magnitude change. And the "fixed," unchangeable aspects of the gingko, coelacanth fish, and many other organisms are fully explainable as exemplary of horizontal, limited-range, micro-evolution-magnitude change.[2]

Are Evolution and Creation Necessarily Mutually Exclusive?

Yes. In view of proper definitions of the terms, evolution and creation are necessarily mutually exclusive.

Creation, meaning the creative acts of God, the Creator of all things, definitely involves and necessarily en-

ists. I consider their attempts to argue for a special creation between 10,000 and 6000 B.C. to be a total misreading of the evidence. Their work is essentially negative, and their reconstructions are harder to believe than the evolution they are opposing. Where their work crosses my field of expertise, the Hebrew Scriptures, they offer me instead of an ancient document a perennially valid description of the way things came to be.

Everyone who works with the idea of evolution admits that there are gaps in the theory. Darwin recognized the sparseness of fossil evidence and bemoaned it.[4] And even though much more evidence has come to light since Darwin's day, the famous gaps persist.[5] Evolution says that there has been a development from simpler to more complex forms, even to the changing of one species into another. Much circumstantial evidence exists.

An interesting variation on evolution has emerged from the work of French scientist L. Vialleton. He posits three

YES

NO

tails the supernatural. All finite human beings are completely unable to explain the origin of the cosmos, life on the earth, or human beings in any fully naturalistic manner. As stated, such concepts of first origin are singularities that occurred in the past, in the prehistorical. Therefore careful, proper application of methods and procedures of repeated observation, experimentation, and explanation is fully impossible.

It is true that some authorities maintain that evolution and creation are not mutually exclusive. But they do so at great risk of loss of rigor of intelligent, rational investigation. Such authorities are willing to practice ambiguity in their expressions about evolution. Commonly evolution is taken to mean any change, and some authorities are seemingly unwilling to utilize the prefixes micro- and macro- in any practiced manner in speaking and writing about evolution. Hence semantic confusion is perpetrated and compounded in most treatments of origin questions in the mass media — and even in prestigious scientific journals.

Perpetuation of ambiguous use of the term "evolution" and repeated failure to employ the practical prefixes micro- and macro- results too commonly in

kinds of evolution: (1) micro-evolution, which is limited to a "slow variation" among the lower forms of life (sub-species, species and genera) operating continuously; (2) macro-evolution, also continuous but limited to genera and families; and (3) mega-evolution, a discontinuous quantum evolution concerning the higher systematic groupings such as families, orders, and above. (Sometimes in evolutionary circles macro- and mega-evolution are equated.)[6]

These distinctions offer hope of harmonizing science and the Bible only to those who view the Bible as God's last word on science rather than as God's first word on salvation (among others). In other words, one who reads Genesis as literal fact rather than as doxological metaphor could

YES possibly harmonize Genesis 1 with the evolutionary theory by accepting a microscopic, molecular evolution while de-

---

NO uncritical mixing of theism with practical atheism as well as of supernatural concepts (creative acts of God) with supposed natural concepts (actually macro-evolution magnitude of change). Thus the contradictory, illogical combinations of "theistic evolution" and "progressive creationism" have been coined.

Is There a Difference Between Evolution and Evolutionism?

Yes. There is a significant difference between these terms.

The term "evolution" is employed repeatedly by professional scientists in metaphysical expressions about first-origin questions. As stated, they do so essentially as natural philosophers who commonly fail to use the prefixes macro- and micro-. In contrast the term "evolutionism" is a rubric for a most widely accepted and utilized worldview *(Zeitgeist* or *Weltanschauung)* as a philosophy or frame of reference to organize one's outlook about all reality.

When evolution is employed so as to convey the meaning of changes in the distant past (macro-evolution), then only imaginative narratives are put forth about how existing conditions of the present might have come into existence.

nying any change "after its kind." This way out does not appeal to me because I see no need of harmonizing God's two books, the book of nature and the book of Scripture.[7]

I turn now to an analysis of Genesis 1, that marvelous metaphor of the world's origin.

1. *Genesis 1:1-2.* These verses clearly state that God had a pre-existent something to work with. The principle taught here is not a creation out of nothing but out of chaos. But Christian theology teaches (and the modern, believing mind insists) that God created all things out of nothing. Is this a contradiction? No, it is a development of doctrine. The ancient Near Eastern mind either could not grasp, or did not need, a creation-out-of-nothing. The Babylonian "creation epic," *Enuma elish,* likewise begins its account with pre-existent matter.

In order to do justice to Genesis 1, one should hear it fairly, against the background of its day. One does the Bible an injustice when he imposes modern ideas upon it. Thanks to the archaeological unearthings of the last hun-

YES

NO

Such after-the-fact formulations have been specifically presented for adoption by nonscientists since around 1859. These formulations have been represented as "scientific" substitutes for the traditional, theistically oriented worldview accepted for long centuries and summarized succinctly as the explanation that God was the Creator of all things.

And corollary to that concept was the idea believed by the seventeenth-century founders (physical and biological scientists) of professional scientific endeavor that human beings are specially created in the image of God. Therefore those founding scientists believed that they could utilize God-given abilities to study the natural environment around them, to study the creation of God. That worldview is most appropriately labeled creationism (special creationism).

Today, however, a type of total evolutionism is *the* worldview or frame of reference by which to organize one's outlook about all reality. Thus certain astrophysicists, reductionist biochemists, and biological macroevolutionists are encouraging nonscientists (young and old) to accept a substitute worldview most appropri-

dred years or so we are better able to hear the Bible in its ancient setting.

Here in chart form are the points of comparison and contrast listed by Heidel:[8]

BABYLONIAN "CREATION EPIC"	GENESIS CREATION ACCOUNT
1. Divine spirit and cosmic matter are coexistent and coeternal	1. Divine spirit creates cosmic matter and exists independently of it
2. Primeval chaos; *Tiamat* enveloped in darkness	2. The earth a desolate waste, with darkness covering the deep *(tĕhôm)*
3. Light emanating from the gods	3. Light created
4. The creation of the firmament	4. The creation of the firmament
5. The creation of the dry land	5. The creation of the dry land
6. The creation of the luminaries	6. The creation of the luminaries
7. The creation of the human race	7. The creation of the human race
8. The gods rest and celebrate	8. God rests and sanctifies the seventh day

YES

NO

ately labeled total evolutionism, which may be elucidated broadly under the subtitles of stellar (cosmic) evolution, molecular (chemical) evolution, organic (biological) evolution, and human (societal) evolution.

Total evolutionism is the overarching worldview that has increased in popularity since 1859, when Charles Darwin and his fellow unbelievers began to popularize the evolutionary view that has become so much a part of the twentieth-century effort to "un-God" the universe.[3] Regrettably the worldview of total evolutionism is based upon evidence of circumstantial similarities of unexplained origin found in living and nonliving things. Proponents of total evolutionism must practice exclusive implementation of the comparative method of reasoning.[4]

Could There Have Been Evolution in Certain Areas and Not in Others?

Using careful delineation of the meaning of change associated with the term "evolution," we must answer

The most remarkable coincidence between Genesis 1:2 and *Enuma elish* is the biblical word for "the deep" and the Babylonian word *Tiamat*. Tiamat is the female monster-goddess who tries to make all the younger gods subservient. Marduk, the god of the city of Babylon, manages to kill Tiamat, and her dismembered body serves as the foundation and sky of the world. What we perhaps have in "the deep"—*tĕhôm*—is a demythologized relic of the old polytheistic creation myth. The proper point of comparison of the biblical creation account is not the textbooks of modern science but the similar accounts of peoples who lived and worshiped and wrote in the ancient Near East.

2. *Genesis 1:3-5*. The creation of light on the first day becomes a problem for interfacing with modern astronomy **YES**

NO

"No" if broad-range, unlimited change of macro-evolution magnitude is intended.

Concepts of broad-range, unlimited, vertical change (macro-evolution) between easily recognized groups of animals (or plants) are fully imagined or supposed. Macro-evolutionists are completely dependent upon the comparative method as applied to evidence of circumstantial similarities. And vertical, macro-evolution changes are unobserved, unobservable, and untestable genetically. Furthermore all suggestions that macro-evolution occurred in the past between animals (or plants) before existence of human beings are in complete violation of laws of genetics. In other words proponents of macro-evolution in living things are, in effect, denying the laws of Mendel, the laws of genetics. Actually, only genetic variation within limits of some easily recognized group of living organisms is observed, is observable, is testable.

And, in point of fact, all individuals in the human race, regardless of height, weight, or color, are members of one easily recognized group. Human beings are human beings are human beings. And human beings are in no way genetically related to any other living (or dead) organism.

Admittedly there is evidence of circumstantial similarities between human beings and easily recognized animal groups. But such circumstantial similarities are

because we know that the light and power on earth is largely due to the sun's rays, past or present. And the sun is not created until the fourth day. There have been many interpretations of this strange state of affairs. One of them is to see in the light of the first day the beginning of a symmetry that the author may have preserved:

Day one:	light	Day four:	the lights: sun, moon and stars
Day two:	firmament	Day five:	birds to fly across the firmament; fish
Day three:	dry land and vegetation	Day six:	animals and humans to live on the dry land and off the vegetation

It is possible that the author was more interested in symmetry than in science. Another interpretation is that the author is thinking phenomenologically—that is, the author is describing what happens every day before the sun appears: It gets light. But whatever the interpretation of the

YES

NO

of completely unknown, unexplained genetic origin. No professional scientist can provide any genetic evidence that human beings "evolved" from anthropoid origin. Any discussion of supposed anthropogenesis is nothing but special pleading without repeatable observational evidence of genetic significance.

The one fully documented scientific finding from all breeding results is that each easily recognized plant group and each easily recognized animal group, including human beings, is distinct and discrete. Only genetic variation within limits of all known, easily recognized groups of organisms is documented scientifically.

Are "Theistic Evolution" and "Progressive Creationism" Helpful Concepts?

Involved in an answer to this question is the fact that a variety of meanings has been associated with these terms for several decades. That variety depends upon the degree of involvement by God, the Creator, that proponents of these concepts set forth.

Such variability cannot be discussed at length here. Suffice it to state that some authors suggest that God

creation of light on the first day, it does not fit easily into a rigidly scientific understanding of the cosmos.

3. *Genesis 1:6-8.* The designation of that which divided the waters is happily rendered in various English translations as "firmament." The rendering is felicitous (1) because it accurately translates the Hebrew *rāqîaʿ* ("something firmly beaten out") and (2) because it yields the ancient notion that what we call the atmosphere was solid—hard enough to hold back the "waters above the firmament."

Again, phenomenologically, as with the light prior to and separate from the sun, one can understand the ancient mindset. The blue curvature of the sky could appear to hold back more water than is in the clouds. Moderns, however, are altogether sure that there is no water beyond the atmosphere ("firmament") of planet earth. This is a clue to the understanding of Genesis 1 in its entirety: It is an ancient metaphor in praise of the creator God.

4. *Genesis 1:9-13.* In these verses land is separated from the water under the heavens. The land is called Earth and the waters are called Seas. The phrase that concerns

YES

NO

created and then endowed all things with the capacity for complete macro-evolution magnitude of change. Others propose that God was involved only in the installation of the soul of each human being, whereas still others suggest that God intervened in the natural environment whenever major changes in living things and living conditions were necessary. The latter position may be identified as "threshold evolution" and used as a synonym for "progressive creationism" (also known as "religious evolution"). For the purposes of this chapter, remaining discourse will center upon the term "theistic evolution."

Proponents of "theistic evolution" are basically evolutionists. Support for this assertion is found in the grammatical structure of the terminology. The word "theistic" is used as an adjective that is descriptive of the word "evolution." A "theistic evolutionist" is one who desires, in some manner or degree, to add God to so-called naturalistic concepts, such as an explosion of dense matter, or sudden and spontaneous appearance

us is the one that says the vegetation is to reproduce itself "after its kind." This phrase runs directly counter to a central claim of evolution—namely, the mutation of species.[9] Beside restating the above point that the author of Genesis 1 is describing reality as perceived, I would add that the slowness of change in many areas of evolution yields the appearance of permanence. We now know that the stars, including our sun, are slowly burning themselves up into extinction. But the number of years it will take is literally astronomical. These stellar bodies will burn themselves out in tens of billions of years. It surely will happen, but it happens so slowly that one hardly notices. The stars appear to be eternal. The fossil evidence involving long-transformed species is incomplete but nonetheless compelling.

5. *Genesis 1:14-19.* Day four of this creation account deals with the creation of sun, moon, and stars. The text begins with God saying, "Let there be lights in the firmament of the heavens." The firmament, we learned from verses 6-8, is the blue sky we also call the atmosphere. The author of Genesis observes that the sun, moon, and

YES stars appear to be "in the firmament." On a hot summer

NO of living substance, or emergence of human beings from animal ancestry.

Belief in "theistic evolution" is dependent upon atheistic evolution. In order for the evolutionist to have a position into which that person then adds God, the Creator (in whatever manner or degree asserted), a definite preliminary acceptance of so-called macroevolution magnitude of change of supposed naturalistic phenomena is required. The "theistic evolutionist" must first, then, be an evolutionist and secondarily become a "theistic evolutionist" by personal selection of some involvement of God, the Creator of all things.

Thus "theistic evolution" is a hybrid belief entailing attempted combination of the supernatural with some type of presumed natural phenomena. Also "progressive creationism," "threshold evolution" and "religious evolution" are hybrid beliefs.

A type of analogy is drawn by "theistic evolutionists," implicitly or explicitly,[5] between identified laws of na-

afternoon it sometimes does appear that the sun is on this side of the blue.

This section also shows that the author's interest is not in the details of creation in and of themselves. Having little interest in the "how" of creation, the author shows considerable interest in its "why." The lights are "for signs and for seasons and for days and years" (verse 14). The heavenly bodies are not gods, as the polytheistic cultures around Israel thought, but servants to assist people in reckoning time—especially cultic time, sacred time (cf. especially Israel's festival of the new moon, 1 Sam 20:24; Amos 8:5).

This anti-polytheistic demythologizing becomes more explicit in verse 16, where the sun and the moon are called "the greater light" and "the lesser light." The author does not use the Hebrew words šemeš ("sun") and yārēaḥ ("moon") because they sound too much like the names of the Babylonian sun-god Shamash and the Canaanite moon-god Yarikh.

Finally, the author reveals the same attitude by adding: "He made the stars also." Those luminaries worshiped by

YES

---

ture and long-standing laws of society, such as the following:

NO

Laws of nature	Laws of society
1. Descriptions of order	1. Prescriptions, prohibitions
2. Apply to things incapable of any volition (choice)	2. Govern responsible beings with choice of options
3. No moral connotation	3. Lead to implication of criminality for those who break them
4. Identified, discovered	4. Passed or decreed by human beings
5. Mainly a choice among average readings	5. Stated with precision as basis for just punishment for infraction

Clearly, natural laws are descriptive whereas societal laws are prescriptive. Natural laws do not prescribe or determine "why" things interact or interrelate. Natural laws are merely man-derived descriptions of "how" aspects of the existing natural environment interact or

the Babylonians as life-controlling gods are passed off in Genesis with something akin to "Oh yes, our God made 'your' stars too!"

As understandable as this mention of stars is against the backdrop of the ancient Near East, it becomes unintelligible if it vies for respectability as a modern scientific statement. Unless the astronomers are misleading us, one can go out at night and see stars that are millions of light years away. If so, then those stars were created millions of years ago. This causes insurmountable difficulties for a chronology that, taking biblical dating literally, arrives at a date between 10,000 and 6000 B.C. for the origin of the cosmos. One could say, of course, that God created the stars with their beams of light already reaching the earth. But there is an old and useful theological phrase that would apply to such an attempt: *Miracula non multiplicanda sunt* ("Miracles must not be multiplied").

6. *Genesis 1:20-23.* When verse 20 has God saying, "Let the waters bring forth swarms of living creatures," I am almost tempted to read back into these words insights

YES

NO

interrelate. Natural laws do not govern. They are only descriptions.

From all this discussion comes the need for the reader to avoid the danger of a too-willing or too-uncritical acceptance (ignoring) of contradiction, compromise, and inconsistency in one's thinking. Quite specifically, contradiction, compromise and inconsistent thinking are entailed in formulations of "theistic evolutionists." Belief in the supernatural and belief in prehistoric supposed naturalistic phenomena are mixed by "theistic evolutionists."

A second danger to be avoided is accepting human ideas about first origins in a preferential manner over the unchanging and unchangeable statements on first origins in Genesis. Quite often ancient myths, such as the Babylonian "creation epic" *(Enuma elish)*, or metaphysical speculative narratives about first origins offered by professional scientists are even given equality with the long-standing traditional authority of Scripture. Involved in this second danger is the potential confusion between men's interpretations of God's Word

gleaned from modern paleontologists. But if I disallow the creationists to read their concepts back into the Bible, I must do the same for the evolutionists.

7. *Genesis 1:24-25.* In the first part of the sixth day God creates the animals "according to their kind." In addition to what was said above on verses 9-13, I note that the fossil evidence does not support this. "Kinds" have changed. It does not take us too long to develop breeds of dogs for various purposes. Just think of what we could do if we had a few million years.

8. *Genesis 1:26-31.* "Let us make man in our image . . . . So God created humans in his own image." "Humankind and the gorilla have a common ancestor." The juxtaposition of these two sentences strikes at the heart of the evolution-versus-creation controversy. It strikes rather close to home for the reader, who is invariably a human being.

The scientists have a word for it: anthropogenesis. The human being evolved like the animals. Humans are ani-

YES

---

and men's observations of God's world.[6]

NO

Clear distinction must be made between measurements and descriptions of the existing cosmos, between analysis and comparison of living substance and inanimate matter, and between study and identification of unique conceptual, symbolic behavior of human beings and just perceptual behavior and response to signals by anthropoid organisms.

Professional scientists do not measure the size of the universe, do not observe appearance of first life on the earth, do not observe appearance of human beings on the earth, do not measure the age of the universe, do not measure the age of the earth, and do not measure the age of any rock. With regard to the latter three points about time, scientists offer only their estimates of some aspect of prehistory. All such statements about prehistoric time and conditions are identifiable as metaphysical statements by modern natural philosophers.

"Theistic evolutionists" in particular have evidently been intimidated with regard to vast periods of time claimed by scientists. "Theistic evolutionists" have too

mals. They are in the animal kingdom. Here is how the biologists categorize us:

Phylum	Vertebrate
Class	Mammalia
Order	Hominoidea
Family	Hominidea
Genus	Homo
Species	Sapiens

Are we special, or are we not? The biologist emphasizes that we are not radically different from other living creatures. What makes us different from the animals biologically is the size of our brains. The Genesis author, as before, is not interested in the "how" as much as in the "that." According to Genesis, what is special about humans is being made in the image of God and having authority over the animal world.

Is it possible to be a theist and accept the theory of evolution? Yes. The options are rather to be a theistic evolutionist or an atheistic one. In either case, evolution stays. The creationist approach will not stand close scrutiny either by scientists or by experts in ancient Near Eastern studies.

The real difference is between the atheistic evolutionist,

YES who operates consistently with a random nonpurposive-

NO uncritically accepted the time scale of stellar (cosmic) evolution and the dates of supposed molecular (chemical) evolution and organic (biological) evolution as well as the time scale of interpretations of fossil materials.

Yet there is no scientific calibration of prehistoric time, nor any record of the fossils, as if an observer had prepared scientific notes about extensive deposition of sediments. No one has witnessed any process of sedimentation in the magnitude exposed most exemplarily in the Grand Canyon. Many statements about prehistoric time, or a presumed fossil record, partake of imaginative narratives.

No, "theistic evolution" and "progressive creationism" are not helpful concepts. These concepts involve compromise, contradiction, and inconsistent thinking. Use of them means that the reader will risk being uncritically enticed to accept supposed naturalistic (ma-

ness to all evolutionary change, and the theist, who holds to a directedness and purposefulness of the development of life through the eons.

None of this should be too difficult for the Christian, the basis of whose faith rests on the most marvelous mutation of all: resurrection.

To conclude: The creation process is best described by the evolutionary theory. The evolutionary theory can be held to without belief in a higher being. But the believer can freely operate with and endorse the same theory without doing damage to his faith.

On the other hand, there are all sorts of discrepancies between the biblical accounts of creation and the evolutionary theory. That is only to be expected of descriptions of reality coming from cultures separated from each other by two and a half millennia or more.

Here is how one believing scientist put it: "There is grandeur in this view of life, with its several powers, having been originally breathed by the Creator into few forms or into one; and that, whilst this planet has gone cycling on according to the fixed law of gravity, from so simple a begin-

YES

NO

terialistic) substitutions for Christian theism based on Scripture. Most worthy of special note with regard to origin questions is the warning in Colossians 2:8, the admonition in 1 Kings 18:21, and the advice in Psalm 118:8.

Conclusions

Only by consistent use of the term "macro-evolution" versus "micro-evolution" will semantic confusion be avoided.

Only by recognition that "evolution" and "creation" are mutually exclusive will semantic confusion be avoided.

Only by distinguishing the difference between "evolution" and "evolutionism" will semantic confusion be avoided.

Only by differentiating "evolution" from genetic variation will semantic confusion be avoided.

Only by avoidance of the contradiction, compro-

YES

ning endless forms most beautiful and most wonderful have been, and are being evolved."
    The believing scientist? Charles Darwin.[10]

NO

mise, and inconsistency of trying to add God, the Creator, as attempted by "theistic evolutionists" (and "progressive creationists") will clarification be gained.

ENDNOTES

YES

1. W. Countryman, *Biblical Authority or Biblical Tyranny: Scripture and the Christian Pilgrimage* (Philadelphia: Fortress, 1981) 10.

2. T. Dobzhansky, "Evolution," in *Encyclopedia Americana* (1979), 10, 734.

3. S. J. Gould prefers to call evolution a fact, reserving the word "theory" for the mechanisms of evolution; cf. his essay "Evolution as Fact and Theory" in *Science and Creationism* (ed. A. Montagu: Oxford: University Press, 1984) 117–25; but cf. C. Patterson, *Evolution* (London: British Museum, 1978) 146: "The theory of evolution is . . . neither fully scientific, like physics, for example, nor unscientific, like history. Although it has no laws, it does have rules, and it does make general predictions about the properties of organisms. It therefore lays itself open to disproof."

4. E.g., chapter 10 of C. Darwin, *The Origin of Species,* is entitled "On the Imperfection of the Geological Record."

5. R. Collin, *Evolution* (New York: Hawthorn, 1959) 116; C. McGowan, *In the Beginning . . . A Scientist Shows Why the Creationists Are Wrong* (Buffalo: Prometheus, 1984) 95, 119.

6. Collin, *Evolution,* 57, 92.

7. R. M. Frye, "The Two Books of God," in *Is God a Creationist: The Religious Case Against Creation Science* (ed. Frye; New York: Scribner's, 1983). Frye traces this very helpful concept back through Francis Bacon to Augustine.

8. A. Heidel, *The Babylonian Genesis* (Chicago: University Press, 1951) 129.

9. McGowan, *In the Beginning,* 36–37; P. Luykx, "Mutation," in *Encyclopedia Americana* (1979), 19, 680: "Over the course of many generations a new favorable combination of genes may become established as the norm. In this way a new species may arise."

10. The last sentence of the conclusion to *The Origin of Species.*

NO

1. At this point proper scientific theories should be identified as carefully formulated sets of ideas that scientists have developed over the centuries about the natural environment, about the creation, all around

them. Outstanding examples of proper scientific theories are the atomic theory, kinetic-molecular theory and gene theory. These scientific theories have been generated from prior awareness of aspects of the natural environment. Each theory is a set of postulates about the existence, relationship, and activity of imagined entities (atoms, electrons, molecules, or genes—DNA and/or RNA—and there is much indirect evidence for the existence of each). Also from a proper scientific theory before-the-fact predictions (expectations) are made about aspects of the natural environment. Such predictions are then tested and retested, directly or indirectly. Thus tangible support (or denial) of aspects of a scientific theory is gained. Practitioners of methods and procedures associated with proper scientific theories are not limited to use of the comparative method of reasoning upon which evolutionists must depend.

2. Note the discussion of "living fossils" in J. N. Moore, *How To Teach Origins (Without ACLU Interference)* (Milford: Mott Media, 1983) 209–10.

3. See N. C. Gillespie, *Charles Darwin and the Problem of Creation* (Chicago: University Press, 1979) 15; J. C. Greene, *Science, Ideology, and World View* (Berkeley: University of California, 1981).

4. Total evolutionism is foundational to many modern-day, twentieth-century "-isms." A partial list might include scientific socialism, Nazi fascism, communism, materialism, naturalism, imperialism, Freudianism, behaviorism, and secular humanism.

5. Either explicit or implicit in the thinking of "theistic evolutionists" is acceptance of the concept that the universe is governed by or controlled by natural laws. Natural laws (or laws of nature) have been identified most successfully by both physical and biological scientists over the last few centuries. The point of view that natural laws govern the universe was developed from much successful description of interactions and interrelationships of aspects of the natural environment. As can be shown through analysis of historical events, that point of view was basic to an outlook of more and more deterministic thinking in the nineteenth and early twentieth centuries. Many leading thinkers in those times became known as deists and came to supplant the earlier leadership of confirmed Christian theists. In a sense, then, "theistic evolution" was proposed as a way of putting together the two points of view of Christian theism and naturalism, which is a practice of compromise, contradiction, and inconsistent thinking.

6. For documentation of the fact that modern science is based on the Christian worldview see S. L. Jaki, *The Road to Science and the Ways to God* (Chicago: University Press, 1978); *The Origin of Science and the Science of Its Origin* (South Bend: Regnery/Gateway, 1978); *Science and Creation: From Eternal Cycles to Oscillating Universe* (New York: Science History Publications, 1974); H. Butterfield, *The Origins of Modern Science* (New York: Bell, 1962); R. R. E. D. Clark, *Science and Christianity—A Partnership* (Mountain View: Pacific Press, 1972); R. Hooykaas, *Religion and the Rise of Modern Science* (Grand Rapids: Eerdmans, 1972); E. M. Klaaren, *Religious Origins of Modern Science* (Grand Rapids: Eerdmans, 1977). Further corroboration that modern science grew out of Judeo-Christian traditions has been stressed by both A. N. Whitehead, *Science and the Modern World* (New York: Macmillan, 1926), and J. R. Oppenheimer, "On Science and Culture," *Encounter* (October 1962).

5   Is the Doctrine of the

Trinity Implied in the Genesis Creation Account?

YES: EUGENE H. MERRILL

Genesis 1 anticipates and implies the doctrine of the Trinity, a truth whose mature expression must admittedly be found in the New Testament and in the confessions of the early Church. The approach will be to examine the matter (1) theologically—that is, in terms of a total biblical theology in which the Old Testament and New Testament are mutually informing; (2) hermeneutically—that is, with proper consideration of the canons of interpretation, which require among other things that Scripture be taken in con-

NO: ALAN J. HAUSER

The doctrine of the Trinity is not implied in Genesis 1. Before I begin my argument, however, I want to make three preliminary observations:

1. *The issue of whether the doctrine of the Trinity is implied in Genesis 1 does not have any substantive impact on the broader issue of the validity of the doctrine.* Jews and Christians, both of whom take Genesis 1 seriously, have completely opposite stances regarding the doctrine of the Trinity. These stances are taken on the

text, that it be compared with other Scripture, and that it be understood against the principle of progressive revelation; and (3) grammatically and exegetically—that is, with careful attention to comparative lexicography, etymology, usage of words, form, and syntax.

Theological Evidence

The term "biblical theology" must, to the evangelical at least, convey certain significances including the divine origin of the Old Testament and New Testament, their basic unity as a result of common authorship and design, and a common stream or streams of revelation that may become individually perceivable at different stages of sacred history, that may run parallel at times or always, but that can never contradict one another.[1]

If the foregoing assumptions are correct, one may expect the roots of New Testament theology to be found in the Old Testament—though certainly not always explicitly, or necessarily in the same form. A case for this can be

YES

NO

basis of presuppositions, texts, and arguments that lie far beyond the bounds of Genesis 1. Since there are so many other factors on the basis of which one can affirm or deny the doctrine of the Trinity, it should be obvious that a Christian can simultaneously affirm the doctrine and yet deny that it is implied in Genesis 1.

2. *The doctrine of the Trinity is a relatively "late" doctrine.* That is, the process of defining the essential aspects of the doctrine involved considerable debate as late as the Council of Nicea (A.D. 325), the Council of Constantinople (381) and the Council of Chalcedon (451). These councils made explicit the basic elements of the doctrine, such as the co-equality of the three Persons, the distinction between the Persons, and the generation of the Son from the Father. By comparison to these developed statements the New Testament must be said to allude to the doctrine in an implicit and veiled manner, with passages like John 14 providing statements and ideas that could later be employed and expanded by theologians in the early Church as they formulated the doctrine.[1]

Furthermore, when one looks at the Old Testament it becomes clear that there are no discernible references

made for individual doctrines such as creation, hamartiology, soteriology, eschatology, and so on.[2] If one grants that this is true of those teachings that reflect the activity of God, what may be said of those that concern his nature, his person, his very being? Is it conceivable that a truth so basic to theology as the Godhead itself could find its origins only in the New Testament?

Analogically, the answer to this question would seem to be a resounding "No." But analogy cannot serve as proof. It remains now to examine the biblical data themselves to see if they teach the doctrine of a triune God, particularly in Genesis 1. This will require, first of all, careful attention to commonly accepted hermeneutical principle and procedure.

YES

NO

to the Trinity. Claimed allusions to the Trinity became perceptible by hindsight only after the Church councils had defined the doctrine. Without the perspective of the Church councils and the Church fathers who formulated the creeds, it is inconceivable that we could even speak of a doctrine of the Trinity in the Old Testament. In other words, it would not be possible to state the doctrine even in skeleton form on the basis of passages chosen only from the Old Testament. An important principle of biblical interpretation is that one must always be careful to distinguish the perspective and milieu of the writer and of his contemporary audience from the perspective and viewpoint of later interpreters. One can attribute to a writer's words only those nuances and meanings it would be reasonable to claim he could have thought, given the temporal, spatial, social, and intellectual limitations existing in the context in which the writer lived. This leads to my third observation.

3. *No word or phrase is context-neutral.* That is, it does not convey a particular meaning or nuance devoid of a context. Even if no context is given, as when a single word is uttered, the hearer or reader will automatically provide a context and use it as a frame of reference for understanding the word. In most cases the hearer/reader is able to grasp the context in which the

Hermeneutical Evidence

That the doctrine of the Trinity—the eternal existence of God in the persons of the Father, Son and Holy Spirit—is a fundamental and universally recognized truth of the Christian Church cannot be denied. But this is only because the Church since New Testament times has found that truth implicitly if not explicitly taught in the New Testament. Over and over again Jesus claimed deity,[3] and that claim was invariably supported by apostolic witness.[4] Likewise, the Holy Spirit is clearly identified not only as a spirit from God but also as God himself.[5] Finally, there are already at least tentative formulations of the tri-unity of God in the New Testament statements that articulate his tri-personality in one divine essence.[6]

Granting all this, one must still demonstrate that the New Testament witness to the nature of God is the full fruitage of a revelation that finds its roots and stem in the Old Testa-

YES

NO

speaker/writer uses a word or phrase, and the appropriate meaning is conveyed. But in some cases, even though a context is provided, the hearer/reader will ignore that context and instead provide one more suited to what he knows or expects.[2] When that happens, the hearer/reader's understanding of the words may substantially disrupt the meaning the speaker/writer intended to convey.

As I will show below in regard to the use of the word "spirit" in Genesis 1, one must always be careful not to force a word to carry too many nuances and implications in one specific textual context. Even though a particular biblical word may carry a number of different meanings when we survey its use in many passages throughout the Old Testament, no one passage is likely to carry all these meanings. We need to study the basic thrust and flow of the passage being examined to determine which meaning is most appropriate to that passage, rather than simply assuming that because a meaning appears elsewhere it will also be appropriate here. If one is not careful to follow this rule of interpretation, almost anything can be read into a passage.

We now turn to Genesis 1. Consider verse 2: "And the earth was without form and void, and darkness was

ment. It might theoretically be possible that nothing was known of the essence and person of God until the dawning of New Testament revelation. But, as suggested above, this is so patently improbable as to require little refutation. If, as many theologians maintain quite correctly, God himself is a dominant theme of biblical theology,[7] is it even possible that he would have said little or nothing about the ontological basis for his activity in history and redemption? Would he have created man to be in his image and likeness without communicating something of what that means in terms of his own personhood?

The pursuit of these questions leads to a consideration of the nature and progress of revelation. It is rather evident from even a superficial study of any biblical truth that it does not appear full-blown at its first moment of revelation. No matter what the doctrine, one can easily see that it was **YES** revealed gradually, over a period of time, and progressively. Every generation of biblical history was given the op-

---

NO upon the face of the deep. And an awesome wind stirred the face of the waters." Three Hebrew words provide the key to understanding this verse.

The most important of these is *rûaḥ,* which may be translated as "wind," "breath," or "spirit,"[3] depending on which passage we are considering of the several hundred passages in which it appears. I will defer the discussion of the meaning "spirit" to a later point in this paper, focusing now on the other two meanings.

The word *rûaḥ* can mean "breath," as in Genesis 6:17; 7:15; 7:22, where it refers to the breath that is in all flesh. It can also refer to the breath of God, as in Psalm 18:15, where the blast of God's nostrils scatters the enemy and shakes the world, or as in Job 4:9, where the breath of God's nostrils causes the wicked to perish. Unlike the breath of all flesh, the breath of God is clearly a powerful force, one that can shake the cosmos. Combined in the idea of the "breath of God" are the analogies of breath (as in human breath) and of a powerful wind (as in a tornado or hurricane).

The word *rûaḥ* also often means "wind," as in the four winds that blow from the four quarters of heaven (Jer. 49:36; Dan. 7:2; 11:4). These winds God is said to

portunity at least to participate in the ever-increasing divine self-disclosure. Truth known in germinal form in primeval times was elaborated to the patriarchs, further clarified to Moses and the poets and sages, brilliantly and increasingly expounded to the prophets, and in its fullness laid bare to the apostolic Church.

This process, known commonly as progressive revelation, touches the underlying hermeneutical issue involved in a study such as this—namely, that theological truth as central as that of the essence and nature of God himself is part and parcel of a developmental process that has its origin at the beginning of revelation itself and its culmination in revelation's final witness. To use the analogy of Geerhardus Vos[8] and other scholars, the progressive revelation of truth must be viewed as an organic process with the finality of its expression being comparable to the mighty oak tree with its towering trunk, stately branches, and beautiful

YES

NO

bring out of his treasuries and to dispense (Ps. 135:7; Jer. 10:13). In Numbers 11:31 the Lord sends forth a wind that brings quail from over the sea into the Israelite camp. In Genesis 3:8 God walks in the garden in the cool (windy) part of the day. In 8:1 God sends forth a wind to dry up the waters of the flood. In these and numerous other passages, *rûaḥ* clearly refers to a wind sent by God.

"Wind," not "spirit," is the best translation of *rûaḥ* in Genesis 1:2.[4] After the initial, encompassing statement in verse 1 that "in the beginning God created the heavens and the earth," verse 2 focuses on the chaotic condition of the world before God began to give it order and structure. This chaos is expressed through three vivid images: (1) The earth was without form and void; (2) there was darkness over the water; and (3) an awesome wind was blowing over the face of the water.[5]

As anyone who has ever been in a storm at sea knows, a powerful wind can enrage the waters, and the ensuing chaos can consume ship and crew alike (cf. Jonah 1–2). Thus the image of the strong wind completes the picture of chaos in verse 2. Any proposal that *rûaḥ* be translated as "spirit" and taken to refer to the spirit of God would disrupt this picture of chaos. One might ar-

foliage. But such truth, like the oak, did not arrive at maturity by creative fiat. Rather, it grew to its massive proportions only gradually, originating in a tiny acorn and from that unpromising beginning expanding through successive accretions from stage to stage until at last it achieved its mature expression.

One could not, however, define an acorn as an oak tree, nor could he say that the oak tree is only a large variety of acorn. Similarly one must not confuse the full-blown New Testament teaching of the Trinity with what is only nascently and implicitly in the Old Testament. On the other hand, the acorn is potentially an oak tree, because there is nothing in the final product that is fundamentally alien to or even added to the seed. In other words, the acorn is the microcosm of the oak, and the oak is the macrocosm inherent in the acorn.

YES In theological/hermeneutical terms the New Testament

NO gue that the spirit of God is mentioned at the end of verse 2 as a way of foreshadowing the creative activity that is coming. But then one would have to wonder why the writer, having mentioned the spirit of God in verse 2, never mentions it again in all of Genesis 1, instead referring consistently to the Creator simply as "God."

This lack of even a second reference to the spirit of God constitutes a serious problem in a passage that repeatedly stresses the image of a dynamic, creative God giving order and form to the world. It would seem natural to expect additional references to the spirit of God if indeed that was the meaning of *rûaḥ* in verse 2. The lack of a second reference to an awesome wind stirring the waters presents no such problem, since the image of chaos in verse 2 constitutes a preface to God's various acts of creation, which make order out of chaos.[6]

The second Hebrew word to be studied in verse 2 is *'ĕlōhîm*, "God(s)." While one might argue that the use of this term immediately after *rûaḥ* indicates that the third person of the Trinity is meant ("spirit of God"), such an argument is not sensitive enough to the range of meanings for both words. Not only can *rûaḥ* mean "wind," as I have just argued; *'ĕlōhîm* can mean "awesome" or "powerful." "Wind of God" would then mean

doctrine of the Trinity, while "leafed-out" and mature, is essentially nothing more, nothing less, nothing else than that same doctrine in the Old Testament. At least one must say as a Christian interpreter that the notion of a triune God exists potentially in the Old Testament whether or not it would be recognizable as such without the subsequent New Testament revelation. It is therefore necessary to see if the text of the Old Testament will support the theological and hermeneutical assumptions proposed above. If the oak tree of full revelation of the Godhead is in the New Testament, and if the New Testament is a progressive development of Old Testament themes, one ought to be able to dissect the "acorns" of the doctrine in the Old Testament to see if the alleged potentiality is actually there.

Exegetical Evidence

The procedure to be followed in this section is to examine a few major texts bearing on the subject and to do so

YES

NO

not a part of God or a divine person but rather a powerful wind sent from God.

For example, when the wind of the Lord comes up from the wilderness (Hos. 13:15) the springs and fountains of the land are soon dried up. Or when Job accuses God of having forsaken him, he says (30:22) that God lifts him up on the wind, makes him ride on it, and tosses him about in the storm. Thus the context of Genesis 1, and especially of verse 2 with its emphasis on chaos, makes the translation "awesome wind" or "wind of God" much more reasonable than "spirit of God."

The third Hebrew word to be studied in verse 2 supports this contextual argument. The verb *rāḥap* appears in only two other passages. In Jeremiah 23:9 it describes the shaking of Jeremiah's bones in fear as he contemplates the destruction God will send against the wicked prophets. In Deuteronomy 32:11 the verb refers to the fluttering of an eagle over its young. In both cases the verb expresses agitated activity, hence my translation in Genesis 1:2: "stirred."[7] "Hovered" or "brooded," as in the translation "the spirit of God hovered over the waters," is too passive a translation when one considers

chronologically and canonically, thus bringing to bear the theological and hermeneutical principles just suggested. This requires attention first to the very passage under discussion: Genesis 1. But after the other relevant texts have been considered, Genesis 1 will once more and finally be addressed retrospectively to determine whether there is genuine evidence for the Trinity there.

Scholars of all persuasions have been intrigued through the ages by the plurality of the divine name *'ĕlōhîm*, "God," one of the most common designations for the God of Israel. The term is not so much a name, of course, as it is an appellative describing deity, but its plurality when referring to the God of Israel and not only to gods in general is none the less significant.[9] In fact, there are almost no parallels to this in all the other literatures of the ancient Near Eastern world.

YES   Jewish tradition has generally explained the form

NO   the verb's usage in the other two passages. "Stirred" expresses the agitation of the waters due to the activity of the awesome wind. This translation fits nicely with the chaotic picture presented throughout verse 2.

Even if one dismisses these arguments for translating the words in verse 2 as "an awesome wind stirred the face of the waters" and insists on translating "the spirit of God moved (or hovered) over the face of the waters," it does not follow that "spirit of God" must refer to the third person of the Trinity. In our contemporary context, after almost two thousand years of Christian history during which the doctrine of the Trinity has been developed in detail as a key teaching of the Church, it is almost automatic for most readers to understand "spirit of God" to refer to the Holy Spirit. As mentioned earlier, people will consistently place terms or phrases into a context with which they are familiar. That does not mean, however, that a close study of the phrase "spirit of God" in the Old Testament will support such an interpretation.

Let us briefly examine the use of "spirit of God" in the Old Testament. The first part of the phrase, "spirit of," is commonly used in the construct state in Hebrew to denote the motivating force or dynamic power of a person

'ĕlōhîm as a "plural of majesty" or something similar.[10] This is a legitimate grammatical way of viewing the word, for there are other instances in which grammatical plurality expresses something other than number. Since the God of the Old Testament is transcendent and infinitely powerful, holy, and mysterious, it is only fitting that he be described in ways that transcend the limitations of grammar, including the singular noun form.

Some scholars have explained the phenomenon by suggesting that the plurality is a vestige of a time when Israel's theological ancestors were polytheistic. Though the ancestors abandoned their notions of multiple deities in the process of their evolutionary religious understanding, they retained the terminology of polytheism, at least in this instance. The epithet 'ĕlōhîm, then, is a carry-over from primitive times—though in the Old Testament it no longer conveyed any notion of plurality other than grammatical.[11]

The major problem with such a view is that it finds no

YES

NO

or of God. In 2 Chronicles 36:22 we are told that "the Lord stirred up the spirit of Cyrus king of Persia" to issue a proclamation allowing worshipers of Israel's God to rebuild his temple (cf. Ezra 1:1). In 1 Chronicles 5:26 God stirs up "the spirit of Pul king of Assyria—that is, the spirit of Tiglath-Pileser king of Assyria" to carry away some of the tribes of Israel.

In these instances "spirit of" does not denote an entity in any way separate from the person but rather the active, forceful power of that person (cf. also Gen. 45:27; 2 Kgs. 2:15; 1 Sam. 30:12; Hag. 1:14). Why should we presume that it is different when the object of the phrase "spirit of" is God? When we are told in Judges 14:6 that "the spirit of the Lord came mightily upon" Samson, and that Samson tore apart the lion, does this mean that the Holy Spirit seized Samson? What is meant instead is that God's power came upon Samson and gave him strength (see also, for example, Judg. 6:34; 11:29). There is no hint of a separate Person within the Godhead from the Father acting upon the individual. This is true consistently in the many Old Testament texts where someone is seized by the spirit of God (see, for example, 2 Kgs. 2:16; 1 Sam. 10:6; 11:6).

parallel in extra-biblical religion and literature. Why should only the Hebrews have failed to discard the plural number when referring to their one God when no other peoples of the ancient Near Eastern world regularly retained the plural when describing any one of their gods as an individual? For this and other reasons this option has been universally rejected.

The other idea—that *'ĕlōhîm* speaks of a plural of majesty—is possible, but only insofar as it deals with the grammatical plural alone. What must be considered in addition is the context in which this plural form is used when referring to God as a single being. It is sufficient to note only Genesis 1 in this connection. In verse 26 the text says, "Let us make man in our image, in our likeness." The Hebrew here has one verb in the plural, (*na'ăśeh*, "let us make") and two nouns with plural suffixes (*bĕṣalmēnû*, "in our image"; *kidmûtēnû*, "in our likeness"). Since the subject is

YES

NO   Allow me to summarize my analysis of Genesis 1:2. It is best to translate the words in question as "an awesome wind stirred the face of the waters," since this fits best in the immediate context. However, even if one translates "spirit of God" this does not automatically mean that the "Holy Spirit" is meant, as a close examination of the usage of "spirit of God" in the Old Testament has shown.

We now turn to Genesis 1:26, the other verse sometimes taken to imply the Trinity: "And God said, 'Let us make man in our image, after our likeness.'" The phrase "Let us make" and the two plural possessive pronouns "our" are commonly referred to by those who see here an indication of the Trinity. However, as is often the case when a passage is translated, care must be taken not to misinterpret the subtleties and nuances of the original language. The key to understanding the verse is the word for God, *'ĕlōhîm*. This Hebrew word is plural (the singular form being *'ēl* or *'ĕlōah*). The use of the plural form is not unusual, since there are many cases in the Old Testament where the plural noun *'ĕlōhîm* is used when clearly only one God is meant.

For example, in Genesis 20:13 Abraham says to Abimelech king of Gerar, "When God caused me to

ʾĕlōhîm it is clear that God, who normally is perceived to be singular, is here at least cast in the plural not only grammatically but functionally.

Jewish tradition generally maintains that the plural is to be explained as God taking counsel together with the angelic assembly in the work of creation.[12] Against this is the clear scriptural affirmation that only God creates and that the angels, as created beings, cannot be creators with him.

Another suggestion is that the language of Genesis 1:26 is the language of polite discourse in which the subject modestly uses the "we" when in fact he means "I." Such a use is, indeed, common in modern western literature, but there is no evidence for it elsewhere in the Old Testament[13] or in the vast literatures of the ancient Near East. To see it here smacks of special pleading.

There are two other passages in Genesis where the "we" or "us" occurs with the divine name ʾĕlōhîm—namely,

YES

NO

wander from my father's house. . . ." The Hebrew word for God is plural, but even more significantly the verb *hitʿû,* "caused to wander," is in the third person plural in Hebrew. Even though the passage clearly intends to denote only one God, the use of the plural noun has even caused the verb to be plural.

This is also true in Genesis 35:7, which says that Jacob built an altar and called the place "El Bethel, because there God appeared to him." Again we have the plural form for God, ʾĕlōhîm, and again we have a third person plural form of the Hebrew verb (*niglû,* "appeared"). It is not commonly argued that these passages allude to the Trinity. Why then should it be argued that Genesis 1:26 does? The only difference in the Hebrew text of 1:26 is that the plural in the noun, ʾĕlōhîm, and in the verb, *naʿăśeh* ("Let us make"), has been extended to the two nouns *ṣelem* ("image") and *dĕmût* ("likeness"), both of which carry the plural suffix *-nû* ("our").

Here again it is a case of the context in which a passage is read. If one reads Genesis 1:26 in the context of grammatical usages common in the Old Testament it is quite clear that only one speaker is meant, with no implication of the concept of the Trinity, even though plu-

3:22 and 11:7. In the former passage man, having sinned, is said to be "like some of us." That is, man in some sense has become like God. Surely the divine lament is not that man has become like an angel or some other creature. It was Satan's argument, in fact, that man would be like *ʾĕlōhîm* were he to eat of the forbidden fruit (3:5). Similarly, following the construction of the tower of Babel the Lord came down to witness man's hubris and then proclaimed in holy indignation, "Come, let us go down and confuse their language." Again, it is hardly conceivable that the Lord is invoking the assistance of the angels or anyone else. It is he alone who creates, commands, and judges his creation. It is he alone who speaks and who does so on occasion as a subject described by grammatically plural terminology.

The plurality of the divine Person of Genesis 1 is further supported by the role of the Spirit of God, who was "hovering over" the surface of the waters at the time of the creation of the cosmos (1:2). Though it must be admitted that this is highly figurative language and that the spirit could be only an extension of God rather than a separate personality, the plurality of the pronouns, as argued above, would

YES lend substance to the fact that the Spirit at least is to be un-

---

NO ral forms are used.[8] If on the other hand this passage is read in the context of Christian theology, some would see it reasonable to argue that the plurals point to the Trinity. But it is important to note that—even if we suspend momentarily the grammatical point about the use of plural forms—the use of a plural noun, a plural verb, and plural possessive pronouns would not in and of itself denote the Trinity. Plural forms simply indicate two or more, and there is nothing to specify three.

Another example might explain the plural forms. The Old Testament frequently presents the idea of the divine council (for example, 1 Kgs. 22; Job 1) in which numerous heavenly beings appear before God. One could thus explain Genesis 1:26 as God speaking in the presence of the heavenly council. Were it not the case that the frequent use of the plural noun for God already provides an appropriate explanation for the plurals in 1:26, as explained above, one could make a far better

derstood as a Person of God co-laboring with *ĕlōhîm* in the work of creation. To see trinity here is to go beyond the evidence, but the likelihood of duality is certainly preparatory to the conception of God Three-in-One.

Perhaps most striking of all Old Testament passages is one that, ironically, is seldom cited in support of the tri-unity of God. This is found in the early Israelite confession of Deuteronomy 6:4–5. The relevant phrase reads: "The Lord our God, the Lord is one." The word "one" (Hebrew *'ehād*), a word that is composite in its nuance and that implies one through many or many in one,[14] is an adjectival form related to the verb *yāhad*, "be united."[15] Other Hebrew derivatives are *yahad*, "unitedness"; *yahdāw*, "together"; and *yāhîd*, "only, solitary."[16] It is clear that the fundamental meaning of the root is that of a unity brought about by the joining of particulars. Thus the numeral "one," where applied to God, may denote among other things a oneness of originally separate elements.

The implication of this passage is that *'ehād*, at least ety-

YES

NO

case, based on the context of the Old Testament itself, for explaining the plurals as a reference to the divine council than as a reference to the Trinity. Thus we conclude that these plurals can be understood to refer to the different persons of the Trinity only if that concept is read into the passage and only if the plurals are made to carry meanings and implications that run counter to similar usages elsewhere in the Old Testament.

In light of these arguments that the doctrine of the Trinity is not implied in Genesis 1, how are we to understand passages like John 1, Colossians 1, and Hebrews 1, all of which refer to the presence of the Word (Son) at creation?[9] Does our discussion of the Genesis 1 passages invalidate the claim made in these New Testament passages?

One could begin by noting that Genesis 1:2 does not refer to the Son and is therefore beside the point in discussions of these three New Testament passages.[10] But the fundamental question regarding the relationship of Genesis 1 to the New Testament passages lies deeper and revolves around the issue of proper methods of interpretation.

mologically, teaches that the Lord is a unity. This is not to say that wherever the numeral is used in the Old Testament a unity of particulars is in mind, for words have a semantic development that often departs from their etymological meaning. In Deuteronomy 6:4, a statement highly charged with theological content in light of its confessional character, it is not at all unreasonable to assume that the historical, etymological meaning is in view. This is particularly likely given the divine intentionality—namely, the selection of a theologically loaded term to convey at once the uniqueness and solitariness of the Lord and the multipersonality of the Godhead.

The final Old Testament text to which attention can be given is Isaiah 48:16, the author's translation of which is as follows: "Draw near to me, hear this: From the beginning I have not spoken in secret; from the time it [first] happened I was there; and now Yahweh the Lord has sent me, and his Spirit [also has sent me]." The context beginning with verse 12 introduces the speaker as "the first and last" (cf. Rev. 1:8, 17; 22:13). He created the heavens and the

YES

NO   Many people appear to operate under the assumption that a doctrine or teaching professed by the Christian Church and/or delineated in the New Testament must already be visible in the Old Testament. It is true that in some cases a direct connection can be shown between an Old Testament teaching and a teaching later in evidence in Christianity, as in the case of the requirement that God alone be worshiped. But in many other cases it is not obvious that the Old Testament clearly anticipates and delineates a New Testament teaching.

For example, while Christians in hindsight look back to the Old Testament and find many passages that can be understood to point to Jesus as the Christ, these Old Testament passages by themselves do not give details that point specifically and exclusively to Jesus of Nazareth as the one who was to be the Christ. He is never mentioned by name in the Old Testament, as he ought to have been if Old Testament writers had a clear picture of his time and work. His incarnation is a unique and in some ways unanticipated event. Jesus' disciples,

earth (verse 13; cf. John 1:3; Col. 1:16; Heb. 1:2) and called and enabled Cyrus to deliver Israel from Babylonian exile (verses 14-15; cf. 44:24-45:1). And verse 16 suggests that this speaker has been sent by the Lord and the Holy Spirit.[17]

The language of this passage, together with that of those cited from the New Testament, clearly identifies this person as Jesus Christ. In a remarkable juxtaposition of the three persons of the Godhead, our Lord is seen prophetically as being sent by both the Father and the Spirit. This mission of the messianic Savior is clear from both Testaments (Isa. 61:1; Mark 9:37; Luke 4:18, 43; 9:48; 10:16; John 3:17; 6:29, 57; 7:29; 8:42; 10:36; 11:42; 17:3, 8, 18, 21, 23, 25; 20:21; 1 John 4:9-10, 14). Though one could wish for a clearer Old Testament theological formula, such as that in 2 Corinthians 13:14, there is no way to think of the coexistence of the speaker with God from creation itself without thinking of him as forming part of the Godhead.

The suggestion made earlier that Genesis 1 contains in embryonic form the doctrine of the Trinity seems well supported in light of subsequent Old Testament and New Testament passages where there is little or no room for doubt. By no method could one argue such a point if he had only Genesis 1 at his disposal. But by no means can one deny

YES

NO

all of whom were Jews and therefore presumably had a basic knowledge of the Old Testament, did not begin to understand what or who Jesus was until Pentecost, after Jesus' earthly career was over.[11]

It is natural for Christians to claim that God chose to reveal himself in Jesus at the right time in human history (Gal. 4:4). But before that time, and even during his ministry, Jesus of Nazareth's calling as the Christ who would die and rise again was obscure.[12]

Why should one assume it would be any different with the doctrine of the Trinity? It would seem perfectly reasonable for a Christian to believe that God chose to reveal to us the doctrine of the Trinity at a time he deemed appropriate, and that before that time God chose to reveal himself in less specific ways. Even though no one before the time of the early Church was led to speak clearly and directly of the doctrine of the Trinity, this

the preparation for, if not the reality of, the doctrine there if he takes seriously the unity of the divine revelation and the immutability of the divine Person.

Conclusion

This study has proceeded from the premise that every doctrinal truth of the New Testament (including the Trinity) finds its roots in the Old Testament. A corollary to this is that it is inconceivable either that God's nature could have undergone transformation from one era to the next or that the biblical revelation concerning that nature could or would be totally silent even in its earliest stages, including Genesis 1.

This theological assumption presupposes the unity of the Testaments, carries with it the hermeneutical principle of progressive revelation, and implies the expectation that the more complete New Testament teaching concerning the Trinity elucidates that of the Old Testament and, in any case, cannot contradict it. That the Old Testament does not present a systematic trinitarian concept of God cannot be

YES

NO

need not be seen as detracting from the validity of the later doctrine. But when we examine a particular Old Testament passage such as Genesis 1, we must be careful to distinguish the writer's basic intention and meaning from concepts and beliefs that later generations used as a means of reinterpreting the past and making it compatible with their own frame of reference. We must be careful not to allow the lack of clear reference to the Trinity in Genesis 1 to tempt us to try to force the Old Testament to say what it does not say.

This study of Genesis 1 has shown that the concept of the Trinity could not have been in the mind of the writer or the writer's audience. Any attempt to interpret this passage must take into account the context and age in which the passage was written, along with common points of grammar and word usage in the Old Testament. Above all, the interpreter must be sensitive to the considerable gap between the perspectives and beliefs in evidence in the Old Testament and those in evidence in the New Testament and in subsequent Christian interpreters.

denied, but it is clear that the Old Testament is not anti-trinitarian. In fact, those texts (including Genesis 1) that touch at all upon ontological questions bear unanimous testimony to the glorious fact that the Lord of Israel is God the Father, God the Son, and God the Holy Spirit of the Church.

ENDNOTES

YES

1. For these and other ideas as to the nature of biblical theology see G. F. Hasel, *Old Testament Theology: Basic Issues in the Current Debate* (rev. ed.; Grand Rapids: Eerdmans, 1982) 169–83.

2. This concerns the continuity/discontinuity aspect of the relationship of the Testaments, a matter surveyed fully by D. L. Baker, *Two Testaments: One Bible* (Downers Grove: InterVarsity, 1977).

3. Cf. Matt. 26:63–64; John 10:30; 14:9; 17:11, 22.

4. Cf. Phil. 2:6; Col. 1:15; Heb. 1:3.

5. Acts 5:3–4; 1 Cor. 3:16; 6:19; 12:4–5; Heb. 9:14.

6. Matt. 28:19; 2 Cor. 13:14; 1 Pet. 1:2.

7. So e. g. Hasel, *Theology*, 140, and the scholars noted in n. 121. The present writer holds to a somewhat narrower center—the sovereignty of God and his kingdom—but this does not affect the following argument.

8. G. Vos, *Biblical Theology* (Grand Rapids: Eerdmans, 1954) 15–17.

9. See H. Ringgren, "*'ĕlōhîm*," in *Theological Dictionary of the Old Testament* (ed. G. J. Botterweck and H. Ringgren; Grand Rapids: Eerdmans, 1974), 1, 267–84.

10. E. Kautzsch and A. E. Cowley, *Gesenius' Hebrew Grammar* (Oxford: Clarendon, 1957) sec. 124g N2.

11. W. O. E. Oesterley and T. H. Robinson, *Hebrew Religion: Its Origin and Development* (New York: Macmillan, 1937) 127.

12. So Ibn Ezra, Rashi, *et al.*, cited by J. Skinner, *Genesis* (New York: Scribner's, 1910) 31.

13. *Gesenius*, sec. 124g N2. Gesenius describes it as a "plural of self-deliberation," a view accepted also by C. Westermann, *Genesis 1–11: A Commentary* (Minneapolis: Augsburg, 1984) 145. The only text cited by both scholars in support of this use of the plural is Isa. 6:8, a passage that could as easily be used in support of the plurality of the Godhead, especially in light of the so-called *trisagion* ("holy, holy, holy").

14. H. Wolf, "*'eḥād*," in *Theological Wordbook of the Old Testament* (ed. R. L. Harris, G. L. Archer, Jr., and B. K. Waltke; Chicago: Moody, 1980) 30.

15. The basic root is probably *ḥd* (as in Aramaic *ḥd*) to which was prefixed prosthetic *aleph*. Since the Aramaic verb *yaḥēd*, clearly a de-

nominative of *ḥad*, means "to unite," one might argue by analogy that the Hebrew verb *yāḥad* is also denominative of *'eḥād* and so etymologically means to join separate elements together into a united whole. See F. Brown, S. R. Driver and C. A. Briggs, *A Hebrew and English Lexicon of the Old Testament* (Oxford: Clarendon, 1962) 402.

16. Ibid., 402–03.

17. The proposed rendering of the verse would suit the poetic parallelism and thus supply the ellipsis of the second line of the second couplet: "And his Spirit [also sent me]." The Spirit, along with Yahweh, is then an agent of sending the speaker. See N. Snaith, *The Distinctive Ideas of the Old Testament* (London: Epworth, 1960) 158.

NO

1. While the church eventually came to view as heretical many of the positions presented by early Christian writers about the nature of Christ, his person and work, the relationship of the Father to the Son, etc., most of these nonorthodox positions are not specifically and unequivocally ruled out by the New Testament itself. Many of those whose teachings were later declared unorthodox maintained that certain New Testament passages supported their views and argued, sometimes eloquently, in support of such claims. They could not have done so if the New Testament were so clear in delineating the doctrine of the Trinity that positions other than those eventually spelled out by the councils were automatically ruled out. We do well to remember that, on balance, most heretics were not evil persons who deliberately tried to pervert the teachings of the New Testament. Many of them were sincere and well-intentioned interpreters who advocated theological positions that the Church, in its wisdom, eventually came to view as wrong.

2. There is an excellent example in Mark 15:33–36 of the way in which different people will place the same words in different contexts of understanding. There the evangelist quotes the dying Jesus as crying out "Eloi, Eloi, lama sabachthani?" ("My God, my God, why have you forsaken me?"). The evangelist, writing for a Christian audience, leads his readers to understand Jesus' words as an expression of the spirit of affliction described in Psalm 22. Those standing by the cross, however, understand the same words in the context of their suspicion that Jesus was a messianic revolutionary who planned a rebellion against Rome and conclude that Jesus still expects help from Elijah, who the Jewish community thought would come immediately before the Messiah. (Note that a shortened form of Elijah's name, Eli, which in Hebrew means "my God," sounds very much like Eloi. The bystanders could therefore understand Jesus' words either as a cry that God had forsaken him, or as a last-minute plea to Elijah for help: "Elijah, Elijah, why have you forsaken me?") Thus the same words are understood in two very different ways by persons who place them in different contexts of meaning.

3. See R. Young, *Analytical Concordance to the Bible* (Grand Rapids: Eerdmans, 1970) 114, 924, 1057; see also p. 41 of the Index-Lexicon to the Old Testament.

4. The debate over whether to translate *rûaḥ* as "spirit" or "wind" has a long history. A number of early Church fathers favored "spirit"; Tertullian vacillated; Ephraem and Theodoret favored "wind." See W. H.

McClellan, "The Meaning of Ruaḥ 'Elohim in Genesis 1, 2," *Biblica* 15 (1936) 519–20. H. M. Orlinsky, "The Plain Meaning of RUᴬḤ in Gen. 1. 2," *Jewish Quarterly Review* 48, 174–80, cites numerous commentators (Saadia, Ibn Ezra, Rashbam) who argue for "wind," and he cites Targum Onqelos and the Septuagint as also preferring "wind" (disagreeing in regard to the Septuagint with McClellan, 519, who argues that the Septuagint is no more specific than is the Hebrew).

5. See G. von Rad's discussion of the image of chaos at the beginning of Genesis 1; *Genesis: A Commentary* (Philadelphia: Westminster, 1961) 47–48.

6. U. Cassuto, *A Commentary on the Book of Genesis: Part I* (Jerusalem: Magnes, 1961) 24, dismisses the arguments of commentators who propose "powerful wind" as a translation. Cassuto mistakenly assumes that such a wind would have to be understood as the force that separates the upper waters from the lower waters (verses 6–7) or the lower waters from the dry land (verses 9–10). As I have shown, however, the wind is rather to be understood as an element of the chaos described in verse 2.

7. See E. A. Speiser, *Genesis: Introduction, Translation, and Notes* (Garden City: Doubleday, 1964) 5, for a discussion of the Ugaritic cognate. See also von Rad, *Genesis,* 47.

8. Speiser translates the first part of verse 26 as follows: "Then God said, 'I will make man in my image, after my likeness'"—thus rendering the plural forms of the Hebrew as singular forms in English in order to convey their proper sense (*Genesis,* 4, 7).

9. Note that in these passages the doctrine of the Trinity is not clearly spelled out. There are only individual statements and ideas, which were later incorporated into the Church's doctrine.

10. We should also note that it is quite a leap from the plural noun and verb in Gen. 1:26 (if, for the sake of argumentation only, one were to entertain the idea that the plurals might point to more than one Person of the Godhead) to any claimed, clear reference to the Word in Genesis 1.

11. For examples of the disciples' misunderstanding of Jesus see Mark 8:27–33; Matt. 26:51–54; Luke 24:1–27; Matt. 11:2–3.

12. The Jews did not fail to recognize Jesus as the Christ (Messiah) because they were poor interpreters of Scripture. Rather, the Old Testament is open-ended enough that the Jewish community could formulate expectations of the Christ very different from those that Christianity came to adopt.

6 Was Cain's Offering

Rejected by God Because It Was Not a Blood Sacrifice?

YES: HERSCHEL H. HOBBS

"And the Lord [Yahweh, Jehovah] had respect [looked with favor] unto Abel and his offering: but unto Cain and his offering he had not respect [did not look with favor]" (Gen. 4:4-5 KJV).

Jehovah looked with favor upon or accepted Abel and his offering, but he did not look with favor upon—he rejected—Cain and his offering. Why was this done—in both cases? We do not know. But Cain and Abel knew. The reason in each case is related to the other, but in contrast.

NO: JOEL D. HECK

Why was Cain's offering rejected by God, while Abel's offering was accepted (Gen. 4:3–5)? Was it because Abel brought a blood sacrifice, while Cain brought a sacrifice of grain? Was it that both men were expected to offer a blood sacrifice, but Cain ignored or rejected that requirement? Or was there some other reason for the rejection of Cain's offering? This essay contends that the issue was not blood sacrifice. Cain's offering was rejected because of his attitude, which

130

Interpreters hold to various views as to Jehovah's different responses to the two offerings. The Bible does not give
the reason. G. Henton Davies summarizes the principal
different views:

> The preference may have been due to (a) a different disposition of
> spirit in the brothers; (b) the material of the offering, flesh and fat not
> fruit; (c) the method of the offering—the first-fruits by presentation
> only [the text does not say first-fruits, only fruit], the firstling, by sacri-
> fice, that is, by death, and presentation. This means only a blood ritual
> was acceptable.[1]

As to disposition, George Livingston says that "Cain
could not take second place to anyone."[2] Commenting on
the same thing Clyde Francisco says:

YES

NO

made his offering unacceptable.

There are two major groups of people who claim that
the presence or absence of blood was a key factor. First,
blood is the issue for some of those scholars who do not
read the story of Cain and Abel in Genesis 4:1–16 as
straightforward history. For them the account is myth,
legend, folk story, or something similar.[1]

Second, there are many others, most of them laypeo-
ple, who think that blood sacrifice was the issue. We
may cite Henry Morris as a representative of this viewpoint.[2]

A study of this issue must involve a careful reading of
the text, a reading that neither assumes information
not stated nor ignores information that is stated. The
text must speak for itself. We turn now to Genesis
4:2b–7, since it is these verses that speak most directly
to the point.

The Genesis Account

1. *"Now Abel kept flocks, and Cain worked the soil"*
(4:2b).[3] Following the announcement of the births of
Cain and Abel in verses 1–2a, the author lists their occupations. No reasons are given for their choices of occupation, even though some have suggested that Abel
withdrew from working the soil after God cursed the
ground because of Adam's sin (3:17–19).[4] There is no
suggestion that one occupation was inferior to the
other.[5] Indeed, as Keil and Delitzsch have pointed out,

A valuable clue is seen in the mention of *firstlings* in Abel's offering. There is a corresponding "firstfruits" used of produce in the Old Testament . . . . The absence of the corresponding term in reference to Cain is conspicuous . . . . In contrast to Abel's best, Cain simply brought God something. It was not that it was poor quality [as the Talmud teaches]; it was not his *best*.

Cain was grateful to God for a successful year of farming; he wanted to thank him for his help; so he brought him a present. Abel in giving God his best . . . witnessed to his total dependence upon God, his indebtedness to him. Cain thanked God for serving him. Abel confessed himself to be a servant of God.[3]

YES   It is evident from these comments that those cited, for the most part, hold to views other than the second one in

---

NO   the two occupations can never be entirely separated from one another.[6]

The appearance of both occupations is, in fact, a natural result of the cursing of the ground. The two occupations simply divide the work assigned to Adam in 2:15.[7] The animals will no longer cooperate so well with man (see 2:19–20; 3:21), nor will the earth so easily yield crops (see 2:15; 3:17–19, 23). Caretakers of both are needed.

Even the order in which the names of the brothers occur suggests no superiority or inferiority. The alternating (or chiastic) sequence of the names in verses 1–5 (Cain, Abel; Abel, Cain; Cain, Abel; Abel, Cain),[8] apparently for literary effect, gives first position to each brother twice and suggests no preference on the part of the writer for either man.

Scholars who do not view this story as history have tended to read back into it the rivalries between the pastoral and agricultural, the nomadic and sedentary, ways of life.[9] They say that the purpose of the story is to explain why shepherds and farmers do not get along well. This point of view assumes that the story is created out of cultural conflict rather than revealed truth from God. There is certainly no evidence in the text itself that demands this interpretation.

Some would go on to say that the rejection of Cain by God is intended to show the superiority of the nomadic, pastoral life to the settled, agricultural life.[10] The author of this chapter, they would say, was partial to shepherd-

Davies' partial list. However, the counting of people holding to a view, while impressive, does not rule out other positions. Opinions are to be weighed, not counted. The purpose of this essay is to present briefly the case for a "blood sacrifice" as the basis of Jehovah's rejection of Cain and his offering.

As previously noted, the Genesis account within itself is not clear as to the reason for the Lord's rejection of Cain and his offering. Thus we can only speculate or seek to interpret in light of other biblical passages.

The one definitive statement about Abel's offering is found in Hebrews 11:4: "By faith Abel offered unto God a more excellent sacrifice than Cain, by which he obtained

YES

NO

ing, so he conveyed his preferences by this story,[11] which depicted God's preference for a blood sacrifice. Such an interpretation is guilty of reading something into the text that is not there. More seriously, it labors under the misconception that Genesis 4 is not history.

There are those who think that Abel's choice of occupation had to do with the usefulness of sheep for sacrifice, since atonement ("covering") required the shedding of blood. They would relate this to 3:21, where the blood of animals is shed in order to provide a "covering" or garment for Adam and Eve.[12] Then they would read 4:2b–7 as the story of a sacrifice made to atone for the sins of Cain and Abel, a sacrifice that required the shedding of blood. Since Cain did not offer the blood of an animal, he sinned against God. However, the text does not say that in this verse or anywhere else. Furthermore, there is no connection between the account of God clothing Adam and Eve in 3:21 and the story of Cain's sacrifice in 4:2b–7.

In verse 2, mention is made of the two occupations simply to provide the reader with some background to explain why Cain and Abel brought the sacrifices they did. They brought sacrifices appropriate to their occupations.

2. *"In the course of time Cain brought some of the fruits of the soil as an offering to the Lord"* (verse 3). Most commentators agree that the opening phrase refers to an indefinite length of time that had transpired

witness that he was righteous, God testifying of his gifts: and by it he being dead yet speaketh" (KJV). Though being dead, yet "he continues to speak" *(lalei)*. Certainly he keeps on speaking to future generations as to the validity of faith. May it not also include speaking to the present problem? The best interpreter of the Bible is the Bible itself. But, of course, the element of human weakness enters the picture as human beings seek to interpret the interpretation. For this reason conscientious interpreters often arrive at differing conclusions.

YES

It was "by faith" that Abel offered a "more excellent sacri-

NO

after the beginning of their respective occupations. Whether this was the first such sacrifice cannot be determined from the text.

Just what is intended by the phrase "the fruits of the soil"? Many insist that the context suggests that Cain brought the choicest fruits. Since it is clearly stated that Abel brought the best of his flock, the firstborn or firstlings, they assume that Cain would have done no less.[13] Moreoever, the Hebrew word for "offering," *minḥâ,* used in verse 3 of Cain's gift, they say correctly, is used of both Cain's offering and Abel's offering in verses 4b–5a. Many of the rabbinical writings disagreed, suggesting that Cain brought produce of the poorest kind, in some cases specifying flax seed as the offering.[14] Were the rabbis correct?

It is certain that "offering," *minḥâ,* does not always refer to a blood sacrifice. It is used in its general sense in, e.g., Numbers 16:15; Judges 6:18; I Samuel 2:17 to mean "gift, present, offering." It is used in that same sense here.[15] Later, both grain offerings and blood offerings were acceptable under the Mosaic law. It should not surprise us that the same was true at the time of Cain and Abel.

However, the important point is the contrast between the phrase "some of the fruits" (verse 3) and the phrase "some of the firstborn" (verse 4). The former phrase is a general reference, while the latter refers to the choicest part of the flock.

3. *"But Abel brought fat portions from some of the firstborn of his flock. The Lord looked with favor on*

fice" than *(para)* Cain. A. T. Robertson says "literally, 'more sacrifice' (comparative of *polys,* much)."[4] This evidently means more in quality, not quantity. For this reason "he had witness borne" *(emartyrēthē,* passive voice) concerning him "to be righteous" *(einai dikaios).* Arndt and Gingrich cite Hebrews 11:4 as an example of the Old Testament concept of "righteous" in the religious sense of "not violating the sovereignty of God, and keeping his laws."[5]

Now all this Abel did by "faith." Faith in what or in whom? Obviously it is faith in God's sovereignty and his laws. God's sovereignty means that he can act within him-

YES

NO

Abel and his offering, but on Cain and his offering he did not look with favor" (verses 4–5b). The RSV translates more literally in this verse: "Abel brought of the firstlings of his flock and of their fat portions. And the Lord had regard for Abel and his offering."[16] Notice that the additional phrase "and of their fat portions" emphasizes the nature of Abel's offering. The fat portions were later seen as the choicest portions of the animal, and they are probably seen that way here as well. Mention of the fat portions makes it clear that the animal was killed, but it also emphasizes the nature of Abel's offering. The additional phrase, in my opinion, was intended to draw the reader's attention to the difference between the two sacrifices.[17] E. A. Speiser writes that this phrase offers a clear contrast between the unstinted offering of Abel and the minimal contribution of Cain.[18] If, as pointed out earlier, the author of Genesis 4 intends to indicate that Cain and Abel brought sacrifices appropriate to their ways of life, the rejection of Cain's sacrifice is not likely to be due to the absence of a blood sacrifice. It may, however, be due to the attitude of Cain as reflected in the poorer quality of the sacrifice.[19]

There are three major explanations for the rejection of Cain's sacrifice. Some scholars claim that the reason is to be found in God; Cain did nothing wrong, since his sacrifice was of the same quality as Abel's.[20] In reality, they would say, there is no reason given for the rejection of Cain's sacrifice, so we must attribute the rejection to the sovereign will of God.

self without the advice or consent of anyone outside himself, and in keeping with his benevolent will and purpose—which brings us back to the Genesis account.

The first example of this in the spiritual sense is Jehovah's expressed will concerning the forbidden fruit. Through their disobedience, for the first time Adam and Eve realized that they were naked. In their effort to cover themselves they made aprons out of leaves, the fruit of the ground. Since their awareness of nakedness followed their sin, there is between them a direct relationship of cause and effect. Therefore there is reason to see in their aprons an effort to cover their sin.

YES

NO

One variation of this viewpoint sees the text explaining the rejection as God's preference (or, if Genesis is seen as a purely human work and not a divine one, as preference of certain men) for the shepherd over the farmer, the nomad over the sedentary agriculturalist, that which grows spontaneously over that which has to be cultivated.[21] However, Genesis 27:27 shows that God has blessed the land and its produce just as much as animals and their keepers. Furthermore, such an interpretation gives us a jaundiced view of God. He does not show favoritism (Acts 10:34).

In the view of Gerhard von Rad, the story shows God's preference for a blood sacrifice—but von Rad denies that Cain's actions or attitude had anything to do with his rejection. He places acceptance and rejection completely within God's free will and removes it from man.[22] Claus Westermann writes similarly: "It is saying something about the immutable; it happens so."[23] Although it is usually not specifically stated, many who hold this view would see here the rivalry between Israel and Judah, the Northern Kingdom and the Southern Kingdom (after the split of the nation in 931 B.C.), the former of which consisted primarily of grain farmers and the latter of which consisted primarily of shepherds. In either case the reason is to be found in God.

The second major explanation is that the reason for rejection is to be found in Cain's attitude. This viewpoint has two major variations. One is that the sinful attitude of Cain resulted in his failure to bring the re-

Eventually Jehovah made "coats of skin, and clothed them." This implies the death of an innocent victim—a blood sacrifice, if you please—in order to cover the couple's sin. We are not told what animal was the victim.

In the case of Abel and Cain, some interpreters hold that sin was not involved in their offerings. Actually, the Bible leaves this an open question. To argue from silence is the weakest of all arguments in logic. So this position rests on an uncertain foundation. Simply because the Bible does not say what was the nature of the offering, no one is justified in saying what the Bible would have said had it been more specific. Neither can one argue dogmatically on the

YES

NO

quired blood sacrifice. The other is that the sinful attitude of Cain (pride—perhaps over his position as firstborn?) resulted in his failure to bring the best of his crop.[24] Even though he prefers the first major explanation, Westermann points out the great importance of the sacrifice of firstfruits in primitive cultures.[25] That importance supports the idea that the issue in Genesis 4 involved firstfruits.

Certainly one of the messages that dominates the entire Bible is that God has no pleasure in mere outward forms. He desires the sincere attitude of the heart. Indeed, some have suggested that Hosea 6:6 summarizes the entire prophetic message of the Old Testament: "For I desire mercy, not sacrifice, and acknowledgment of God rather than burnt offerings." The New Testament witness also supports this point of view, and we will turn to that later.

The third major viewpoint is that the text is silent. No reason is given for God's acceptance or rejection, because that is not the concern of the writer. The concern is Cain's response to God's rejection, not the reason for the rejection.[26]

The connection with blood sacrifice is maintained by Morris, who suggests that God had instructed Cain and Abel "about the necessity of substitutionary sacrifice as a prerequisite to approaching God."[27] Morris goes on to maintain that this instruction was probably given when the Lord killed some animals and made garments of skin for Adam and Eve (3:21). Whereas Cain had previ-

basis of various offerings prescribed later in the Mosaic code.[6] Donald Grey Barnhouse is correct in saying, "Later God demanded the fruit. . . . But the blood must come first."[7]

However, in light of Genesis 3:7, 21 certain suggestions are in order. Insofar as the biblical record up to this point is concerned, there is no hint of any offering other than a blood sacrifice for sin.[8] To see any other is to color the account with later developments. Also it is entirely possible that Adam and Eve related their experience to their sons. Before there were written records, the ancients orally passed their history on from one generation to another. Even had this not been done in the case under consider-

YES

NO

ously purchased sheep from Abel, he resented this dependence upon his brother, rebelled, and refused to make the necessary purchase on this occasion. Instead, he brought the fruit of the ground.[28]

However, the text of 4:2b–7 nowhere states that substitutionary sacrifice was here required by God, that this was a sacrifice intended to atone for sin, that Cain had previously purchased sheep from Abel, or even that Cain and Abel had previously offered any sacrifices. Furthermore, 3:21 does not speak of sacrifice, only of the making of garments from skins. It is possible that God used the skins of animals that had died, perhaps even the skins of the first casualties in the animal world as a result of the fall. However, even if it be granted that God or man may have slain animals in order to make skins, there is no hint that such a slaying involved a sacrifice to God.

Little needs to be said regarding how Cain became aware of the rejection of his sacrifice. Some have suggested that fire consumed Abel's offering but not Cain's.[29] Some say that smoke ascended from Abel's offering.[30] Some say that there was a visible sign in the sacrifice itself.[31] Some say that Abel prospered thereafter but Cain did not.[32] Some say that God appeared only at the offering place of Abel, but the text suggests the same place for the offering of both Cain and Abel.[33] After all the speculation has been made, however, we must admit that the text simply does not say. Nor is it

ation, Jehovah himself could have revealed to these brothers his will about animal sacrifice.

However the knowledge came to them, we can suppose that they knew this. "By faith" Abel obeyed Jehovah's sovereign commandment. As a shepherd he brought "the firstlings of his flock and of the fat thereof." It was not necessarily the firstborn of the flock. This related to Israel's deliverance from Egypt. Apparently it was the best of the flock. Furthermore, it included "the fat thereof." Later Jehovah revealed to Moses that all the fat of a sacrificial animal belonged to him. It was burned as an offering to God.[9] The fat **YES**

---

important for us to know, particularly for the purposes **NO**
of this essay.

Another piece of evidence regarding the reason for Cain's rejection is the wording of verses 4b and 5a. The Lord looked favorably on "Abel and his offering," but he looked unfavorably on "Cain and his offering." God first directs himself to the person and then to the offering. There is an intimate relationship between the person and his gift. This shows further that the attitude of the individual is the determining factor.[34]

4. *"So Cain was very angry, and his face was downcast. Then the Lord said to Cain, 'Why are you angry? Why is your face downcast?'"* (verses 5b–6). Does the reaction of Cain to the Lord's rejection give us any additional information? There are those who say that Cain's angry response indicates that he was in the wrong frame of mind when he offered his sacrifice.[35] Leupold thinks that the falling of Cain's glance meant that he did not want to look God in the eye (if God appeared to him in some visible way).[36]

On the other hand, there are those who state that Cain's reaction was normal and did not imply that his attitude toward the sacrifice had been bad.[37]

Human experience suggests that anger and a downcast face can be the result of an earlier sin or an unjust accusation from another person. And yet, while the reaction need not imply Cain's improper attitude at the time of the sacrifice, it is likely that the context of the entire Cain and Abel story points in this direction. One of the most important messages of this chapter is that

was the richest part of an animal and belonged to God. Apparently Abel knew this (by revelation also?) long before the Lord revealed it to Moses. Knowing these things, "righteous" Abel obeyed God absolutely.

We may assume that Cain had the same knowledge his brother possessed. But the picture of him in Genesis is that of a headstrong person. He also would bring an offering. But no matter what Jehovah had said or his brother did, he would make an offering of his own choosing. He pitted his own will against the sovereign will of the Lord. He was like those who say they do not like a "bloody" religion. But Jehovah does—and he alone sets the requirement. Man is

YES

NO

sin, if unconfessed and unforgiven, can lead to greater and greater sin. Cain's sinful attitude led to an inferior quality of sacrifice, which in turn led to anger rather than repentance after the Lord's rejection of the sacrifice. This then led to murder.

We find God operating in this passage much as he did with Adam and Eve in the previous chapter. In both chapters God asks a question of the person who had sinned (3:9, "Where are you?"; 4:6, "Why are you angry?"), not to gain information (he already knew where and why) but to lead the person to repentance and restoration to God's favor.[38]

5. *"If you do what is right, will you not be accepted? But if you do not do what is right, sin is crouching at the door; it desires to have you, but you must master it"* (verse 7). The precise translation of this verse and its meaning is a subject of much debate. In fact, one Old Testament scholar calls this the most obscure verse in the entire book of Genesis.[39] I will not attempt here to explain the various viewpoints on each word or phrase of the verse. Instead I will offer my understanding of the verse, one that coincides with that of most commentators and with the NIV translation above.

Here God continues to speak to Cain, telling him that the cause of his dissatisfaction lies in himself. The problem is Cain's attitude.[40] The verse does not speak to the blood sacrifice issue. Whether it is a poor attitude leading to a bloodless sacrifice, as Morris suggests, or a

free to choose, but he is also responsible for his choices.
At the same time Barnhouse is correct in saying:

> We must not think of Cain as an iniquitous man at first, but as a cultured gentleman who thought that polished fruit was more esthetic than a blood sacrifice and who wished to consider the holiness of beauty rather than the beauty of holiness. I think of Cain when I see a man faultlessly attired walking down Fifth Avenue in the Easter parade after attending a church service where the bodily resurrection of Jesus Christ is denied.[10]

Cain said that as a farmer he grew vegetables and fruit. If it was good enough for him, it was good enough for Jehovah. It is not necessary to hold that he brought inferior products. The absence of "firstlings" implies that he simply brought the good but not necessarily the best.

Some insist that as a farmer he had no flocks but that he

YES

NO

poor attitude leading to the failure to bring his best offering, we cannot tell from this verse. The point is that Cain can prevent alienation from God, whether that be in future sacrifices or in his future relationship with God in general, by turning from the wrong and doing what is right.[41]

Sin is pictured as a dangerous, crouching animal, ready to pounce upon its prey, control it, and bring it to even greater ruin. As the final clause suggests, however, Cain can master the problem. Should Cain choose to dwell on his discontent, he could be heading for more serious problems. As stated previously the succeeding verses, which tell the story of Abel's murder, suggest that a major purpose of the author of this chapter is to point out the problem of one sin leading to another and to suggest the importance of nipping the problem in the bud.

S. R. Driver calls the chapter "a striking example of the manner in which the propensity to sin may be transmitted, in even an aggravated form, from one generation to another."[42] The problem of sin, which first affected husband and wife, has now also affected the brother-brother relationship.[43]

The New Testament Evidence

What does the New Testament say about the Cain and Abel story? There are two passages in particular

brought what he had. True. But he could have exchanged some of his produce for an animal from Abel's flock. He simply did not do it.

The tragic result was that his offering was rejected. The seemingly best of human reason is futile if it runs counter to the revelation of God. Like most people who choose to go their own way in spite of God's will, he did not blame himself for the consequences. In reality he blamed Jehovah himself. But he vented his wrath upon his brother.

By way of summary, the book of Genesis is a book of beginnings, as the name implies. It tells of the origin of all things,[11] both material and spiritual. It presents the creation of man in God's image. It talks about man's sin and the consequences of such. The *Protevangelium* (Gen. 3:15) speaks of the victory through suffering of "the seed of the woman" over the serpent, Satan. "Coats of skin" dimly speaks of the sacrifice of the supremely sinless Victim for the sins of men. While it is not so called, it speaks of sacrifice as depicted in Abel's offering. The flood presents a new

YES

NO

that lend support to the view expressed above, although they do not help us to decide between the issue of blood sacrifice or firstfruits. In Hebrews 11:4 the writer states: "By faith Abel offered God a better sacrifice than Cain did. By faith he was commended as a righteous man, when God spoke well of his offerings." Here the inspired writer tells us that Abel's attitude was one of faith and that it was this faith that made his sacrifice better than Cain's.

The other passage is 1 John 3:12: "Do not be like Cain, who belonged to the evil one and murdered his brother. And why did he murder him? Because his own actions were evil and his brother's were righteous." Most commentators agree that the evil actions of Cain that led to murder were the actions involved in the offering of his sacrifice. Cain had a fundamental moral problem that rendered his sacrifice unacceptable.

Conclusion

The picture that we have from the New Testament is consistent with the conclusions drawn in the explanation of the Old Testament text itself. Cain's sacrifice was

beginning. Through the ages Jehovah chose one man, Abraham, through whom his redemptive purpose should run.

Beyond Genesis lies the exodus, a priest-nation, and the system of sacrifices that is but the "shadow of good things to come" (Heb. 10:1). The reality of the "shadow" is Jesus Christ, who gave his life, his blood, as a sacrifice on behalf of all, the Savior of all who believe in him as Savior.

Flowing out of eternity and depicted in the accepted sacrifice of Abel is the saving purpose of the eternal God. The author of Hebrews voiced eternal truth when he wrote that "without shedding of blood is no remission" (Heb. 9:22). Like Cain and his offering, God rejects all else.

YES

NO

rejected by God, because Cain's sinful attitude was reflected in the poor quality of his sacrifice. As is so often the case in modern human experience, poor attitude and poor actions corresponded to one another. However, it was not a matter of one sacrifice being a blood sacrifice and the other not. Unlike his brother, Cain did not bring the best of his crop because he did not approach the sacrifice with the attitude of faith in God.

ENDNOTES

YES

1. G. H. Davies in *The Broadman Bible Commentary* (Nashville: Broadman, 1969), 1, 144.

2. G. H. Livingston in *The Beacon Bible Commentary* (Kansas City: Beacon Hill, 1969), 1, 49.

3. C. T. Francisco in *The Broadman Bible Commentary* (rev. ed.; Nashville: Broadman, 1973), 1, 133. For further comment see M. O. Evans in *The International Standard Bible Encyclopedia* (Grand Rapids: Eerdmans, 1949), 1, 5; see also 1, 538–39.

4. A. T. Robertson, *Word Pictures in the New Testament* (Nashville: Broadman, 1932), 5, 419. See also W. F. Arndt and F. W. Gingrich, *A Greek-English Lexicon of the New Testament* (Chicago: University Press, 1957), 695.

5. Arndt and Gingrich, *Greek-English Lexicon*, 194.

6. Lev. 19:24.

7. D. G. Barnhouse, *Genesis* (Grand Rapids: Zondervan, 1970), 1, 30–31.

8. It is this writer's position that Genesis records true history and was written in the order it appears in the canon, not at a late date and reflecting the offerings of worship later prescribed in the Mosaic code.

9. Exod. 29:13, 22; Lev. 4:8–9.

10. Barnhouse, *Genesis*, 1, 37.

11. See H. H. Hobbs, *The Origin of All Things* (Waco: Word, 1975).

NO

1. For example A. Ehrenzweig, "Kain und Lamech," *Zeitschrift für die Alttestamentliche Wissenschaft* 35 (1915) 1–11; H. Gressmann, "Sage und Geschichte in den Patriarchenerzählungen," *Zeitschrift für die Alttestamentliche Wissenschaft* 30 (1910) 34; O. Gruppe, "Kain," *Zeitschrift für die Alttestamentliche Wissenschaft* 39 (1921) 71; H. Gunkel, *The Book of Genesis* (1904) 43; G. von Rad, *Genesis* (2d ed.; Philadelphia: Westminster, 1973) 104; H. Weinheimer, "Zu Genesis Kap. 2 und Kap. 4," *Zeitschrift für die Alttestamentliche Wissenschaft* 32 (1912) 38.

2. H. M. Morris, *The Genesis Record* (Grand Rapids: Baker, 1976) 135–37.

3. Unless otherwise noted, the *New International Version* is the translation used whenever a verse is quoted in its entirety.

4. So Rashi, according to A. ben Isaiah and B. Sharfman, *The Pentateuch and Rashi's Commentary on Genesis* (Brooklyn: S. S. & R., 1949) 38.

5. U. Cassuto, *A Commentary on the Book of Genesis, Part I: From Adam to Noah, Genesis I–VI 8* (Jerusalem: Magnes, 1978) 203; F. Delitzsch, *A New Commentary on Genesis* (Edinburgh: T. and T. Clark, 1899), 1, 179; D. Kidner, *Genesis: An Introduction and Commentary* (Downers Grove: InterVarsity, 1967) 74; C. F. Keil and F. Delitzsch, *The Pentateuch* (Grand Rapids: Eerdmans, n.d.), 1, 109; H. C. Leupold, *Exposition of Genesis* (Grand Rapids: Baker, 1942), 1, 192; Morris, *Genesis Record*, 135; C. Westermann, *Genesis 1–11: A Commentary* (Minneapolis: Augsburg, 1984) 294.

6. Keil and Delitzsch, *Pentateuch*, 1, 109.

7. W. Brueggemann, *Genesis* (Atlanta: John Knox, 1982) 55–56.

8. Westermann, *Genesis 1–11*, 294.

9. For example C. R. Brown, *The Story Books of the Early Hebrews* (Boston: Pilgrim, 1919) 9. On this point see Kidner, *Genesis*, 74. A. Bentzen calls the story about Cain and Abel an etiological legend— that is, a story compiled to explain the existence of a later phenomenon, in this case the hostility between shepherds and farmers (*Introduction to the Old Testament* [Copenhagen: G. E. C. Gad, 1948], 1, 237, cited in L. M. Hopfe, "A History of the Interpretation of Genesis 4:1–16 and its Relevance for Biblical Hermeneutics" [unpublished doctoral dissertation; Ann Arbor: University Microfilms, 1965] 116). For B. Vawter the story is not history, nor does it explain the hostility between shepherds and farmers. It has the purpose of conveying the religious message that man must be on his guard against sin (*A Path Through Genesis* [New York: Sheed & Ward, 1956] 72).

10. I. Hunt, *The Book of Genesis: Part 1 with a Commentary* (New York: Paulist, 1960) 18; B. Vawter, *On Genesis: A New Reading* (Garden City: Doubleday, 1977) 94; E. A. Speiser, *Genesis* (2d ed.; Garden City:

Doubleday, 1964) 31; Weinheimer, "Zu Genesis," 33–40.

11. The assignment of this chapter to "J," the "Yahwist" (e.g. S. R. Driver, *The Book of Genesis* [New York: Edwin S. Gorham, 1904] 44–75), further suggests that critical scholars view the chapter as written from a southern or Judahite point of view in opposition to the northern or Israelite point of view for the purpose of advancing the claims of the southern kingdom after the division of 931 B.C. as the true people of God.

12. J. P. Lange, *Genesis* (Grand Rapids: Zondervan, 1960), 1, 255, on Delitzsch and Hofmann; Morris, *Genesis Record,* 135.

13. O. Procksch, *Die Genesis* (2d and 3d ed.; Leipzig: A. Deicherische, 1924) 46; J. Skinner, *Genesis* (2d ed.; Edinburgh: T. and T. Clark, 1930) 104; Gunkel and most modern commentators according to Cassuto, *Commentary,* 205.

14. The Targum of Pseudo-Jonathan reads: "It came to pass after some time, on the fourteenth of Nisan, that Cain brought of the produce of the land, of the seed of the flax, an offering of first fruits to the Lord." See also Cassuto, *Commentary,* 205; ben Isaiah and Sharfman, *Pentateuch,* 38; Brueggemann, *Genesis,* 132, 137.

15.Westermann, *Genesis 1–11,* 295; Leupold, *Exposition,* 194; Delitzsch, *New Commentary,* 180; G. Ch. Aalders, *Genesis* (Grand Rapids: Zondervan, 1981), 1, 120; Kidner, *Genesis,* 75; Skinner, *Genesis,* 103–04.

16. Procksch, *Die Genesis,* 44–45, would repunctuate the word *ûmèhelbêhen* to read "and from their milk," *ûmèhalabhen.* But "firstborn and milk" would be an unnatural pair.

17. So also M. G. Kline, "Genesis," in *New Bible Commentary* (3d ed.; Grand Rapids: Eerdmans, 1970) 86; Lange, *Genesis,* 256; Cassuto, *Commentary,* 205–06; Jewish Publication Society of America (JPSA) translation; J. H. Hertz, ed., *The Pentateuch and Haftorahs* (1st ed.; London: Soncino, 1975) 14. M. Maimonides (1135–1204), a representative medieval Jewish interpreter, writes: "If all kinds were valid for meal offerings, why did the Sages rank their quality? So that one would know which was the very best, which were equal in value and which was the least valuable. Behold, it is said in the Torah: And Abel, he also brought of the firstlings of his flock and of the fat thereof. And the Lord had respect unto Abel and to his offering" (*The Code of Maimonides: Book Eight, The Book of Temple Service* [New Haven: Yale University, 1957], 8, 10).

18. Speiser, *Genesis,* 30.

19. The Hebrew phrase *gam-hû'* is ambiguous. It could indicate a contrast or a similarity between Cain and Abel. For a representative viewpoint on each side see Leupold, *Genesis,* 195–96; M. Luther, *Lectures on Genesis: Chapters 1–5* (ed. J. Pelikan; St. Louis: Concordia, 1958), 1, 251.

20. J. Goldin, "The Youngest Son or Where Does Genesis 38 Belong?", *Journal of Biblical Literature* 96 (1977) 33 n. 36; Brueggemann, *Genesis,* 56; von Rad, *Genesis,* 104; Vawter, *On Genesis,* 95; Westermann, *Genesis 1–11,* 296.

21. Josephus was a proponent of this view, writing that "Abel . . . paid heed to virtue; he led the life of a shepherd. Cain, on the contrary, was thoroughly depraved and had an eye only to gain: he was the first to think of plowing the soil" (*Antiquities* 1.52). See also Goldin, "Youngest

Son," 32–33 n. 36; Gruppe, "Kain," 71; Gunkel according to Leupold, *Exposition*, 195; Gressmann, "Sage," 27; Skinner, *Genesis*, 105–06; Weinheimer, "Zu Genesis," 38; S. Levin, "The More Savory Offering: A Key to the Problem of Gen 4:3–5," *Journal of Biblical Literature* 98 (1979) 85; Ehrlich according to E. König, *Die Genesis* (Gütersloh: C. Bertelsmann, 1919) 276; R. H. Pfeiffer, *Introduction to the Old Testament* (New York: Harper, 1941) 162.

22. Von Rad, *Genesis*, 104.

23. Westermann, *Genesis 1–11*, 296.

24. So Oehler according to Keil and Delitzsch, *Pentateuch*, 1, 111; Philo and some rabbinical writings according to Goldin, "Youngest Son," 32–33 n. 36; Kline, "Genesis," 86; Hertz, *Pentateuch*, 14; JPSA translation; Cassuto, *Commentary*, 205; Lange, *Genesis*, 256; Leupold, *Exposition*, 196; Driver, *Genesis*, 64–65; Luther, *Genesis*, 1, 250; Delitzsch, *New Commentary*, 181; Kidner, *Genesis*, 75; Dillmann according to Procksch, *Die Genesis*, 47; Keil and Delitzsch, *Pentateuch*, 1, 110. There are other variations. Halevy suggested that since the earth had been cursed because of Adam's sin, Cain stood to lose out. Jacob, Tuch and others claimed that the objective worth of animal sacrifices was greater than vegetable offerings, so Cain made a wrong choice (Cassuto, *Commentary*, 207; Skinner, *Genesis*, 105). According to Aalders, *Genesis*, 120–21, an ancient Jewish interpretation was that Cain failed to observe the proper ritual, a viewpoint that rests on predating the Mosaic law to the time immediately after the events in Eden. Those explanations that resort to editorial reworking, saying that a writer took over an early tale and edited it, provide no satisfying solutions and create more problems than they solve; see e.g. M. S. Enslin, "Cain and Prometheus," *Journal of Biblical Literature* 86 (1967) 88. Some early Church fathers, e.g. Origen, Chrysostom (Hopfe, "A History," 86–87, 90) and later the Venerable Bede (673–735) (Hopfe, "A History," 100), cite Cain's attitude as the problem, but they do not say whether it resulted in the failure to offer firstfruits or the failure to offer a blood sacrifice.

25. Westermann, *Genesis 1–11*, 295.

26. R. Davidson, *Genesis 1–11* (Cambridge: University Press, 1973) 52; A. J. Hauser, "Linguistic and Thematic Links Between Genesis 4:1–16 and Genesis 2–3," *Journal of the Evangelical Theological Society* 23 (1980) 300.

27. Morris, *Genesis Record*, 136–37. Although von Rad sees blood sacrifice as more pleasing to God, he does not blame Cain's attitude. It was a rejection displayed entirely apart from man, totally within the free will of God (*Genesis*, 104). See n. 1 above for other proponents of the blood sacrifice approach. The views of Philo (49 B.C.–A.D. 20) and Josephus were influential in the early Church and on later Jewish commentators. Philo read Genesis 4 allegorically. Josephus (A.D. 37–100) likewise did not explain the text in its normal grammatical sense (Hopfe, "A History," 46–54). The reading in the Targum of Pseudo-Jonathan in part explains the origin of this viewpoint, since that Targum understands the offerings as the celebration of a primitive Passover. The Targum states that the offerings took place on the fourteenth of Nisan, the time for the celebration of Passover; so Hopfe, "A History," 28. Hopfe goes on to warn us, however, that Jewish commentators often interpreted "sentences, phrases, and words without concern for their context or histori-

cal occasion" (43). In other words, they occasionally took liberties with the text.

28. Morris, *Genesis Record*, 136–37. In this, Morris is repeating many of the arguments stated a century earlier by J. C. K. von Hofmann in his *Scripture Proofs* according to Lange, *Genesis*, 256.

29. For example ben Isaiah and Sharfman, *Pentateuch*, 38; Luther, *Genesis*, 1, 252; Jerome, Rashi (1105), Ibn Ezra (c. 1167), Theodotion, late haggadic Midrashim, J. Gerhard, F. Delitzsch.

30. Ewald, Strack according to Skinner, *Genesis*, 104–05; Bertholet according to Westermann, *Genesis 1–11*, 297.

31. Von Rad, *Genesis*, 105; Gunkel according to Cassuto, *Commentary*, 207.

32. Calvin according to Skinner, *Genesis*, 104–05; Brock-Utne, Cassuto, Ehrlich according to Westermann, *Genesis 1–11*, 297.

33. Knobel, Vilmar according to König, *Die Genesis*, 275; Schumann according to Lange, *Genesis*, 256; Skinner, Jacob according to Cassuto, *Commentary*, 207.

34. Luther, *Genesis*, 1, 257; Leupold, *Exposition*, 196; König, *Die Genesis*, 276.

35. Driver, *Genesis*, 64–65; Dillmann according to Westermann, *Genesis 1–11*, 297–98.

36. Leupold, *Exposition*, 198. Unfortunately Cain's downcast face has in some circles been attributed to Satanic ancestry. According to the Targum of Pseudo-Jonathan (4:2), Cain was conceived via Sammael (i.e. the Satan) whereas Abel was conceived via Adam (J. Bowker, *The Targums and Rabbinic Literature* [Cambridge: University Press, 1969] 132; E. Levine, "Syriac Version of Genesis 4:1–16," *Vetus Testamentum* 26 [1976] 73).

37. Skinner, *Genesis*, 106; Westermann, *Genesis 1–11*, 298.

38. So Westermann, *Genesis 1–11*, 299; von Rad, *Genesis*, 105; Driver, *Genesis*, 65; Delitzsch, *New Commentary*, 181; Aalders, *Genesis*, 121–22; Kidner, *Genesis*, 75; J. J. Davis, *Paradise to Prison* (Grand Rapids: Baker, 1975) 99; Cassuto, *Commentary*, 208; Leupold, *Exposition*, 199.

39. Procksch, *Die Genesis*, 47.

40. So Davidson, *Genesis 1–11*, 52.

41. Whether the word "lifting up," *śĕ'ēt*, refers to the elevation of the countenance (a smile?), acceptance in the sight of God, or forgiveness, the result is the same: reconciliation with God as a result of a proper attitude and, no doubt, repentance over the previous bad attitude. Menahem ben Yashar offers the attractive interpretation that *śĕ'ēt* designates the special position and dignity of the oldest son. When Cain offered a sacrifice of poor quality, he lost this special position. He would translate verse 7a something like this: "If you do what is right, is not the right of the firstborn yours?" For his complete argument see "Zu Gen 4:7," *Zeitschrift für die Alttestamentliche Wissenschaft* 94 (1982) 635–37, in the light of U. Woller, "Zu Gen 4:7," *Zeitschrift für die Alttestamentliche Wissenschaft* 91 (1979) 436.

42. Driver, *Genesis*, 62.

43. Again, whether the word *rôbēṣ*, "crouching," refers to a demon, real or imagined, as some suggest, or is a metaphor of a ravenous beast lying in wait, the result is the same: Sin has the potential of destroying Cain. This writer's preference is for the latter view.

7 *Were There People Before Adam and Eve?*

YES: H. WADE SEAFORD, JR.

A curious Frenchman was fascinated with the unnaturally shaped stones collected from surrounding farms. Certainly they were not fashioned by local artisans, nor had Isaac de la Peyrere ever seen drawings of these petrous forms in the literature at his disposal. The answer seemed clear: They must have been made by men who lived before Adam. Born in 1596 of Huguenot stock, Peyrere was steeped in biblical knowledge, which he used to interpret Genesis in a most unorthodox manner. Adam was not the

NO: GEORGE KUFELDT

In order to ask this question, one must assume that the biblical creation accounts in Genesis 1 and 2 refer to the creation of one initial human couple, one male and one female, who became the parents of the entire human race. While chapter 2 may be taken to describe the creation of an initial human couple, its real purpose seems to be to show the divinely-intended mutual complementariness and equality of male and female within human society. Its differing order of creation (man, ani-

148

first human being but the first Jew. Since Romans 5:13 states that "sin indeed was in the world before the law was given," there must have been many people—sinful people—living before Adam and Eve. They were the Gentiles, the origin of whom is described in Genesis 1. In 1655 Peyrere published his views in *Praeadamitae*. Although it went through five printings that same year and became the basis for a Christian sect, it was condemned by authorities—Catholic, Jewish, and Protestant—and ordered to be burned publicly. Peyrere himself barely escaped the Inquisition.[1] Preadamites were obviously unpopular.

Nearly two centuries later the climate of opinion had not changed much. This time it was a French customs official, Jacques Boucher de Perthes, who was fascinated by the mysterious stones, which we know today as Old Stone Age tools, especially abundant in French deposits. Unsuccessfully he endeavored to convince the intelligentsia that these were evidence of a very ancient culture. In England some

YES

NO

mals, and then woman) seems to stress that its primary emphasis is on the rationale for the human sociosexual relationship and not the origin of the species.

The account of the creation of human beings in chapter 1, however, is very different, as seen in 1:27: "So God created man (Hebrew, *'ādām*) in his own image, in the image of God he created him; male and female he created them" (NIV). At issue is the significance and meaning of the Hebrew term *'ādām*. It is certain that its meaning here is not a personal name since it has the definite article: "the" *'ādām*. Since the text says that God created "the" *'ādām* male and female, it is apparent that *'ādām* is to be construed as a collective noun, to be interpreted something like "mankind, humankind, human race." In fact the obvious pun in Genesis 2:5—"there was no man *('ādām)* to till the ground/earth *('ādāmâ)*"—interprets *'ādām* as "earthling," also without gender specificity. Theologically, *'ādām* is "Everyman/Everywoman."

When the text is taken just as it stands, it leaves completely open the question whether God created "the" *'ādām* as a single male and female couple or

decades earlier John Frere had promoted the same idea, with similar discouraging results.

Another century or so has passed. Although I do not foresee a public burning, or what I have to say being rejected out of hand by the scientific community, there are still those who would not agree that human beings existed before Adam and Eve. The vast literature of the "scientific creationist" movement attests to this.

When I say "existed before Adam and Eve," I am interpreting provisionally the opening chapters of Genesis literally—i.e., assuming that the initial pair really lived in the ecological and cultural setting described in the creation story. Let us consider this setting.

Perusing the biblical account in Genesis 1:11—4:20, we note that on the third day God commanded the earth to yield seed-bearing plants and fruit trees. These were to provide food for human consumption (1:29; 2:8-9, 16). Before this time the earth was not yielding food because there was no rain nor any person to "work the ground" (2:5, NIV). Therefore man was created for the purpose of

YES "tilling and caring for the garden" (2:15, NEB). Cultivated

---

NO many male and female couples. It simply states that God created mankind, the human race. One must read into chapter 1 the idea that God created only one male and female human couple who then became the parents of the whole human race, an "Adamic race." One is forced to confess that the origins of the human race are as much a mystery to the believer in the Bible as they are to the nonbelieving scientist, except that the believer knows the Who if not the how.

But if one accepts the interpretation that the human race began with one man, Adam, it is only a short step to theorizing about existing conditions before this father of the Adamic race came upon the scene. Such theorizing began in earnest about a hundred and fifty years ago in response to the developing science of geology and its discovery of fossil remains, which seemed to contradict the traditional dating of creation. This dating had placed creation at 4004 B.C. and was the result of the genealogical calculations of the Irish archbishop James Ussher (1581–1656). He had worked out a chro-

plants provisioned the larder of Adam and his spouse.

There was yet another dimension to human subsistence. Since Adam was a lonely soul, eating only seeds and fruit, God (on the sixth day of chapter 1) made from the soil an array of wild and domesticated animals and birds, bringing them to Adam to name (2:18-20). The serpent receives special treatment for its dastardly deed, being distinguished from both wild and domesticated animals (3:14). It is described as "more crafty than any of the wild animals" (3:1, NIV).[2]

Fortunately for the domestic economy, Adam and Eve's progeny complemented one another. Cain continued his father's occupation of tilling the soil, while Abel pastured the livestock. Eventually, however, this felicitous arrangement deteriorated into fatal strife between cattleman and sodbuster (4:8-11). As a result of Cain's murder of Abel, the tiller was banished to a wandering existence, obviously inimical to his occupation. Like Esau of later days Cain managed to wrangle something of a reprieve, which in his case took the form of a passport, protecting him from getting his just deserts from people he would meet on his journeys (4:12-15).

Apparently the writer of this account did not hesitate to suggest that there were other people around. That modern **YES**

NO

nology for the entire Bible, and these dates were virtually canonized since they were printed in English Bibles for centuries.

The continuing development of the science of geology with its resultant pushing back of the date of the beginnings of the universe made the 4004 B.C. date for creation an impossibility. Consequently Bible students and believers were faced with the admission of a contradiction between Genesis and geology "or (i) try to overturn geology completely or (ii) seek a different interpretation of Genesis."[1]

The first theory of harmonization of geology and Genesis suggested that geological formations and fossil remains were the result of the catastrophic flood described in the Bible. But continuing geological studies showed that the fantastic rock formations everywhere on the surface of the earth could not be reasonably ex-

wags make a conundrum of it could indicate a cultural incongruity in the communication process. For the original
author(s), it appears that the matter is inconsequential to
relating the narrative.

As if to emphasize the inconsequentiality of an inhabited
world already existing in the days of Adam's son, the text
bluntly states that Cain found a wife. Whether it was the
marriage or the unprofitable wandering, Cain finally settled
down and took up city building. Within six generations of
this urban[3] project the amenities of civilization were available, among them sophisticated music and metallurgy (including ironworking; 4:17-22).

Such an ecological/cultural setting is well known to students of prehistory and the early development of civilization.[4] The time of cultivating the ground and raising
domesticated animals would suggest a date after ten thousand years ago, when food production became widespread in the Near East. But there is some evidence that
the art of domesticating plants and animals was known
twice that long ago. Domesticated food was the economic

YES

NO

plained by a flood of only a year's duration. Geologists
concluded that such formations were possible only
after thousands if not millions of years of geological
change and construction. Geology and geologists
needed more time, but how was more time to be found
within the confines of the Genesis account?

One answer came through what has become known
as "the gap theory,"[2] a theory that permeates much
evangelical thought even to this day. This theory says
that Genesis 1:1 describes creation, which was then
followed by a catastrophe (1:2) that was the result of
Lucifer's rebellion and consequent judgment against
him and the earth. The catastrophe or gap lasted for
many millions of years, during which time the earth
was left alone and the various geological formations
took place. Finally, somewhere around 4004 B.C. God
recreated the earth in six literal twenty-four-hour days
as described in Genesis 1:3–31. According to this theory, "Genesis 1 contains an original creation, a judgment and ruination, and then a recreation."[3]

Fully accepting the theory, C. I. Scofield wrote of the

basis for the development of civilization and urbanism by 3300 B.C. Copper metallurgy is known from the seventh millennium B.C., bronze (a copper alloy) from the fourth, and iron from the second.

The picture I have just drawn is hardly novel. Harold Lindsell, for example, states:

> For nearly three centuries the accepted chronology of the Bible was based upon the assumption that Adam commenced his career around 4004 B.C. This chronology was worked out by Archbishop Ussher in the 17th century. Recent scientific advances, including the carbon dating method, make the Ussher chronology impossible. Many scholars accept interpretations of the biblical text which allow for substantial chronological gaps in the genealogical lists of Gen 5, 11, thus allowing for an age of man much greater than that suggested by Ussher. Bronze did not become common until 3300-3000 B.C. Tubal-cain, the 8th generation from Adam, according to this verse was *the forger of all in-*

YES

NO

catastrophic judgment or gap: "It was animal life which perished, the traces of which remain as fossils. Relegate fossils to the primitive creation, and no conflict of science with the Genesis cosmogony remains."[4]

According to the catastrophe or gap theory, Genesis 1:1 describes an original creation, including the creation of a race of human beings. With the destruction of the earth that followed the revolt of Lucifer, this original race of people was destroyed also. When, according to the theory, God created the world as we know it (1:3–31), including mankind or 'ādām (1:27), the original but now destroyed human race was identified as "the pre-Adamic race."

It should be clear to any serious student of the Bible that the Bible knows nothing at all of any "pre-Adamic race." This idea is the unfortunate result of sincere but wholly misguided efforts to reconcile the Bible with science, forgetting that the Bible is not a textbook on science and so does not require reconciliation with science.

Does the Idea of a Pre-Adamic Race Threaten the Doctrine of Original Sin?

Since, as has been discussed above, there is no basis in either the Bible or science for the theory of a pre-Adamic race, the question falls in and of itself. The

struments of bronze and iron. This, along with scientific data, makes it evident that the biblical chronologies have tremendous gaps in them.[5]

Among the main catalysts for the rise of cities were economic and demographic forces. Population had probably reached an estimated five million worldwide by ten thousand years ago, and by 4000 B.C. it had jumped to something like 86,500,000.[6] Cain had every reason to worry about running into bounty hunters. And as for finding a wife, he must have had a variety of maidens from which to choose. His investment in urban real estate would have assured the erstwhile farmer a steady income once again.

The ecological and cultural data contained in Genesis 1:11—4:20, if compared to established archaeological knowledge, places the events somewhere between ten thousand and two thousand years ago. An account referring to iron metallurgy could have been written, at the earliest, in the second millennium and would obviously contain elements of earlier origins—for example, domesticated food. However, let us say that even though iron metallurgy occurs within eight generations of Adam, using one of Lindsell's gaps we could place Adam at the dawn of the Neolithic Age (plus or minus a few thousand years). This would be somewhere around ten thousand years ago.

But if the ecological and cultural setting is interpreted literally, what of the implication that Adam and Eve were the first humans? Lindsell clearly states that "all human life de-

YES

NO

question may have even less validity when one pursues the related question of whether the doctrine of original sin is really taught in the Old Testament at all, and specifically in Genesis 3. To begin with, the doctrine of original sin stands or falls on the basis of whether one accepts the idea of an Adam and Eve who became the parents of us all. In expounding his doctrine of original sin, the apostle Paul bases his whole argument on this idea (see Rom. 5:14; 1 Cor. 15:22, 45; 1 Tim. 2:13-14).

Still, in his discussion Paul not only avoids using the term "original sin" but is not emphasizing sin—original or otherwise—as much as he is emphasizing the redemption that Christ came to bring. He moves quickly and decisively from the sinner to the Savior. Even if one accepts the idea of a literal Adam and Eve whose sin

rives from Adam and Eve,"[7] and this represents the beliefs of half of American adults.[8] But if that be the case, what about the evidence for human culture covering two million years with definable increments of development from a rude beginning to the sophisticated age of Tubal-Cain? With a population at the beginning of the Neolithic Age of five million, the culture of the Old World was a going concern at the time of a literal Adam.

Here is the impasse: If I try to be literal about the setting, I find it impossible to be literal about the traditional primeval protagonists being the first pair. To make things work out I would have to interpret the Neolithic Adam and Eve as allegorical characters that refer to some earlier date when humans came on the scene, the setting for which the author of Genesis knew nothing about.

At first blush such maneuvering might seem to harmonize theology with archaeology, but we are not yet out of the impasse. Did a human pair, whether literal or allegorical, ever produce a whole new species completely unrelated to antecedent populations? When could such an event have occurred? Those agreeing with Lindsell would apparently answer: "At the beginning, of course." But

YES

NO

plunged the whole human race into sin by passing on this corrupted nature through the procreative process, one must still ask the question: "If I sin because of Adam's sin, then why did Adam sin?" After all, the idea of original sin includes the idea of Adam's prior innocence, whereas his descendants are born with corrupted natures.

If on the other hand one rejects the idea of a literal Adam and Eve the doctrine of original sin falls, but this still does not and need not cancel the fact of sin in the world and in the human race. The evidence of it is all around us and within us. If the garden story in Genesis 3 cannot be used to blame human sinfulness on an original Adam, what is the significance of the story? When it is seen as the story of Every Sin—the description of the source, process, and consequence of every sin that has ever been committed in the history of mankind—it takes away all our alibis and confronts us directly with personal responsibility for our every sin. Instead of a

when has humankind been anything other than a population? Let us turn to the paleontological record to consider
the question of original pair versus population, and to the
related question: "When did humans become humans?"

There is overwhelming, staggering evidence that humans inhabited the world millennia before the Neolithic/
Iron Age setting of the creation story. The mode of
subsistence for at least a million and a half years before and
up to the Neolithic era was hunting and foraging. Certainly
humans ate fruit from trees, as Adam is said to have done.
But there were no domesticated plants or animals. Hunting was a principal source of protein. There were no towns,
much less cities. And man, like Cain at least in one respect,
was a wanderer. Can we call those who lived before a Neolithic Adam and Eve "people"?

Going back to the first evidence of life forms that were
differentiated from other hominoids[9] in a human direction
we encounter the australopithecines of Africa, which
emerged by five million years ago and which endured an
incredible three million years. It is obvious from the thousands of fragments found that these creatures habitually
walked on their hind limbs as indicated by foot form, knee,

YES

NO

story of original sin that corrupts all mankind afterward, it simply says that sin is original to the human
condition, and so we are all sinners by choice. Only the
human animal can sin, because he is a spiritual creature. Because mankind is human and spiritual, the desire to "be like God" is endemic to the human race.

Would Other Human Beings Apart from Adam's Race Be Outside of God's Plan of Salvation for Mankind?

Again, the possible answers to this question hinge on
one's assumptions concerning the origins of the human
race. If one assumes a literal Adam and Eve who have
fallen and so have passed on this taint of sin to all their
descendants, logic must dictate that God's plan of redemption, especially as described by the apostle Paul,
applies only to Adam's and Eve's descendants. Any
other human beings who might exist must exist on
other planets and so have no genetic connection with

thigh angle, pelvic structure, vertebral column curvature and base of the skull. Although their teeth were human, their skulls were distressingly (from our point of view) small. This, together with their protruding faces, might cause some to question their humanity.

In fact many of the scholars who were accustomed to dealing with these matters called them apes—though curious ones—for at least two decades after their discovery in 1924.[10] They are now placed in the same biological family as we, although not in the same genus. Among the known facts about australopithecines is their existence in populations in various parts of Africa.

Two million years ago most populations of redoubtable australopithecines were replaced by populations of *Homo habilis*. Brains had increased from pint-size to pint-and-a-half-size, lending to the head some semblance of human form. Since the first purposely chipped stone tools were found in deposits at least two million years old, it is assumed that habilines made them. With the exception of the larger skull, it has not been established that habilines were too different from late australopithecines.

Were these "people"? If australopithecines were not

YES

___

NO

the human race on planet earth, the only human race the Bible knows.

Further, any "non-Adamic" extraterrestrial human race must by definition be assumed to have pre-fall Adamic innocence and sinlessness—unless, of course, one assumes that this extraterrestrial race has had its own "Adam" who fell. In that case they would be considered to come under the biblical conditions and promise of salvation, being part of the "world" (John 3:16). (Any who might argue that the term *kosmos* in John 3:16 includes only that part of the world known to the people of New Testament times and so excludes other planets as places of habitation must realize that the New Testament knows nothing of the Far East or the western hemisphere.)

On the other hand, if one assumes that any extraterrestrial human race is untainted by any kind of "Adamic fall," one must still assume, on the basis of our human experience and history, that such a human race—

(after all, no normal humans ever have pint-size brains), then can the first toolmakers claim the title? If these were people, is there evidence that they emerged (were created) abruptly, one man and one woman, to produce all the African populations? Besides such an event being a biological fantasy, their close relation to australopithecines in time and form attests the impossibility of it. Were these people, or do we await better things to come?

By 1.7 million years ago Africa was inhabited by another species of the genus *Homo* called *erectus*. These rugged "preadamites" became skillful hunters. With the convenience of fire and other cultural amenities they soon inhabited most of the Old World: Africa, Asia, Europe, Indonesia. Undoubtedly he (or, more likely, she) plucked fruit, but there were only wild animals for him to name, none of the domestic variety with which Adam contended. Head size—capacious enough for about a quart of brains—of *Homo erectus* averaged larger than that of the first toolmakers, overlapping in its upper range some of the smaller, modern *Homo sapiens* heads.

YES   There is tenuous evidence, if one exercises great imagination, that *erectus* practiced a ritual related perhaps to

NO   because it is human—probably has sinned too. Each such extraterrestrial human being must have succumbed to the desire to "be like God" since sin is original to the human condition. Having sinned, every extraterrestrial human being, being created by God and being a part of his world, must be considered to come under both God's judgment for sin and God's plan of salvation from sin.

Where Did Cain Get His Wife?

This is probably the most frequently asked question concerning the Bible. It obviously stems from the traditional interpretation of *'ādām* as the literal original human being who became the father of the whole human race. Cain, then, is seen as one of the sons of the original human pair, and so part of a very limited human society since there is yet only one family. Where could Cain get a wife under such conditions? Umberto Cassuto gave a very straightforward answer: "One of his

elephant hunting. If so he was a religious being, unlike any of his predecessors—at least as far as the evidence goes. Surely these are "people"! With brains the size of the French literary genius Anatole France (who had an exceptionally small head), and with a possible proclivity for using hunting magic, *Homo erectus* is a prime candidate for being "people."

In order to proceed with caution, however, in attempting to determine who are people and who are not, it should be mentioned that *erectus* would not have looked like any human being I have ever seen, nor was his skull like any modern one I have examined. The face jutted forward, making the nose appear flatter than ours. The chin lacked an eminence. Foreheads were sometimes virtually nonexistent, and the grotesquely (by Hollywood standards) protruding brows would add authority to any horror movie.

Were the widely scattered *Homo erectus* populations "people"? If so, could they have arisen from a single human couple? Hardly. They were too much like their predecessors. Over the million-year span of their existence it is estimated that they increased to one million souls.[11] One developmental event that might give them status as peo-

YES

NO

sisters, of course, is meant (v. 4: *and he had other sons and daughters*); this explanation is given by all the commentators from Talmudic times to our own day."[5] Why did the text omit this explanation? J. H. Hertz comments: "The marriage of brother and sister was quite common in primitive times, but the Hebrew people looked upon it with such abhorrence (cf. Lev. xviii, 9) that Scripture makes no reference to the identity of the wife in this passage."[6]

If, however, one assumes that "the narrative of Cain has typical significance,"[7] and that "'Man' is not just Adam and Eve, but also Cain and Abel,"[8] the question about the source of Cain's wife becomes nonessential. Cain represents "Man" in community or social relationships. Just as the story in the garden (Gen. 3) is the story of every sin of Everyman/Everywoman, so the story of Cain's murder of his brother, Abel, "furnishes a typical example of the manner in which sin gains dominion over a man; and the psychological analysis of

ple, more than any other, occurred toward the end of their earthly career about a half million years ago. Some populations of *erectus* looked more and more like *Homo sapiens*. In fact it has been a matter of discussion whether these later populations were late *erectus* or early *sapiens*. If the later ones are people, perhaps someone will say the earlier ones were not. If so, where did the transition occur? When did humans begin? Maybe we should wait for bona fide *Homo sapiens* before we start talking about people.

Surely all *Homo sapiens* are people. But let us not be too hasty in our judgment. If we use looks as our main criterion, early *Homo sapiens* did not look much like Neolithic people. They still had rugged, not overly large skulls. Some of them did, however, have chin buttons, which gave them a more dignified look (according to modern standards) than *erectus*. Ranging from Africa, Europe, China and Indonesia, these distant relatives still bore the stamp of their predecessors, but we must claim them as our own genus and species. It should be noted that they were still hunters and gatherers. They did not cultivate their foods.

YES Around 75,000 years ago a large-brain edition of these rugged individuals emerged in Europe and southwest

---

NO the process (vv. 7, 8) is very complete."[9] By interpreting Cain as "Man" in community or social relationships, one is saved from the fruitless speculation that "Cain" is really a people or tribe—e.g., the Kenites, the tribe of Moses' father-in-law Jethro. More importantly, to recognize oneself in Cain as "Everyman/Everywoman" is to be alert to the subtleties of temptation to sin: that gross acts of sin have their origins in our attitudes and thinking.

What Is the Best Way to Account for Cain's Fear That "Whoever Finds Me Will Kill Me"?

This question is somewhat analogous to the prior question concerning the identity of Cain's wife, for who could have been there if we take the story literally? Driver comments: "According to the existing Book of Genesis, it is plain that there could have been no one. The inconsistency is one of which, however, the narra-

Asia. These were the notorious Neanderthals, who, it should be established, never had dinosaurs for pets, since the latter had become extinct 65,000,000 years earlier when not even a primeval australopithecine was on the scene. These Neanderthals were smart, having developed a relatively advanced technology and manifesting sensitivity in burying their loved ones. It cannot be gainsaid that these were humans indeed, but humans that did not suddenly appear on the face of the earth.

Formally designated *Homo sapiens neanderthalensis*, their genus goes back to *Homo habilis*, two million years before. They did not have domesticated foods, but they were intelligent hunters who practiced religious rituals. Neanderthals must have been "people."

By forty thousand years ago, early modern humans had finally established themselves. Although still stalwart hunters who displayed the anatomical marks of their heritage, they can be considered full-fledged *Homo sapiens sapiens*, the genus, species and subspecies to which you and I belong. Titillatingly, some appeared on the coasts of the Sea of Galilee—a stone's throw, as it were, from Eden. But the literally understood Adam and Eve of Genesis were not among them. The Neolithic was over 25,000 years in the future.

Were there people before Adam and Eve? If we interpret the ecological and cultural setting of Genesis 1:11—4:20 **YES**

NO

tor (or compiler) is evidently unconscious."[10] If the story is taken literally, a number of conjectural answers could be and have been proposed: wild animals, members of a "pre-Adamic race" who might still exist, or other members of the original family whose names have not been given to us (Gen. 5:4). All these answers fail again, however, to understand that Cain's fear is the expression of the guilt common to the human being who has violated human relationships and who realizes that he deserves some kind of retaliation for his sin.

Since "he is speaking in an utterly unreflective manner,"[11] he illustrates the guilt and panic felt by most people when the reality of their sin against another person is realized. The "whoever," the "people out there," exist first in the mind of the panic-stricken, guilty person who

literally, the answer has to be "Yes." When did these people become "people"? Regretfully, I must disappoint your expectations for now. But I will be ready with an answer when you can tell me how many angels can stand on the point of a pin! One thing is sure: These human and/or human-like forms occurred in successive populations, presumably related to each other. [12]

Can we understand the Genesis account as an allegory, written by persons—for example, Moses—who used the ecological and cultural setting with which they were acquainted to tell the story of human alienation from God and of God's redemptive purpose? If we wish to claim Adam and Eve as symbolic progenitors of the entire human race, we must consider them as representing an event occurring thousands or millions of years before the setting in which the text of Genesis places them.

YES Unfortunately for the literally-minded exegete, if the set-

---

NO has violated another person. Thus they are very real to him, even though his fears may not be realized later.

Why Would Cain Need to Build a City (Gen. 4:17) for Only Himself, a Wife and a Son?

The story of Cain's building a city is part of the continuing primeval events described in Genesis 1–11. Cassuto has observed that Israel's neighbors used to attribute the development of culture to their gods. This deification of the supermen of the past was vigorously opposed by the Torah, which "teaches that human culture was created only by mortals, by ordinary human beings, who were no different from the rest of mankind."[12] This characterization certainly would apply to Cain. By identifying Cain as the builder of the first city, the Biblical writer may be emphasizing that "the building of cities was something that happened prior to and outside its own history. . . . Neither Israel nor its ancestors had any part in it."[13]

This does not mean that Israelite tradition saw cities and urban culture as inherently evil and sinful. The Rechabites in Jeremiah 35 are noteworthy only because they are a vocal minority. In fact the history of Israel seems to point to the idea that cities and the ad-

ting is an anachronism for the beginning of the human race the figurative biological feat of the protagonists is equally incapable of literal interpretation. The paleontological record thoroughly establishes that one population is always preceded by another, making the idea of a single pair of humans procreating an entire species unthinkable.

A literalistic interpretation of the creation story generates insurmountable problems for contemporary Christians who are acquainted with scientific knowledge. The human species did not begin in the ecological and cultural setting described in the opening chapters of Genesis. There were many populations of people before Adam and Eve, as literally understood. Only by allegorical interpretation can theology be noncontradictive to archaeology, biochemistry, biology, and paleoanthropology.

If in some time-warp fantasy I could be brought face to face with the author(s) of Genesis to put forth such burning questions as "When did Adam and Eve live?" "Did any people live before them?" "Were they really the progenitors of the human species?"—if I could, indeed, muster the courage to ask the questions, in my mind's eye I can see the pathos on Moses' face as he replies, "I see you didn't get my point!"

YES

NO

vancement of civilization are a positive part of human history. Did not God choose the city of Jerusalem as his dwelling place?

As part of the primeval story, Cain again seems to typify human culture and its progress. As with the problems of where Cain got his wife and who Cain was afraid of, the biblical writer is not conscious of any inconsistency or possible missing details. He simply thought of cities as he knew them. In his concern to identify Cain as the first city-builder and his descendants as the originators of the various aspects of civilized culture (Gen. 4:20–22), he apparently overlooked the problem that occurs to us: Three people do not make a city. When Cain is viewed as "Man" in community or social relationships, the idea of his building a city for himself, his wife and his son fits perfectly.

An underlying emphasis in the Old Testament is on the basic social unit, the family, consisting of father, mother and child. Any city is a multiplication of the basic social unit, the family. What better symbol than Cain, who typifies human culture in its earliest stages, as the builder of a city, a typical city?

ENDNOTES

YES

1. "Preadamites," *Encyclopaedia Britannica* (1962), 18, 425; I. Robinson, "Isaac de la Peyrere and the Recall of the Jews," *Jewish Social Studies* 40 (1978) 117–30; B. G. Campbell, *Humankind Emerging* (Boston: Little, Brown, 1985).

2. An interesting set of opposites is part of the fabric of these chapters: God and serpent, serpent and wild animals, wild and domestic animals, agriculture and pastoralism, acceptable and forbidden fruit, innocence and nocence. Man and woman stand in sharp contrast to all these opposites. They are "one flesh" (Gen. 2:24b).

3. In the archaeological record, urbanism and civilization (see n. 4) are part of the same feature. The biblical account does not say that they are chronologically different either. Just because the sixth generation happened to be proficient in the arts is not to say that the arts did not exist until that time.

4. For anthropologists, civilization is a sociocultural, demographic phenomenon that occurs in human history some millennia following the advent of food production. Its characteristics include, for example, social stratification, occupational specialization, bureaucracy, populous aggregates, writing, monumental architecture, and irrigation. Some of these characteristics may not be present in all cases.

5. Note on Gen. 4:22 in *Harper Study Bible* (ed. H. Lindsell; New York: Harper, 1964) 11.

6. E. S. Deevey, Jr., "The Human Population," *Scientific American* 203/3 (1960) 195–204.

7. Ibid., 5 footnote.

8. "The Christianity Today—Gallup Poll: An Overview," *Christianity Today* (1979) 14.

9. Hominoids are members of the taxonomic category Hominoidea. This is a superfamily of the order Primates, which includes three families: Hylobatidae, Pongidae (based on recent biochemical evidence, some would prefer to distinguish as a separate group the Panidae) and Hominidae. The australopithecines and all the chronospecies of the genus *Homo*—e.g., *erectus, sapiens*—belong to the latter taxon, apes to the former two (or three).

10. Taxonomy, the procedure for classifying living forms, depends upon ever-accumulating evidence. In 1924 the criteria for delineating the family Hominidae did not include the mixture of traits manifested by the intermediate australopithecines, since before that date no one knew such a creature ever existed. It took a couple of decades to point out the

predominance of human characteristics over ape-like ones. The early situation was further clouded by a limited number of remains. For example, some anatomical evidence for bipedalism was present but inconclusive.

11. Deevey, "Human Population," 196.

12. The fossil record shows that mankind has always been a single biological unit, whether family (as in the days of *Australopithecus*), genus (since the time of *Homo habilis*), or species for the last 250,000 years or so. The unity of mankind is what I understand the creation story is about as well. The idea of two unrelated creations, preadamites and adamites, is biologically untenable. The paleontological events responsible for the emergence of human beings were too singular, too precarious, to imagine that the process could have occurred twice. For this reason, despite the undoubted existence throughout the cosmos of many planets capable of earthlike environments, it is beyond my imagination to think that *Homo sapiens* can exist anywhere else. However, the universe is very big, my mind is very small, and the Creator's ways are "inscrutable" (Rom. 11:33b, RSV).

NO

1. B. Ramm, *The Christian View of Science and Scripture* (Grand Rapids: Eerdmans, 1955) 177.

2. Ibid., 195. Ramm gives a good historical survey of the gap theory and its shortcomings.

3. Ibid., 197–98.

4. *The Scofield Reference Bible* (ed. C. I. Scofield; New York: Oxford University, 1917) 4.

5. U. Cassuto, *A Commentary on the Book of Genesis, Part I: From Adam to Noah. Genesis I–VI 8* (Jerusalem: Magnes, 1961) 229.

6. J. H. Hertz, *The Pentateuch and Haftorahs: Hebrew Text, English Translation and Commentary* (London: Soncino, 1952) 15.

7. S. R. Driver, *The Book of Genesis* (3d ed.; London: Methuen, 1904) 68.

8. C. Westermann, *Genesis 1–11: A Commentary* (Minneapolis: Augsburg, 1984) 318.

9. Driver, *Book of Genesis,* 68.

10. Ibid., 67.

11. Westermann, *Genesis 1–11*, 311.

12. Cassuto, *Commentary,* 230.

13. Westermann, *Genesis 1–11*, 327.

8   *Did People Live to Be*

Hundreds of Years Old Before the Flood?

YES: JAMES A. BORLAND

It is an almost universal human trait to keep track of one's age. Octogenarians are honored, and those few who reach centennial status are frequently reported in the news. On occasion one reads of a Tibetan, or an Indian, or someone else who is well over a hundred years old. I am acquainted with Baptist preacher James Aker, who is 115 and still preaching. These, however, are exceptions. Although the mortality rates have edged downward as medical technology has advanced, men and women in general still cannot

NO: DUANE L. CHRISTENSEN

Any reader of the book of Genesis is immediately struck with the extraordinary ages reported, particularly in chapters 5 and 11. In the ten generations from Adam to Noah the reported ages are as follows:[1]

	Firstborn	Remainder	Total
Adam	130	800	930
Seth	105	807	912
Enosh	90	815	905
Kenan	70	840	910

expect to survive their seventies. Moses' dictum in Psalm 90:10 rings true: "The days of our lives are seventy years; and if by reason of strength they are eighty years, yet their boast is only labor and sorrow. For it is soon cut off, and we fly away" (NKJV).

But the Bible records some rather notable exceptions to man's current relatively short-lived status. The four patriarchs of Israel—Abraham, Isaac, Jacob, and Joseph—lived to be 175, 180, 147 and 110 respectively (Gen. 25:7; 35:28; 47:28; 50:26). Aaron, Moses, and Joshua reached the ages of 123, 120, and 110 (Num. 33:39; Deut. 34:7; Josh. 24:29). These ages are not nearly so startling, however, as those recorded of many of Abraham's ancestors in Genesis 11, the chapter that introduces Abraham. Two years after the Noahic flood, Noah's first grandson was born. Genesis 11:12-32 records that Arphaxad lived 438 years, while the ages of his seven listed descendants down to Abraham's father Terah averaged 280 years.[1]

A similar contrast is made when the Bible records that many antediluvians (people who lived before the flood) reached even far greater ages than Abraham's near-term ancestors. Mentioned in Genesis 5 are nine men who died

YES

NO

Mahalalel	65	830	895
Jared	162	800	962
Enoch	65	300	365
Methuselah	187	782	969
Lamech	182	595	777
Noah	500	450	950

These numbers are not only excessively large but also seem to fall into a discernible pattern, as U. Cassuto has shown: All of the numbers in Genesis 5, along with those for Noah that appear in Genesis 7:11; 9:28-29,

> are either exact multiples of *five*, or else multiples of *five* with the addition of *seven* (one number, the years of Methuselah's life, was twice augmented by seven, one septennium having been added to his age when his eldest son was born, and another to the remaining years of his life). And since there are five such additions (one for Seth, one for Jared, two for Methuselah, one for Lamech), it follows that the sum of the last column is also a multiple of five.[2]

The question emerges as to whether these numbers

between the ages of 777 (Lamech) and 969 (Methuselah). Their average age was 912. Some readers question whether these listed ages are accurate, literal ages of the men mentioned in the text. Do these accounts reflect true history, deliberate falsification, accidental errors in textual transmission, or mere legend?

Were the Pre-Flood Ages Simply Legendary?

One scholar, whose large commentary on Genesis omits all mention of Genesis 5, connects Adam's son Seth (Gen. 4:25-26; 5:3-6) with an "Aramean tribal hero."[2] H. E. Ryle, former dean of Westminster, termed these accounts "popular legend" from "the domain of primitive tradition."[3] More recently a British professor concluded "that the Hebrews, like many other peoples, believed that abnormally long life spans should be attributed to the worthies who lived in the days before the flood."[4] Even Jewish exegete Umberto Cassuto referred to the pre-flood ages as "folk lore."[5] Clyde Francisco maintains that "certainly the biblical writers do not add or subtract from the genealogies they have received," but their sources may have been tainted somewhat "in the process of retelling the story."[6] This view was also popular among some liberal scholars of past generations, as both Whitelaw and Lange note.[7]

YES   No serious evidence, however, suggests that the biblical author meant to record anything other than serious histori-

NO   may have theological meaning rather than simple historical reference.

A tabulation of the succeeding ten generations between Noah and Abram presents a somewhat similar picture:[3]

	Firstborn	Remainder	Total
Shem	100	500	600
Arphaxad	35	403	438
Shelah	30	403	433
Eber	34	430	464
Peleg	30	209	239
Reu	32	207	239
Serug	30	200	230
Nahor	29	119	148
Terah	70	135	205
Abram	100	75	175

cal facts in the Genesis 5 and 11 narratives. The same thing can be said about the other biblical instances that record the ages of individuals, whether it be the age of an Israelite king at his accession or death, or the three times Luke notes Jesus' age (eight days, 2:21; twelve years, 2:42; thirty years, 3:23).

Were the Pre-Flood Ages Errors in Textual Transmission?

Another position concerning the great ages in Seth's family line is that our earliest records are the result of errors in the process of textual transmission.[8] This might be maintained by some in view of the differences in the numbers found in the Hebrew Masoretic Text (MT), Samaritan Pentateuch (SP), and Greek Septuagint (LXX). They do in fact differ, as the following chart reveals.

ANTEDILUVIAN AGES BEFORE THE BIRTH OF THE SON				POSTDILUVIAN AGES BEFORE THE BIRTH OF THE SON			
	MT	SP	LXX		MT	SP	LXX
Adam	130	130	230	Shem (after flood)	2	2	2
Seth	105	105	205	Arphaxad	35	135	135
Enosh	90	90	190	Cainan (only in LXX			
Kenan	70	70	170	and Luke 3:36)	—	—	130
Mahalalel	65	65	165	Shelah	30	130	130
Jared	162	62	162	Eber	34	134	134
Enoch	65	65	165	Peleg	30	130	130
Methuselah	187	67	187	Reu	32	132	132
Lamech	182	53	188	Serug	30	130	130
Noah	500	500	500	Nahor	29	79	79
Years to flood	100	100	100	Terah	70	70	70
Total	1656	1307	2262	Total	292	942	1072

Such differences, however, might be accounted for in several ways. Both the SP and the LXX differ from the MT,

YES

NO

Here a different pattern seems to be present in that the sum of each of the above columns is divisible by seven. After Shem the patriarchs live more than four hundred years for three generations. The next three live somewhat over two hundred years. Both Eber and Terah exceed the limits of their immediate predecessors. They also have special importance, as noted by

but in different ways, perhaps based on particular principles that each followed in making changes in the text.

A careful comparison of the SP and LXX with the MT in
both Genesis 5 and 11 seems to reveal some general ten-
dencies in their differences. "The interval from Adam to the
flood is *shortened* in the Samaritan text by 349 years as
compared with the Hebrew, and in the Septuagint is
lengthened by [606 years]. . . . The interval from the flood
to Abram is *lengthened* in both texts"[9] by 650 years in the
SP and by 780 years in the LXX. One overall result of the
SP was to somewhat even out the amount of time from
Adam to Abraham on either side of the flood.

Another general tendency may have been to even out
the ages at which men fathered a child before the flood and
thereafter, while making sure that Adam's age before the
birth of his son was not exceeded by those antediluvians
(except Noah) who followed him. Thus the SP subtracts
one hundred or more years each from Jared, Methuselah,
and Lamech, resulting in a generally downward progression from Adam to Lamech in the age at the birth of the
next progenitor. The LXX accomplishes much the same by
adding one hundred years to Adam and all others except
Jared, Lamech, Methuselah, and Noah.

For the postdiluvian ages of men at the birth of the next
listed descendant, both the SP and LXX add one hundred
years to each man (except Nahor), perhaps to bring them
somewhat more into conformity with the ages of the antediluvian patriarchs.

Were the Pre-Flood Ages Calculated Differently?

YES

Some have suggested that the pre-flood ages were cal-

NO

Cassuto, in that "Eber is the eponym of the Hebrews
and marks the fourteenth generation from Adam, the
seventh after the seventh."[4] And Terah is the father of
Abram.

In spite of significant research in recent years on the
matter of genealogies, "a satisfactory key to the theological meaning of (the) assumed system has not yet
been found."[5] Marshall D. Johnson has shown rather
convincingly that the present condition of the biblical

culated by a different means than is used today. This argument has both an ancient and a modern version.

In ancient times Varro (116-27 B.C.), a Roman scholar, asserted that the ages of the Hebrew progenitors were given in lunar months rather than solar years.[10] The Hebrew word šānâ ("year") is not a plastic term, but even if it were arbitrarily equated with a month the results would be nonsensical. If each "year" were divided by twelve (approximately) lunar months, Adam would have fostered Seth at age eleven and Enoch would have been only five when he produced Methuselah.

A more recent and novel speculation regarding different calculation methods is that of John Walton. He notes that while the Hebrews used a decimal numbering system and the Sumerians used a sexagesimal system, there may have been an interconnection between the sources for Genesis 5 and the Sumerian king list that resulted in scribes mistaking decimal for sexagesimal figures or vice versa.[11] Walton points out that Ebla's inventory tablets operated under the decimal system but used sexagesimal symbols to record it.[12] However, it is a quantum leap from this observation to the suggestion that both the Hebrews and the Sumerians owed their genealogical tables and king lists to a common source that their scribes hopelessly confused.

Are the Pre-Flood Patriarchs Related to Sumerian King Lists?

Considerable interest has centered around the similarities between the Sumerian pre-flood king lists and the genealogical table of Genesis 5 since both supposedly contained ten names, some of which seemed quite similar. This has led to claims of common sources, indebtedness,

YES

NO

dating probably points to a revision during the Maccabean period with particular focus on the rededication of the temple in Jerusalem in 164 B.C. by the Maccabees, which was calculated to have taken place in the year 4000 A.M.[6] After careful study of five different systems as preserved in the Masoretic Text, the Samaritan Pentateuch, the Septuagint, the Book of Jubilees, and Josephus, Johnson concluded that "all [these] systems

borrowing and the like, frequently based on the list of the Babylonian priest-historian Berossos (d. 260 B.C.).[13]

As more and varied lists were discovered in the past four decades, however, these supposed relationships have largely been abandoned.[14] The most complete chronicling of the many differences between the Sumerian and Genesis lists has been done recently by Gerhard Hasel. He points out the following facts: (1) The names on the two lists are in reality Sumerian and Semitic, respectively, and bear only a superficial resemblance; (2) the numbers on the Sumerian lists are the lengths of reigns whereas the Genesis record has length of life; (3) one gives a line of succession in rule while the other gives a line of genealogical descent; (4) the differences in the numbers are larger by a ratio of almost thirty to one in the Sumerian list over the Genesis list; (5) the Genesis account has ten names whereas recent discoveries show the Sumerian lists to vary from seven to ten names for the antediluvian rulers; (6) Sumer's concern is to show the political concept of unification of the land while Genesis traces ancestors; (7) one is a king list while the other follows the Hebrew literary genre of genealogy; (8) Sumer gives the history of a particular people while Genesis 5 is universal and traces the history of all mankind; (9) Genesis begins with creation while the Sumerian lists start when kingship descended from heaven to

YES

NO

are somehow related, that is, dependent on the same basic tradition."[7]

In his study "On the Chronology of the Old Testament," A. Murtonen has noted that "all of the chronological data given in the Old Testament bear an eschatological character—at least in a certain sense of the word."[8] This paper is an attempt to explore that particular aspect of the theological system of dating within the Old Testament that lies behind the rather confused picture of competing traditions discussed by Johnson. In short, it is an attempt to recover part of that "basic tradition" behind the separate textual witnesses that may well have emerged as early as the sixth century B.C. within the developing canonical process.

Any explanation of the chronological data within Genesis 1–11 must take into account the larger picture

earth; and (10) Genesis ends with Noah, the flood hero, while Sumer concludes with a particular city.[15]

In summary, Hasel concludes that the Sumerian king list and Genesis 5 and 11 show "a complete lack of agreement and relationship . . . manifested through a comparison of names, longevity and reigns, line of descent and royal succession, number of antediluvians, chronographic information, ideology, genre, historical emphasis, and the beginning and end of the respective documents."[16]

Were the Pre-Flood Patriarchs Individuals or Dynasties?

In the nineteenth century skepticism and science both grew as challenges to the biblical claims of creation and inspiration. Theological positions were changed to accommodate the latest claims of Darwinian evolution and uniformitarian geology. Perhaps in an attempt to avoid the conclusion that some antediluvians lived for many centuries, a novel interpretation of Genesis 5 was espoused in the later 1800s and maintains a following even today.[17]

The contention is that the names in Genesis 5 and 11 were used to speak primarily of tribes, clans, or dynasties **YES**

NO

of the Pentateuch as a whole, and perhaps of the entire Old Testament as well. In another paper I have already discussed the ages of Abraham, Isaac, and Jacob according to a single mathematical formula that was noted some years ago by Nahum Sarna.[9] Such a sequence suggests the presence of a fourth person, one who lived 64 years:

	AGE AT DEATH	SUM OF DIGITS
Abraham	$175 = 7 \times 5^2$	$[7+5+5=17]$
Isaac	$180 = 5 \times 6^2$	$[5+6+6=17]$
Jacob	$147 = 3 \times 7^2$	$[3+7+7=17]$
???	$64 = 1 \times 8^2$	$[1+8+8=17]$

A first guess as to the identity of this fourth person would be Jacob's son Joseph; but he lived 110 years. Another possibility is to be found in a closer look at the figure of Jacob/Israel within the Genesis narrative.

Rashi, the great medieval Jewish commentator, worked through the numbers in Genesis with meticulous detail and reached a number of significant conclu-

and only infrequently refer to particular individuals, such as perhaps Enoch and certainly Abraham. This would mean that when the Adam clan had exercised dominion for 130 years, a person was born in the Adam clan who eventually either ruled or was the progenitor of the Seth clan. The Adam clan continued to be powerful for an additional 800 years, and then perhaps the Seth clan took over or perhaps there was a gap before the Seth clan exerted its authority for 912 years.

By means of these assumed consecutive clans with possible lengthy gaps, it is thought that the supposed scientific length of man's existence on the earth might be accounted for. This view is the Siamese twin of the local-flood theory regarding Noah—espoused by Ramm, approved by Davis, and not commented on by Buswell.[18]

The dynastic view has several problems: (1) It is based more on probability than anything else. An allowance is taken as a law, and an exception becomes a rule. (2) Eve bore Cain and Abel (certainly individuals), but when she bore Seth he was a distant dynasty. (3) The text is careful in each instance to note that not only a particular son in the line was born but also brothers and sisters, clearly indicating a personal history. (4) The notation of the age at which a father begat a particular individual (a son) eliminates the

YES

NO

sions. According to his calculations, Jacob left home when he was 63 years of age. But he did not go immediately to Haran. As Rashi put it: "After he had received the blessings he concealed himself in Eber's school for fourteen years."[10] This is a rather typical rabbinic means of pointing out a problem or tension within the received tradition, a bit like the observation in Targum Jonathan on Genesis 22:19 where there is no mention of Isaac in the text when Abraham "returned to his young men" following the events at Moriah. Concerning that occasion the rabbis offered the explanation that "the angels on high led Isaac and brought him to the school of Shem the great, and he was there three years."[11]

Jacob was 63 years of age when he left home, and he served fourteen years in Laban's house before the birth of Joseph (Gen. 30:25). Joseph was 30 years of age when he became ruler in Egypt, and nine years passed

tribe concept for, as Leupold argues, "a complete generation is not thus brought forth within a tribe."[19] (5) If Adam,
Seth, Enoch, Lamech, Noah (notice the personal words
spoken by Lamech at the birth of his son, Gen. 5:29),
Shem (one of the eight on the ark), and Abram were all
individuals,[20] why should not the others be considered the
same? The brief reporting of one's history should not elimi-
nate that one from being considered an individual.

Are Isaac, Jacob, and Joseph to be thought of as dis-
tantly related tribes? Abram certainly was a man, not a
tribe. His father Terah is said to have had three sons:
Haran, Nahor, and Abram. Haran bore Lot, certainly another individual, and Nahor, married to Milcah, produced
Bethuel (Gen. 24:24), the father of Laban and Rebekah. It
should be obvious that Terah's family was but one generation, not a tribe or dynasty. Again, if that is true in Terah's
case, why not for his listed progenitor Nahor?

Another problem with the dynastic view is that even
though there are some gaps in a number of abbreviated genealogical records (Exod. 6:16-20; Matt. 1:8), they are
not extensive. Matthew 1 lists only forty-two names from
Abraham to Christ, a period of about two thousand years.
Counting the three known missing kings (Ahaziah, Joash,
and Amaziah), that would make the space between each

YES

NO

before Jacob came to Egypt. This would make Jacob
116 years of age when he came to Egypt if one assumes
"that the fifty-three years he spent with Laban etc. began immediately after he had left his father."[12] But Jacob himself said to Pharaoh: "[I am] 130 years [old]"
(47:9)—and thus fourteen years are missing. If we follow Rashi's calculations, Jacob left Laban when he was
97 years of age and spent two years en route back to Canaan. At age 99 he wrestled with the angel at the Jabbok, when his name was changed to Israel.

The total of the years Jacob lived with his father
Isaac and his uncle Laban was 63+20=83 years. And
since he died at 147, he lived 64 years in another
"home"—fourteen in "the school of Eber," two years en
route to Palestine, and forty-eight years as Israel in Canaan. The fourth person in the list of patriarchs according to the above mathematical formula would appear

generation only forty-four years—not much room for different tribes and clans to develop and rule. Luke 3 lists fifty-five names from Christ back to Abraham, yielding only thirty-six years between generations. What good reason is there for arbitrarily inserting possible large gaps of time into the additional twenty or twenty-one listed generations that span the gap from Abraham back to Adam? When those names in Genesis 5 are listed in the same context (Luke 3) as the other fifty-five names, why should it be thought that they suddenly became tribes or dynasties while all the others are quite obviously "regular" individuals?

Another major critique of the dynastic or tribal view has been voiced by Gleason Archer. He notes that "Seth is the oldest surviving son of Adam to be mentioned, apart from the exiled Cain, and it is difficult to imagine by what other son Adam's direct line would have descended before the allegedly collateral line of Seth took over."[21]

Why Did the Pre-Flood Patriarchs Live So Long?

YES It is this writer's conviction that the names in Genesis 5 refer to individual men who lived for centuries between the

---

NO to be "Israel," as distinct from Jacob, who lived sixty-four years outside of his father Abraham's and his uncle Laban's house.

C. J. Labuschagne has pointed out that in all cases the sum of the digits used in this mathematical formula add up to the number seventeen.[13] It is possible that an early form of the canon itself was structured in seventeen books—in four groups of four with Deuteronomy as a bridge between the books of the Torah, Former Prophets, Latter Prophets, and Hagiographa, as follows:[14]

Genesis	Leviticus		Joshua	Samuel
Exodus	Numbers		Judges	Kings
		Deuteronomy		
Isaiah	Ezekiel		Job	Proverbs
Jeremiah	"The 12"		Psalms	"Meg"

The designation "Meg" here stands for an early form of what eventually became the Megilloth, the five festal scrolls of Masoretic tradition. Esther apparently did not

creation and the worldwide cataclysm of Noah's flood. There are good reasons to hold this belief.

1. Nothing in the text gives the slightest hint that each pre-flood individual named in Genesis 5 was not the son of the one who is said to have begotten him.

2. The most natural way to read Genesis 5 is as a genealogy intended to give the line of descent from Adam to Noah. That is also how Luke, a superb historian, treats the record in Luke 3. Nor is there reason to posit large gaps in the record. The possibility exists for some minor gaps in the record, as in Exodus 6:20, Matthew 1:8, and Luke 3:36 (cf. Gen. 11:10 LXX). But the gap from Kohath to Amram is a mere three hundred years, not three thousand or thirty thousand years. Matthew's gap is limited to just three kingly generations comprising a total of only seventy years, not seven hundred or seven thousand years.

By analogy, the known gaps place limitations on the number and extent of other possible gaps. A few gaps in the twenty listed names of Genesis 5 and 11 could move the chronology back from Ussher's dates probably no more

YES

NO

become an official part of the Megilloth before Talmudic times.[15]

I have argued elsewhere for the significance of the number 140 in relation to the patriarchs in both Genesis and Job, the number being the sum of the squares of the digits one through seven.[16] Isaac and Rebekah married in Abraham's 140th year, and their marriage lasted 140 years. Jacob was 120 years old at the time of Isaac's death and spent twenty years in Haran with his uncle Laban before his return to Canaan. By one calculation he would thus have been 140 years old at the time he wrestled with the angel at the Jabbok. And, of course, his twin brother Esau would have been 140 years of age as well at that time, which also marked their reunion in Canaan.

Orientation toward time is rather different in modern western civilization compared to that of the ancient Near East. We face the future whereas, as Isaac Kikawada has recently argued, people in that ancient world faced the past.[17] If one wished to know the future, one simply read the events of the past and projected them,

than several hundred or thousand years at the most. The two million years the evolutionary paleontologist requires cannot be accounted for in any event. It would take a gap of one hundred generations (ten omissions for every listed man) in the Genesis 5 account to move man's history back a mere 16,580 years.[22] There is a substantial difference between admitting the possibility of gaps and positing that perhaps as many as 90 percent of the links have been omitted. Nevertheless, even the latter course cannot push back man's existence very far.

3. Why should it be thought incredible that Adam and his descendants to the tenth generation attained great ages prior to the flood? For more than three millennia it was not thought incredible, and it is still probably the majority view among believers today.[23] The following points are a brief recital of reasons why these pre-flood patriarchs may have lived so long.

(1) Human beings were created to live forever. Only sin introduced death as an intruding outside force (Rom. 5:12).

YES

(2) According to premillennial eschatology, in the fu-

NO

as it were, behind him or her into the future. If the future in ancient Israel was thus projected as a "rerun" of the past, perhaps in reverse, which would begin with the appearance of a "new Moses," the picture might be as follows:

Joshua/Joseph → New Israel → Fathers → New Creation

Both Joseph and Joshua lived 110 years, which is curiously the sum of the squares of the digits five through seven.[18] Israel is made up of twelve tribes, and the sum of the squares of the digits one through twelve is 650. The number associated with the fathers is 140 (the sum of the squares of the digits one through seven), and $110 + 650 + 140 = 900$, which is 30^2 or the square of the sum of the squares of the digits one through four. Within the narrative tradition in Genesis, Abraham was 160 years of age at the birth of his grandson Jacob. Isaac was 60 years old when Jacob was born, and Jacob lived with Isaac for sixty-three years and with Laban for twenty years. It is possible that Joseph's descent

ture people will again live for centuries (Isa. 65:17-25).

(3) The gift of long life after the fall would exhibit God's grace to man (or at least to pious men).

(4) In God's wisdom, long lives and fruitful wombs would sooner populate the early earth than otherwise.

(5) Stability in society, as well as piety, could be advanced through the continuity provided by length of days.

(6) Civilization and culture could be, and apparently were, greatly advanced due to the vast accumulation of knowledge made possible because each man lived so long (Gen. 4:20-21; 11:6).

(7) Physical conditions on the earth may have been more conducive to long life in the antediluvian age,[24] and the effects of disease, sin, and pollution may not have been as great then.

Conclusion

The biblical evidence seems to indicate that some people lived to be hundreds of years old before the flood. Theories **YES**

NO

into Egypt at age 17 took place in Isaac's 160th year, at least according to one calculation, namely $60+63+20+17=160$.

Moreover, the number of years between the birth of Shem and Terah is 320, which is two times 160. At any rate, it is interesting to note that $160 \times 900 = 144,000$. Is it possible that this curious number, which becomes the community of the elect within apocalyptic speculation (cf. Rev. 14:1), began in ancient Israel as simply the symbolic lapse of time from the promulgation of the Torah of Moses to the *eschaton,* conceived in terms of a grand reversal of past events in ancient Israel according to the following formula?

Joshua/Joseph $\rightarrow$ New Israel $\rightarrow$ Fathers $\rightarrow$ New Creation

$(110 + 650 + 140) \times 160 = 144,000$

The advent of a new Moses figure would thus lead to the establishment of a future kingdom of Israel. This epoch would be succeeded by an ideal age, corresponding to that of the "fathers" in ancient tradition, which would culminate in a new creation where the people of

arguing that the supposedly great ages were due to legend, errors in textual transmission, different means of calculation, or influence from Sumerian king lists, or that they can be explained as dynasties seem to fall short of the mark— some greatly. The historic view of the Jewish and Christian religions—that human beings did live to great ages—is not only totally defensible but most satisfying intellectually as well.

YES

NO God would eventually become what God intended them to be in the beginning of time.

It is probably not possible to recover the key to the theological meaning of the numbers and ages in Genesis 5 and 11, at least in detail. Nonetheless, it seems likely that the numbers are not to be taken as simply historical report. The mysterious numbers are theological statements that contain within them a look into the future as well as the distant past.

ENDNOTES

YES

1. The Hebrew word translated "begat" means "became the ancestor of." Thus when Arphaxad begat Shelah it means he fathered a son who was either Shelah or a descendant of Shelah. Even if it is assumed that one or more generations may have been omitted from the record of Genesis 11 it probably would not materially affect the average age very appreciably.

2. G. von Rad, *Genesis: A Commentary* (Philadelphia: Westminster, 1961) 112.

3. H. E. Ryle, *The Book of Genesis* (Cambridge: University Press, 1914) 91.

4. R. Davidson, *Genesis 1–11* (Cambridge: University Press, 1973) 62.

5. U. Cassuto, *A Commentary on the Book of Genesis* (Jerusalem: Magnes, 1961).

6. C. T. Francisco, "Genesis," in *The Broadman Bible Commentary* (rev. ed.; ed. C. J. Allen; Nashville: Broadman, 1973), 1, 136.

7. T. Whitelaw, "The Book of Genesis," in *The Pulpit Commentary* (ed. H.D.M. Spence and J. S. Exell; Grand Rapids: Eerdmans, reprint 1963), 1, 94; J. P. Lange, *Genesis* (Grand Rapids: Zondervan, reprint 1960), 1, 270–72.

8. This is the view of Rosenmüller according to Whitelaw, "Genesis," 94. He held that some names had been omitted accidentally during the copying process, thus allowing their ages to be added to the others. But this seems unlikely as Whitelaw argues in view of the "orderly progression from father to son" over ten generations.

9. C. F. Keil and F. Delitzsch, *Biblical Commentary on the Old Testament* (Grand Rapids: Eerdmans; reprint 1966), 1, 122 (italics mine).

10. Varro, *Apud Lactant. Institut.* 1.2, c. 13. J. Gill, *An Exposition of the Old Testament* (London: William Hill Collingridge, 1852), 1, 33, refutes this view thoroughly; see also J. J. Davis, *Paradise to Prison: Studies in Genesis* (Grand Rapids: Baker, 1975) 105–06; Ryle, *Genesis*, 91; J. R. Rice, *"In the Beginning"* (Murfreesboro: Sword of the Lord) 182. More recently Raske held Varro's opinion, and Hensler promoted a variation of the view (each year equaled three months), according to Whitelaw, "Genesis," 94.

11. J. Walton, "The Antediluvian Section of the Sumerian King List and Genesis 5," *Biblical Archaeologist* 44 (Fall 1981) 207–08.

12. Ibid., 208.

13. See G. A. Barton, *Archaeology and the Bible* (7th rev. ed.; Philadelphia: American Sunday-School Union, 1937) 317–26; E. A. Speiser, *Genesis* (Garden City: Doubleday, 1964) 42. See further J. Finegan, *Light from the Ancient Past* (2d ed.; Princeton: University Press, 1959), 1, 29–31, for more on the lists themselves.

14. T. C. Hartman, "Some Thoughts on the Sumerian King List and Genesis 5 and 11B," *Journal of Biblical Literature* 91 (March 1972) 25–32, demonstrates this, drawing largely from W. G. Lambert, "A New Look at the Babylonian Background of Genesis," *Journal of Theological Studies* 16 (1965) 287–300; J. J. Finkelstein, "The Genealogy of the Hammurapi Dynasty," *Journal of Cuneiform Studies* 20 (1966) 95–118; and A. Malamat, "King Lists of the Old Babylonian Period and Biblical Genealogies," *Journal of the American Oriental Society* 88 (1968) 163–73.

15. G. F. Hasel, "The Genealogies of Gen 5 and 11 and Their Alleged Babylonian Background," *Andrews University Seminary Studies* 16 (Autumn 1978) 361–74. See also R. R. Wilson, "The Old Testament Genealogies in Recent Research," *Journal of Biblical Literature* 94 (1975) 169–89.

16. Hasel, "Genealogies," 373.

17. Several statements of this view are J. D. Davis, "Chronology," in *A Dictionary of the Bible* (4th rev. ed.; Grand Rapids: Baker, reprint 1962) 133–34; "Antediluvian Patriarchs," in *International Standard Bible Encyclopaedia* (ed. J. Orr; Grand Rapids: Eerdmans, reprint 1939), 1, 142–43; B. Ramm, *The Christian View of Science and Scripture* (Grand Rapids: Eerdmans, 1954) 341–42; J. O. Buswell, Jr., *A Systematic Theology of the Christian Religion* (Grand Rapids: Zondervan, 1962), 1, 325–43. For a more recent summary and brief bibliography see W. U. Ault, "Antediluvians," in *Zondervan Pictorial Encyclopedia of the Bible* (ed. M. C. Tenney; Grand Rapids: Zondervan, 1975), 1, 172–77.

18. Ramm, *Christian View*, 229–49; Davis, *Dictionary*, 235–38.

19. H. C. Leupold, *Exposition of Genesis* (Grand Rapids: Baker, reprint 1972), 1, 233.

20. See Buswell, *Theology*, 325–43.

21. G. Archer, *A Survey of Old Testament Introduction* (rev. ed.; Chicago: Moody, 1974) 198.

22. This is based on simple mathematics. The average preflood patriarchal generation (without gaps) was 165.8 years (1658 years divided by 10 generations). Thus an additional 100 generations would add 100x165.8 or only 16,580 years. Archer, *Survey*, 197, argues for gaps, but believes that there would be fewer than ten. For an excellently reasoned discussion favoring limited gaps see J. C. Whitcomb, Jr., *The Early Earth* (Grand Rapids: Baker, 1972) 107–11.

23. W. G. Plaut and B. J. Bamberger, *The Torah: A Modern Commentary* (New York: Union of American Hebrew Congregations, 1981) 54–55; Leupold, *Exposition*, 233; Archer, *Survey*, 197; Keil and Delitzsch, *Commentary*, 123–24; Lange, *Genesis*, 270–72; Whitelaw, "Genesis," 94; J. G. Murphy, *A Critical and Exegetical Commentary on the Book of Genesis* (Andover: Draper, 1968) 169–74; G. Bush, *Notes, Critical and Practical on the Book of Genesis* (New York: Ivison, Phinney, 1860) 110–13; Davis, *Paradise*, 104–06; H. M. Morris, *The Genesis Record* (Grand Rapids: Baker, 1976) 143, 152–62.

24. See Morris, *Genesis Record*, 143; G. H. Pember, *Earth's Earliest Ages* (London: Hodder and Stoughton, 1907) 202–04; J. C. Whitcomb, Jr., and H. M. Morris, *The Genesis Flood* (Philadelphia: Presbyterian and Reformed, 1964) 240–42, 253–55, 305–06, 399, 404–05.

NO

1. U. Cassuto, *A Commentary on the Book of Genesis: Part I, From Adam to Noah* (Jerusalem: Magnes, 1961) 260. Cassuto discussed in detail various parallels within Mesopotamian literature where antediluvian and postdiluvian heroes are arranged in similar patterns and achieve amazing longevity. As he put it, "the Babylonian figures far exceed those of the Torah, an average of myriads of years being allotted to each monarch prior to the Deluge" (254).

2. Ibid., 260.

3. U. Cassuto, *A Commentary on the Book of Genesis: Part II, From Noah to Abraham* (Jerusalem: Magnes, 1964) 253.

4. Ibid., 254.

5. J. J. Finkelstein, "Genealogy of the Hammurapi Dynasty," *Journal of Cuneiform Studies* 20 (1966) 95–118; A. Malamat, "King Lists of the Old Babylonian Period and Biblical Genealogies," *Journal of the American Oriental Society* 88 (1968) 163–73; "Tribal Societies: Biblical Genealogies and African Lineage Systems," *Archives européennes de sociologie* 14 (1973) 126–36; M. D. Johnson, *The Purpose of the Biblical Genealogies: With Special Reference to the Setting of the Genealogies of Jesus* (Cambridge: University Press, 1969); K. R. Andriolo, "A Structural Analysis of Genealogy and Worldview in the Old Testament," *American Anthropologist* 75 (1973) 1657–69; J. M. Miller, "The Descendants of Cain: Notes on Genesis 4," *Zeitschrift für die alttestamentliche Wissenschaft* 86 (1974) 164–74; R. R. Wilson, *Genealogy and History in the Biblical World* (New Haven: Yale University, 1977). The quotation is from Johnson, *Purpose*, 261.

6. *Anno Mundi.*

7. Johnson, *Purpose*, 33.

8. A. Murtonen, "On the Chronology of the OT," *Studia Theologica* 8 (1955) 133–37.

9. D. L. Christensen, "Job and the Age of the Patriarchs in Old Testament Narrative," *Perspectives in Religious Studies* 13 (1986). Cf. N. M. Sarna, *Understanding Genesis* (New York: McGraw-Hill, 1966) 84.

10. *Pentateuch with Rashi's Commentary* (ed. A. M. Silberman; London: Shapiro, Vallentine, 1946) 130.

11. J. Bowker, *The Targums and Rabbinic Literature: An Introduction to Jewish Interpretations of Scripture* (Cambridge: University Press, 1969) 226.

12. *Pentateuch* (ed. Silberman), 130.

13. C. J. Labuschagne, "The Literary and Theological Function of Divine Speech in the Pentateuch," *Vetus Testamentum* Supplements 36 (1985) 171.

14. Discussed briefly in "Job and the Age of the Patriarchs" (see n. 9 above).

15. Ibid., and "Josephus and the Twenty-Two-Book Canon of Sacred Scripture," *Journal of the Evangelical Theological Society* 29 (March 1986) 39–48.

16. See n. 9 above.

17. This particular point was stressed in his presidential address, "The Old Testament in Twenty Minutes," which was presented to the Society of Biblical Literature during its Pacific Coast Region annual meetings on March 29, 1985.

18. The number 110 for the age of Joseph is sometimes related to a presumed ideal age in Egyptian literary tradition. See N. Sarna, *Understanding Genesis* (New York: McGraw-Hill, 1966) 226, 231 (nn. 107–108), who mentions twenty-seven such references in Egyptian literature. Even so, it seems preferable to explain the number on the basis of a mathematical schema within the biblical material itself.

9   *Are the "Sons of God"*

in Genesis 6 Angels?

YES: F. B. HUEY, JR.

Most students of Genesis 6:1-4 agree that it is one of the most disputed passages in the Old Testament. It has been described as "a riddle,"[1] "strange,"[2] "difficult,"[3] "unintelligible,"[4] "unsolved,"[5] and "cryptic."[6] The history of its exegesis has been characterized by bitter controversy that seems no closer to resolution by today's scholars than by their ancient counterparts.

In spite of its difficulties and ambiguities, most exegetes who have studied it carefully give the impression that the

NO: JOHN H. WALTON

Genesis 6:1–4 in the history of exegesis has been the source of much frustration. Its brevity and apparent disconnectedness have largely doomed this short narrative to obscurity. Throughout the modern era, three basic traditions of interpretation have existed that find their differences in the way that they understand the distinction between the two groups mentioned in the context: the "sons of God" and the "daughters of men."

problem has been solved. In the middle of the second century A.D., Rabbi Simeon ben Yohai called a curse on anyone who differed with his interpretation.[7] A similar spirit of dogmatism still prevails (though hopefully without the curse on dissenters). Gerhard von Rad wrote: "The question . . . can be considered as finally settled."[8] J. Sidlow Baxter concluded: "Our conviction . . . is finally confirmed by the untenableness of the suggested alternatives."[9] Unfortunately, the interpretations of von Rad and Baxter are poles apart. Von Rad sees the "sons of God" as mythological, supernatural beings,[10] while Baxter insists that they are historical descendants of the godly line of Seth.[11] These are the two most frequently encountered interpretations today, but there are others.

Leroy Birney concludes with many ancient Jewish interpreters that the "sons of God" were rulers.[12] Similarly, Meredith Kline interprets the narrative as marriages between royalty and commoners.[13] H. Freedman describes the "sons of God" as "the sons of princes and judges."[14] It

YES

NO

Survey of the Positions

1. *The first position sees a theological distinction between the two groups.* The sons of God are viewed as the godly Sethites, while the daughters of men are thought to be from the degenerate line of Cain.[1]

2. *The second position sees a material distinction between the two groups.* The sons of God are viewed as supernatural beings (traditionally angels), while the daughters of men are mortals.[2] This is the position supported in the previous essay.

3. *The third position views the distinction as a social one.* The sons of God are viewed as rulers or princes, while the daughters of men are commoners.[3]

Two of the positions have updated formulations that need to be recognized. A variation on the second position may be seen in the many modern commentators who have understood this passage in a mythological context. Some would see the mythological aspect as a vestige from a polytheistic version, while others would understand it as part of a planned polemic on the part of the biblical author. In either case the sons of God, as with those who considered them to be angels, are seen

has even been proposed that the marriages were between Cro-Magnon men and Neanderthal women.[15]

In light of the long history of controversy over Genesis 6:1-4, it is unlikely that the present study will finally settle the issue in favor of a single interpretation of the "sons of God." Its modest purpose, therefore, is to examine the text as objectively as possible to see if the interpretation of the "sons of God" as supernatural beings is a viable alternative.

Liberal or Conservative?

Careful study of scores of interpretations of Genesis 6:1-4 gives the distinct impression that many scholars believe that one's interpretation of this passage reveals whether that person is a conservative or liberal. It is true that many conservative interpreters reject the supernatural-human interpretation.[16] On the other hand, equally conservative scholars insist that the passage describes a union between supernatural beings and human beings.[17] Therefore how

YES

NO

as materially distinct from the daughters of men. In this variation, however, the sons of God are not seen as fallen angels but as rebellious lower-echelon deities. So, for example, Kraeling[4] and Speiser[5] both draw connections to accounts known from Greek mythology, notably that found in Hesiod's *Theogony*. Cassuto[6] and Vawter[7] both make connections to assumed Canaanite roots. Westermann, surveying the history of the discussion, concludes that there can no longer be any doubt that "sons of god" just means "gods."[8] The purpose of the Genesis author is still viewed by these scholars as an affirmation of man's mortality,[9] and the offense is still seen as an unacceptable intermixing between worlds that were meant to remain separate.

A second revised formulation has built upon position three. The rabbis had contended that the sons of God were members of royalty because the term $\check{e}l\bar{o}h\hat{i}m$ is used to designate royalty in several passages.[10] Meredith Kline has suggested that this was not simply a matter of semantics but that divine kingship was in the author's mind.[11] Based on the work of Frankfort, Johnson, Engnell, and others, the institution of sacred kingship had become widely accepted. Kline viewed these

one understands Genesis 6:1-4 does not necessarily label that person as liberal or conservative.

Robert C. Newman has pointed out that the controversial passage creates a paradox for exegetes. Liberal scholars who usually are associated with denial of the supernatural generally accept Genesis 6:1-4 as an account of a liaison between divine beings and humans, whereas conservative scholars, who believe implicitly in angels, are the ones who tend to disallow any such import to this passage.[18] Willem A. Van Gemeren has brought this inconsistency into clear focus with his unsettling questions:

> Why does the theology in which creation, miracles, the miraculous birth and resurrection of Jesus have a place, prefer a rational explanation of Genesis 6:1-4? . . . Normally, the goal of interpretation has been the elucidation of the word of God so the community of faith may know what to believe and what to do. When, however, the object of interpretation becomes the removal of apparent obstacles to which the passage may give rise, reinterpretation is introduced, and one may wonder how this differs from demythologization . . . . Is the difficulty so great that it *must* be removed as something offensive? Is it possible that theology has taken the place of exegesis?[19]

In acknowledgment of the number of conservative scholars who accept the supernatural interpretation and the questions raised by Van Gemeren, the student ap-

YES

NO

kings as tyrants who terrorized the populace. The offense was understood by Kline as polygamy, which he attempted to establish by connection to the Lamech narrative in Genesis 4:19-24.

This position has gained some popularity and was expanded again by D. J. A. Clines in 1979.[12] Clines was struck by some of the similarities between the description of Gilgamesh and the description of the sons of God in Genesis 6. Gilgamesh is described in the epic as two-thirds god and one-third human. This is not, however, a material distinction and may not even be a social distinction. It is merely a matter of titulary. So Clines observes:

> That Gilgamesh was regarded in the epic as a historical human personage is beyond question; the belief in his divine or semi-divine origins explains his significance and the survival of the story of his deeds from ancient times, as well as his titles and entitlements; it does not mean that the epic poet conceives of him as any more than a man, and a mortal man at that.[13]

proaching Genesis 6:1-4 should rid his mind of the notion that the issue is one of believing the Bible or not believing the Bible or of conservative versus liberal. Rather, the questions that should be asked are: (1) Can "sons of God" mean supernatural beings? (2) Is physical union between supernatural and human beings possible? (3) Is the story historical or mythological? (4) What significance did these marriages have for the deluge that followed? Before attempting to answer such questions, however, attention should be given to determine how the passage has been interpreted through the centuries.[20]

History of Interpretation of Genesis 6:1-4

YES

The earliest Jewish and Christian writers without exception interpreted the "sons of God" of Genesis 6:1-4 as supernatural beings. Granted that antiquity alone does not

NO

Clines saw in this a paradigm for understanding Genesis 6. He suggests that "the 'sons of God' were both regarded as rulers of ancient times, and traditionally ascribed divine or semi-divine origins."[14] In this case we are not dealing with mythology. The traditional ascription of deity to these kings is just that—a matter of tradition, which would not have caused the biblical writer any pains to report. This would be a case of mortal men who have titles and presumptions that classified them in the supernatural realm.

Position two in its traditional form, identifying the sons of God as angels, has been presented and defended in the previous essay. The first task at hand, then, is to indicate the weaknesses in that position. We will then proceed to a defense of position three, moving still further beyond the refinements suggested by Kline and Clines.

Examination of the Identification as "Angels"

The principal defense of the sons of God as angels is comprised of two main points, which are presented succinctly by Cassuto as follows:

Firstly, it is impossible that the words *benoth ha'adam* [daughters of man] in verse 2 should be used in a different sense from that

prove the case, it does suggest that the most literal and obvious interpretation for early exegetes was that of angels. It was only later—when theological objections arose to angels cohabiting with human beings—that alternative interpretations were developed.

The earliest datable exposition of Genesis 6 known is 1 Enoch 6-11, usually dated c. 200 B.C. It clearly identifies the "sons of God" as angels.[21] This interpretation could in fact have originated long before 1 Enoch was written.[22] It continued without challenge for the next three hundred years.

The book of Jubilees (dated no later than 100 B.C.) describes the "sons of God" as angels sent to earth to help mankind. They became consumed with lust, cohabited with women, and fathered a race of giants.[23]

The Testaments of the Twelve Patriarchs, 2 Enoch 18, and 2 Baruch 56 present the angels of Genesis 6 as being punished for their sin.[24] The *Genesis Apocryphon* gives evidence that the Qumran covenanters, shortly before New

YES

NO

which they have in verse 1 *(ha'adam . . . ubenoth)* [*man began to multiply and daughters were born . . .*]; and since in verse 1 the human species as a whole is certainly referred to, it cannot be doubted that in verse 2 it is human beings in general that are intended. Since, moreover, the expression *bene ha'elohim* [sons of God] is employed in antithesis to *benoth ha'adam* [daughters of man], it is clear that the former pertain to beings outside the human sphere. Secondly, wherever *bene (ha)'elohim* or *bene 'elim* [literally, 'sons of Gods'] occurs (Psalms 29:1; 89:7 [Eng. 6]; Job 1:6; 2:1; 38:7; also Deuteronomy 32:8 according to the text of the Septuagint) angels are referred to. When, therefore, we find in our section the expression *bene ha'elohim* without any explanatory addition, we have no right to attribute to it a connotation other than that which it normally has in the Bible.[15]

A secondary line of defense is formed by those who would defer to the long line of supporters of the angels identification throughout the history of interpretation and specifically to the support of that interpretation that is thought to exist in the New Testament.[16] We will consider the textual data first and then the history of interpretation.

1. *Textual support for the "angels" view.* The treatment of the phrase "sons of God" in the history of interpretation provides us with a good example of the

Testament times, adhered to the angel interpretation.[25] Some manuscripts of the Septuagint, including the Codex Alexandrinus (fourth century A.D.), translate "sons of God" as "angels of God."[26]

Other early exponents of the belief that Genesis 6:1-4 describes a supernatural-human union include Philo of Alexandria (early first century A.D.),[27] Flavius Josephus,[28] and Church fathers Justin Martyr, Clement of Alexandria, Tertullian, Lactantius, Irenaeus, Cyprian, and Ambrose.[29] The earliest rejection of the "angel" interpretation that has been found came from Julius Africanus (A.D. c. 160-240), who proposed that the "sons of God" were the "righteous of the line of Seth." From the second century A.D., the Palestinian rabbis rejected the angel-human interpretation.[30]

With Augustine's rejection of the angel interpretation in *De Civitate Dei* 15 (written A.D. 413-26),[31] early Christian exegetes for the most part abandoned the supernatural in-

YES

NO

potential that exists for the misuse of lexical data. It is true that the phrase "sons of God" refers to angels every time that it is used in the Old Testament, but what is the significance of that piece of information? First, we must mention that the phrase only occurs three times in the form that occurs in Genesis 6 (Job 1:6; 2:1; 38:7). This makes for a very small lexical base and cannot be considered sufficient to make broad sweeping statements about exclusiveness in the semantic range of the phrase.

Second, even if there were dozens of occurrences of the phrase with the meaning "angels," determination of semantic range may at times be supplemented by data other than context. In this case we may be informed by the numerous other phrases that utilize the form "son(s) of X" throughout not only the Old Testament but in other ancient Near Eastern languages as well. This formula is used to describe items or individuals of a particular category. It describes "belonging."[17] Of course it must be admitted that from a theoretical point of view it is still possible that the phrase "sons of God" was limited to angels in ancient Hebrew idiom. But the fact of the matter is that such a narrow range cannot be concluded on the basis of the lexical data available to us.

terpretation of Genesis 6:1-4. However, the issue has never been resolved with any degree of unanimity. It continues to surface from time to time, as evidenced by its inclusion in this study of persistent questions about the book of Genesis.

Arguments for the "Sons of God" as Angels

The arguments "for interpreting the sons of God" as angels are numerous and persuasive. At least, in the words of John J. Davis, they are "credible, given the evidence currently available."[32] In the following pages nine major arguments for this view will be examined.

1. *"Sons of God" as angels is the most natural reading.* This observation is supported by the fact that it is the most ancient interpretation of the passage (see discussion above). For at least four hundred years (c. 200 B.C.—A.D. 200) no other interpretations were considered. Antiquity is

YES

NO

For lack of definitive data, "sons of God" must then be treated as one of the formulaic examples of the "sons of X" grouping in Hebrew idiom. This means that the sons of God (ʾĕlōhîm) in some way belong to the class of the ʾĕlōhîm, a word used in Hebrew as a sort of generic term for deity and not limited to the one true God. False gods are also called ʾĕlōhîm. The fact that angels also belong to the category ʾĕlōhîm (since they are called sons of ʾĕlōhîm) suggests to us that any supernatural being could be included in that category.

We further find that humans are occasionally included in the category of ʾĕlōhîm. This is particularly the case in Exodus 22:8-9; Psalm 82:6. This would suggest that the term "sons of ʾĕlōhîm" would include not only all supernatural beings but perhaps also humans who were involved in functions considered to be functions of deity. So the king, judges, and perhaps priests may fall into that category from a theoretical standpoint. This is of course speculative, but the main point is that there is no sound basis for placing strict limitations on the semantic range of the phrase "sons of God."

With regard to the contrast between sons of God and daughters of men requiring that sons of God be outside

not a conclusive argument, but it should not be lightly dismissed.

> May it not be possible that we enlightened, twentieth-century Christians can learn something positive from the ancient exegetes? Perhaps they were right in seeing an angelic incursion in Gen. 6:1-4 and we are wrong in denying it . . . . They might well have reached some valid insights which God preserved by inscripturation in the New Testament.[33]

There are many parallels in ancient Near Eastern literature where "sons of God" means deities.[34] These parallels support the belief that "sons of God" was a commonly understood way of referring to angels in ancient times.

2. *Other interpretations do not agree among themselves.* Those who see the union as between human beings are not agreed among themselves as to the identity of the "sons of God" and the "daughters of men." The most frequent interpretation by these scholars is that of marriages between Sethites and Cainites, but others see it as marriages of kings/aristocrats/rulers/judges/believers with commoners/socially inferior women/unbelievers. Still

YES

NO

the human category, there is little to say. As early as Keil this was shown to be an invalid line of reasoning,[18] and many other commentators have followed in his train. We would agree that there is no reason why the sons of God could not represent a smaller group of mankind who were committing offense in the way that they were marrying women as a whole.

Our conclusion is that there is no element of the text that requires that the sons of God be understood as angels, although we would admit that understanding as one of the possible readings of the text if no other suitable or preferable explanation be found. The interpretation of angels, however, is hardly demanded by the text and therefore needs to be weighed against other options.

2. *Support from the history of interpretation.* Robert Newman has done a study of the history of ancient interpretation of this passage and has demonstrated that earliest extant exegesis (prior to the first century A.D.) was unanimous in favor of identifying the sons of God as angels.[19] From the oldest extant interpretation (found either in the Septuagint or in 1 Enoch) through the

others explain it as marriages between godly people and wicked people (a variation of the Seth-Cain explanation).

The Seth-Cain interpretation rests on flimsy associations, not on the text itself. It also leaves some unanswered questions: What proof is there that all male descendants of Seth were godly and all female descendants of Cain were ungodly (the Achilles' heel of Seth-Cain proponents)? If the Sethites were godly people, why did they do such a wicked thing? Is it reasonable to assume that for perhaps a thousand years after Seth's death all his descendants were godly and that this was the first sin committed by members of his family? Since those who say the marriages were limited to human beings cannot agree among themselves, does it not suggest that they are taking liberties with the text by rationalizing and reading into or out of the text what they want it to say? At least there is agreement on the other side that "sons of God" can mean only one thing: divine beings.

3. *Everywhere else in the Old Testament "sons of God"* **YES**

NO

pseudepigrapha (Jubilees, Testament of the Twelve Patriarchs), Qumran, Philo, Josephus, the Targumim and the Church fathers Newman shows evidence of the angels view. Cassuto adds to that some rabbinic support:

> From allusions in the Talmud (*B. Yoma* 67b; *B. Nidda* 61a) it is clear that also in authoritative Jewish circles they were formerly of the opinion that it was actually to angels that the passages referred, and that even after the rejection of this interpretation, some trace of it still survived and found expression here and there incidentally.[20]

Of course, the fact that any of these pieces of literature endorses a particular interpretation is of interest but certainly not binding. They are primary sources, but not always representative of authoritative interpretation. The importance of these citations for Newman's investigation as well as for ours is the backdrop they provide for attempting to determine the New Testament position on Genesis 6, if such a determination can be made. Newman comes to the conclusion that "the evidence seems strong that the New Testament adopts a supernatural interpretation of Genesis 6:1–4."[21] On the other hand, Keil has spent several pages of a long footnote in an attempt to show that the New Testament

means supernatural beings. In Job 1:6, 2:1, and 38:7 *běnê ̄hā'ělōhîm* ("sons of God") can only mean angels. In Psalm 29:1 and 89:6 *běnê 'ēlîm* probably means angels. The words *bar 'ēlāhîn* are interpreted by Christian exegetes as an angel or Christ himself in Daniel 3:25. If "sons of God" is a technical term for supernatural beings everywhere else in the Old Testament, we are correct in insisting that the meaning should not be changed in one passage.[35] Those who say human beings are called "sons of God" in passages such as Exodus 4:22-23; Deuteronomy 14:1; 32:5; Psalms 73:15; 82:6; Jeremiah 31:20; Hosea 1:10; Malachi 1:6 are taking liberties with the Hebrew text.[36] The exact term "sons of God" does not appear in any of the above-cited verses. Instead "my son," "his sons," "your sons," "a son," etc., appear in these passages.

The interpretation of "sons of God" as kings[37] has serious problems. "Sons of God" is nowhere else used in the Bible

YES

NO

cannot be considered to support the angels view of Genesis 6.[22]

The two primary passages to be considered are 2 Peter 2:4 and Jude 6. Peter mentions a sin committed by the angels but gives no details of that sin. The punishment he mentions is that they are held in chains/pits of darkness reserved for judgment. In Jude the sin is given a phrase of explanation: They did not keep their own domain but abandoned their proper abode. Again, bonds in darkness is the punishment.

What must be determined is whether these angels being punished are considered angels involved in the events of Genesis 6. The other alternative is that they are angels who were involved in the primeval fall of Satan. While it is true, as Newman points out, that the punishment cited in Peter and Jude is the same as the punishment meted out to the angels in 1 Enoch's interpretation of Genesis 6,[23] it must also be admitted with Keil that this same punishment is cited in the book of 1 Enoch on other occasions as being applied to angels.[24]

With regard to the nature of the offense, Keil again seems to have the stronger position as he points out that marriage of human women is not cited by Jude, al-

as a synonym for royalty. It seems strange that it would
have that meaning in only one passage with no further explanation. Furthermore, how can one argue that "sons of
God" means "kings" in Genesis 6:2 when it does not have
that meaning anywhere else in the Old Testament and at
the same time deny that the consistent usage as "angels"
everywhere else in the Old Testament supports that usage
in 6:2?

Van Gemeren argues cogently against interpreting "sons
of God" as kings in Genesis 6:2, even though it may have
that meaning in other ancient literature:

> Though the validity of an interpretation of Scripture may be tested by
> external literary data, we cannot agree with the supposition that a
> theme prominently treated in the Sumero-Babylonian epic tradition
> must have a counterpart in the biblical narrative. There is presently no
> clear evidence that the Sumero-Babylonian tradition knew of a king-
> ship which brought about the Flood.[38]

Granted that "sons of God" in other ancient Near Eastern literature referred to kings, it probably was intended to

YES

NO

though it very easily could have been. Further, to speak
of an act of *porneia* by the angels, as Jude does, would
appear to be inappropriate in describing Genesis 6, for
there the women were taken as wives whereas *porneia*
is usually reserved for extramarital sexual activity.[25]

While the evidence for the existence of the angels
view is clear in ancient exegesis, we do not feel that it
can be firmly established as the view of the New Testament authors. If neither the Old Testament nor the New
Testament demands the identification of the sons of
God as angels, then we ought to do our best to examine
what other alternatives exist. The main weakness of the
angels identification is its lack of convincing evidence.
That fallen angels intermarried with human women at
some point in ancient history is certainly not impossible, but it is incredible. Nevertheless, if the Bible confirmed such an event we would certainly accept it as
truth. Given the lack of firm biblical evidence, however,
it must be admitted that the incredibility of the whole
thing works to its disadvantage. It is the view of this author that a more acceptable identification of the sons of
God may be found in ancient Near Eastern kings. The

support rule by "divine" kings. If so, the term would have been studiously avoided by biblical writers.

Some have argued that "sons of God" in the New Testament as believers justifies the same interpretation for Genesis 6:1-4, but the New Testament equivalence of "sons of God" with believers should not be transferred back to the Old Testament and be assumed to have the same meaning.[39]

4. *Correct exegetical principles require that "men" have the same meaning in 6:2 as in 6:1.* Hā'ādām (translated as "men" in 6:1 though singular in form) must be understood as generic (i.e., the whole of mankind) in its context. It refers to the entire human race, both Sethites and Cainites. It is an unjustified restriction to limit the birth of their daughters to Cainites. The statement of 6:1, "daughters were born to them" (the antecedent of "them" being hā'ādām of 6:1), is clearly intended to serve as a link in 6:2 with "daughters of men" (the same word, hā'ādām). The word hā'ādām could not have one meaning in 6:1 and a different meaning in 6:2. "Daughters" cannot take on a restricted

YES

NO

most helpful information for making that identification is supplied by the well-known Gilgamesh epic.

Sons of God as Paradigm for Royalty

Clines had gone so far as to identify the description of Gilgamesh (part human and part divine) as suitable for understanding the designation "sons of God" in Genesis 6 as pertaining to royalty. He did not pursue the issue of comparison any further. In his perception of the offense, for instance, he is in basic agreement with Kline as he speaks in terms of polygamy or "titan promiscuity."[26] It is at this point, though, that we ought to return to the Gilgamesh epic. It is my thesis that the Gilgamesh epic provides a larger-scale paradigm for Genesis 6 than simply a means for understanding the sons of God, but it is on that issue that we will begin.

1. *Gilgamesh as a "son of God."* The description of Gilgamesh as two-thirds god and one-third man occurs in column 2, line 1 of the first tablet, toward the end of the old hymnic introduction.[27] It is repeated in 9. 2. 14,

meaning in 6:2—namely, Cainites—that it did not have in 6:1. If 6:1 is translated as "when the human race (hā'ādām) began to multiply on the face of the earth, and daughters were born to them," it becomes clear that 6:2 is expressing a contrast between "sons of God" and "daughters of men" that is more than a distinction between godly and wicked people.

Since "sons of God" uniformly has the meaning of supernatural beings elsewhere in the Old Testament, the only hermeneutically sound conclusion is that Genesis 6:2 refers to the union of angelic beings with daughters of human fathers. It is an arbitrary decision to limit the "daughters of men" to the descendants of Cain.[40]

5. *The Bible does not say that angels are sexless and therefore incapable of cohabiting.* Such words as "unthinkable," "impossible," and "preposterous" are frequently

YES

NO

16 following the statement that "his body is the flesh of the gods."[28] Tigay cites a similar description of Tukulti-Ninurta in the Tukulti-Ninurta epic (11. 16–18),[29] so we can see that this attributed divine heritage was not unique to Gilgamesh. Rather, the elements of divine parentage and divine qualities are "typical features of royal inscriptions."[30] The idea of the king as "son" of the gods was not connected to deification (although occasional Mesopotamian kings deified themselves—e.g., Shulgi—or were deified by later generations—e.g., Gilgamesh).

The king may consider himself the son of several different deities (cf. Hammurapi in the prologue of his laws), or he may consider a single deity as both mother and father (cf. Gudea, Cylinder A. 3. 6–7). In some inscriptions this is considered physical parentage (Eannatum being suckled by Ningirsu),[31] while in others it is clearly metaphorical (cf. Asshurbanipal's claim to having been formed in the womb of his mother by the hands of Ashur and Sin).[32] It was part of the royal prerogative to claim divine heritage, however it may have been construed or understood, and it was the duty and practice of the populace to acknowledge at least the claim. Thus we can see that the title "son of god" is easily recognizable as a royal motif.

voiced reactions to the angel interpretation of Genesis 6:1-4. Unger acknowledges that

> the most formidable objection to the angelic interpretation is, perhaps, that angels, as spiritual beings, could not take wives of the daughters of men. Much of the argument hinges on this avowed problem. To deny such a possibility though, at least among the fallen and impure angels, . . . is to assume . . . a degree of knowledge of fallen angelic nature which man does not possess.[41]

The hideousness of the sin of the "sons of God" is that they were doing what was not intended by God, and therefore it was a deliberate act of rebellion. Both men and angels apparently were created with the capacity to obey or disobey God (as evidenced by the fall of man, Genesis 3, and the rebellion of disobedient angels, 2 Pet. 2:4).

Undoubtedly the principal objection to the angel interpretation grows out of the belief that angels are sexless and therefore could not be attracted to human beings. However, the argument that angels are without sex organs[42] and cannot cohabit with human beings depends on a superior

YES

NO

2. *Gilgamesh as a giant.* In the Hittite fragment of the Gilgamesh epic, usually tied into the first couple of columns of tablet one, the height of Gilgamesh is said to be eleven cubits. It is also stated that the storm god gave him heroism.[33] This section is fragmentary in the late version of the epic, but Tigay finds "no reason to doubt that it was present in the Akkadian prototype."[34] Gilgamesh's stature and quality of heroism would be paralleled in Genesis 6 by the inclusion of the *nĕphîlîm* and the *gibbôrîm* of verse 4. Based on Numbers 13:33, the only other occurrence of *nĕphîlîm*, most commentators consider the *nĕphîlîm* to be giants.[35] There has been frequent discussion concerning whether the *nĕphîlîm* are to be identified as the *gibbôrîm* (heroes) or are just contemporaries of them. It is also not clear who are identified as the *gibbôrîm*.

If we view the sons of God marrying the daughters of men not as a one-time breach but as a common practice of the period, it may be that the category of *gibbôrîm* includes both the fathers and the sons born to them (as well as the *nĕphîlîm*). Again Gilgamesh may serve as a paradigm. Along with the other ancient kings he was a *qarrâdu,* a *gibbôr,* one of the mighty

knowledge of angels not found in the Scriptures. Matthew 22:30 (cf. Mark 12:25; Luke 20:35-36) is cited as proof that angels cannot marry. But a careful, unprejudiced reading of that text reveals that Jesus was making an analogy. He was not talking about procreation but about relationships. He was saying that the relationship of resurrected Christians will be different from the relationship experienced in marriage on earth. He was no more saying that angels are sexless than he was teaching that resurrected Christians will be neither male nor female. Also it should be noted that he was talking about angels "in heaven" and not about fallen angels.[43] Thus it was not angels in heaven who took wives in Genesis 6:2 but those who left heaven (cf. Jude 6). It should be further observed that the Bible speaks of male angels (Michael and Gabriel, called "the man Gabriel" in Dan. 9:21) and female angels (Zech. 5:9).

Jude 6 is understood by many as a reference to the fall of angels described in Genesis 6:1-4. Richard Wolff is correct when he says that "the angels in heaven neither marry nor are given in marriage, but this does not automatically ex-

YES

NO

men of old.[36] If the *nĕphîlîm* are giants, Gilgamesh also qualified in that category.

3. *Gilgamesh marrying the daughters of men.* The early description of Gilgamesh relates his oppression of his subjects, the people of Uruk.[37] Lines 27–28 are of particular interest: "Gilgamesh does not release the young woman to [   ], the warrior's daughter, the [man's] spouse."[38] Most have restored the lacuna to read "her lover," though Tigay prefers the restoration "her mother."[39] Whatever the proper restoration, it is at least clear that Gilgamesh is detaining women for some reason. The passage remains vague and needs to be considered along with another section in order to fill in the picture.

When Enkidu comes into Uruk after being taught the graces of civilization, Gilgamesh is on the very threshold of the nuptial chamber, and it is there that the brawl takes place between Gilgamesh and Enkidu. Gilgamesh's intentions in the nuptial chamber are elucidated for us by a statement found in the Old Babylonian ver-

clude the possibility of unnatural relationships of fallen angels."[44]

6. *The text does not state that angels were exempt from judgment.* Another objection to the angel interpretation is that if angels did cohabit with women, only the human race was punished. This, however, is an argument from silence and not from a theological stance. The focus of the Genesis narrative is upon man. Furthermore, it is characteristic of biblical narrative to omit details that might seem important to us (e.g., the name of the pharaoh in Exodus 1; the early life of Elijah). Since the angels initiated the sin, it seems reasonable that a just God would punish them, and there is no reason to doubt that he has done so or will do so. Even if 1 Peter 3:19-20; 2 Peter 2:4-5; Jude 6 do not specifically refer to the punishment of those angels who sinned in Genesis 6:2 (though many scholars insist they do), there is still no reason to doubt that God has punished or will punish them. They may have been punished along with the human race in the deluge. However, the focus of the biblical

YES

NO

sion.[40] It is a description of Gilgamesh given to Enkidu just before he enters Uruk: "He cohabits with the betrothed bride—he first, the husband afterwards."[41] On the basis of this it may be argued[42] that one of the primary elements of Gilgamesh's oppression is his exercise of *jus primae noctis* ("law of the first night"), in which the king has the option of being the first to cohabit with the newly married virgin.[43]

If Genesis 6 is dealing with this type of offense, we can certainly understand the divine anger expressed. It is far worse than Lamech's polygamy, which never seemed quite bad enough a violation to figure so prominently here. On the other hand, simple promiscuity did not seem to suit the language of the text. The Hebrew combination *lāqaḥ nāšîm* ("take wives") is used only of marriage, not the sexual act. In Gilgamesh, then, the fact that he was entering the nuptial chamber when he encountered Enkidu is significant—he was taking wives. Likewise the aspect offered by the phrase "any that they chose" is very fitting in Genesis 6, for in the practice of *jus primae noctis* this was the king's option—to take whichever brides he preferred.

story is to show that God punishes man for his sins. Only a few verses in the Bible speak of Satan's punishment, but many warn of the punishment of people for their sins.

7. *"Sons of God" as angels does not require the conclusion that the narrative is mythological.* Another objection of evangelicals to the angel-human interpretation is undoubtedly based on the knowledge that many scholars who accept this interpretation also consider the whole story to be mythological[45] because it has certain parallels to ancient Sumerian, Akkadian, Hittite, and Ugaritic myths in which gods are attracted to human beings.[46]

Even though many ancient myths have creation and flood stories, however, evangelicals do not reject the historicity of the biblical accounts of creation and the flood. There are myths about gods, but that does not compel us to conclude that the God revealed in the Bible is also mythological. Therefore the historicity of angels marrying women in Genesis 6:2 should not be rejected because similar stories are found in ancient myths.

8. *The cohabitation of angels with women gives the best explanation for the offspring they produced.* Granted that 6:4 is not clearly related to what precedes or follows, it is

YES

NO

4. *Gilgamesh and the limits of mortality.* The epic of Gilgamesh is constructed around the hero's search for immortality. Clines had observed this similarity to Genesis 6:3 in a footnote:

> It is perhaps also significant that like the "sons of God" who find their life expectancy greatly reduced, Gilgamesh, since "he too is flesh" . . . is oppressed by the thought of death and he searches for immortality, only to find it eludes him in the end.[44]

We should not suppose that Gilgamesh's obsession with immortality was unique to him. As the major theme of the epic, it explains the epic's undying popularity and its ubiquitous preservation. Gilgamesh embodies everyone's search for answers concerning life and death, but to an even greater extent demonstrates the frustration of kings—achieving the highest earthly power, yet subject to the common human destiny and indignity. The special frustration that this represents for kings can also be seen reflected in the biblical oracle against the king of Babylon in Isaiah 14.

likely that it is. Otherwise it injects an element that serves no understandable purpose.

Much has been written about the etymology of *nĕphîlîm*, but the present evidence is not sufficient to be conclusive.[47] All agree, however, that they were unusual beings, described as "heroes of old, men of renown" (NIV). If the text clearly stated that they appeared after the union of the "sons of God" with the "daughters of men," then the indisputable conclusion would be that they were the off-spring of these illicit unions. However, it must be admitted that the text seems to say that the Nephilim were on the earth both before and after the events of Genesis 6:2. Cassuto, while acknowledging that the Nephilim existed prior to Genesis 6:4, adds that "after 'those days'—there was a renewal of the phenomenon, whenever angels or demons had relations with humans and begot children by them. 'These' . . . children were the mighty men of old.'"[48]

Whatever else may be argued, the Seth-Cain interpretation sheds no more light on the relationship of Genesis 6:4

YES

NO

Therefore, while immortality is a common concern of mankind, it is of particular interest to kings. This can be seen throughout the ancient Near East in the many varied attempts of kings to insure their immortality in one way or another. The Gilgamesh epic and Genesis 6 have in common individuals who have some reason to hope or expect that mortal limitations can be eliminated. In Genesis 6:3 the exact meaning cannot be determined with precision or surety because of the uncertainties surrounding the translation of *yàdôn*[45] and *bĕšaggàm*.[46] But the general meaning is agreed upon and verifies the similiarity to the Gilgamesh epic.

Conclusions

I have attempted to demonstrate that each element of Genesis 6:1–4, however vague it may be, has a parallel of sorts in the Gilgamesh epic, as follows: (1) Gilgamesh qualifies as a "son of God" by virtue of titulary; (2) as a hero of old he personifies the biblical category of *gibbôrîm,* and as a giant he qualifies as one of the *nĕphîlîm* (if such an understanding of *nĕphîlîm* is considered accurate);[47] (3) through the exercise of *jus pri-*

to the rest of the sixth chapter of Genesis than the angel interpretation.

9. *Angel-human cohabitation is the best explanation for the judgment by flood that followed.* Though no clear statement is made that links the flood narrative that follows in Genesis 6-8 with Genesis 6:1-4, there is every reason to believe that 6:1-4 serves as a prologue to the flood and gives the rationale for it. The verses seem to be structurally and thematically connected to what follows. The sin must have been such a horrible affront to God that only total destruction of the world as it existed could serve as adequate judgment. Would marriage of "godly" Sethites with "ungodly" Cainites have brought such a severe punishment? How many of them would have to be involved to warrant destruction of the entire human race with the exception of one family? Surely God would not destroy the human race because kings married commoners. The cohabitation of rebellious angels with women of the human race offers a

YES

NO

mae noctis Gilgamesh takes wives (whichever ones he wants), and even in the Gilgamesh epic this is used to characterize his unjust behavior; (4) Gilgamesh is frustrated in his attempts to gain immortality.

The accumulation of these parallels, however, does not suggest that the two individual pieces of literature have an organic relationship. The connections are too vague to substantiate such a hypothesis. But I have also tried to demonstrate that the particular elements identified from Gilgamesh are not unique to Gilgamesh. Rather, they epitomize ancient royalty. These are simply royal motifs accumulated around the personage of Gilgamesh.

The suggestion concerning Genesis 6:1-4, then, is that we understand here an accumulation of royal motifs (the same as those that can be observed in Gilgamesh) and that these are intended to epitomize the failures of kingship. This would not disturb the view that Genesis 1-11 is a treatise on the continual attempts of man to break loose of divinely established limitations or to eradicate the boundaries between the human and divine spheres. It rather adds a very attractive progression to that treatise, for now we see move-

better explanation than any other for the heinousness of the sin that resulted in the flood.[49]

Conclusion

This study of a passage that has been disputed for centuries has revealed that both the supernatural-human and human-only interpretations have been espoused by pious people of good faith. "Sons of God" interpreted as angels is not liberal or nonevangelical if one accepts the story as historical and not mythological. "Sons of God" elsewhere in the Old Testament as a technical term for angelic beings makes it a good possibility that the expression has the same meaning in Genesis 6:1–4. This understanding of "sons of God" should not be denied simply because of one's presuppositions (not verified by Scripture) about the nature of angels. It seems evident that the major objection voiced by evangelicals to the angel interpretation is based on the problem of angels cohabiting with human beings, but it has been shown that this objection is based on a faulty interpretation of Jesus' words in Matthew 22:20.

In light of the ambiguities of the text that leave many questions unanswered, and based on evidence examined in this study, it is reasonable to conclude that interpreting **YES** "sons of God" in Genesis 6:2 as angelic beings is a viable alternative indeed.

NO ment from individual offenses (Adam, Cain, Lamech?) through royal offenses (here) to societal offense (flood, tower of Babel).

This is not a case of literary borrowing but of two pieces of literature reflecting a common problem of society. The Gilgamesh epic, by utilizing royal motifs to characterize the uncontrollable monarch, helps us to identify the same problem being treated in Genesis 6.

This interpretation makes sense of the elements of Genesis 6:1–4 in the context of its ancient Near Eastern background. The fact that it fits does not of course prove that it is right. In the case of this difficult passage, however, anything that even fits is worthy of consideration.

ENDNOTES

YES

1. N. H. Tur-Sinai, "The Riddle of Genesis VI.1–4," *Expository Times* 71 (August 1960) 348.

2. H. E. Ryle, *The Book of Genesis* (Cambridge: University Press, 1914) 92; R. Davidson, Genesis *1–11* (Cambridge: University Press, 1973) 69.

3. G. H. Livingston, "Sons of God," in *The Zondervan Pictorial Encyclopedia of the Bible* (ed. M. C. Tenney; Grand Rapids: Zondervan, 1975), 5, 493.

4. A. Pieters, *Notes on Genesis* (Grand Rapids: Eerdmans, 1947) 116.

5. Tur-Sinai, "Riddle," 348.

6. D. Kidner, *Genesis* (Chicago: InterVarsity, 1967) 83.

7. P. S. Alexander, "The Targumim and Early Exegesis of 'Sons of God' in Genesis 6," *Journal of Jewish Studies* 23 (Spring 1972) 61.

8. G. von Rad, *Genesis* (Philadelphia: Westminster, 1961) 110.

9. J. S. Baxter, *Studies in Problem Texts* (Grand Rapids: Zondervan, 1960) 180.

10. Von Rad, *Genesis,* 110.

11. Baxter, *Studies,* 171.

12. L. Birney, "An Exegetical Study of Genesis 6:1–4," *Journal of the Evangelical Theological Society* 13 (Winter 1970) 48, 52.

13. M. G. Kline, "Divine Kingship and Genesis 6:1–4," *Westminster Theological Journal* 24 (May 1962) 194.

14. H. Freedman, "The Book of Genesis," in *The Soncino Chumash* (ed. A. Cohen; London: Soncino, 1947) 25.

15. J. E. Shelley, "The Days Before the Flood," *Bible League Quarterly* 161 (October-December 1939) 94.

16. E.g. G. Ch. Aalders, *Genesis* (Grand Rapids: Zondervan, 1981), 1, 154; Baxter, *Studies,* 170; M. Henry, *Commentary on the Whole Bible* (New York: Revell, n.d.), 1, 51; C. F. Keil and F. Delitzsch, *Biblical Commentary on the Old Testament* (Grand Rapids: Eerdmans, reprint 1959), 1, 127–34; H. C. Leupold, *Exposition of Genesis* (Grand Rapids: Baker, 1942), 1, 250; L. J. Wood, *Genesis: A Study Guide* (Grand Rapids: Zondervan, 1975) 44.

17. E.g. J. M. Boice, *Genesis: An Expositional Commentary, Genesis 1:1—11:32* (Grand Rapids: Zondervan, 1982), 1, 245–49; E. W. Bullinger, *How to Enjoy the Bible* (London: Lamp, 1955 [1907]) 192; A. C. Gaebelein, *The Annotated Bible, The Pentateuch* (Glasgow: Pickering and Inglis, 1913), 1, 29–31; J. MacArthur, "Satan, Is He? Who Is He?" Cassette tape GC 1354 (Panorama City: Word of Grace Communications, 1975); G. H. Pember, *Earth's Earliest Ages* (15th ed.; Suffolk: G. H. Lang, 1942) 130; M. F. Unger, *Biblical Demonology* (Wheaton: Scripture Press, 1952) 45–52.

18. R. C. Newman, "The Ancient Exegesis of Genesis 6:2, 4," *Grace Theological Journal* 5 (Spring 1984) 13.

19. W. A. Van Gemeren, "The Sons of God in Genesis 6:1–4 (An Ex-

ample of Evangelical Demythologization?)," *Westminster Theological Journal* 43 (Spring 1981) 320.

20. The following among the voluminous literature on the history of interpretation of Gen. 6:1–4 are recommended for further study: Alexander, "Targumim," 60–71; G. E. Closen, *Die Sünde der 'Söhne Gottes' (Gen 6:1–4). Ein Beitrag zur Theologie der Genesis* (Rome: Päpstliches Bibelinstitut, 1937); F. Dexinger, *Sturz der Göttersöhne; oder, Engel vor der Sintflut? Versuch eines Neuverständnisses von Genesis 6, 2–4 unter Berücksichtigung der religionsvergleichenden und exegesegeschichtlichen Methode* (Wiener Beiträge zur Theologie 13; Wien: Herder, 1966); Newman, "Ancient," 13–36; D. Poulet, "The Moral Causes of the Flood," *Catholic Biblical Quarterly* 4 (October 1942) 293–303; C. Westermann, *Genesis 1–11: A Commentary* (Minneapolis: Augsburg, 1984) 365–72; L. R. Wickham, "The Sons of God and the Daughters of Men: Genesis vi 2 in Early Christian Exegesis," in *Language and Meaning: Studies in Hebrew Language and Biblical Exegesis* (Leiden: Brill, 1974) 135–47; P. L. Williams, *Who Were the Giants?* (Houston: private printing, 1982).

21. R. H. Charles, trans., *The Book of Enoch* (Oxford: Clarendon, 1912) 13–26. P. D. Hanson, "Rebellion in Heaven, Azazel, and Euhemeristic Heroes in 1 Enoch 6–11," *Journal of Biblical Literature* 96 (June 1977) 195–233, discusses the similarities of Gen. 6:1–4 with 1 Enoch 6–11.

22. Alexander, "Targumim," 60.

23. *The Book of Jubilees* (ed. R. H. Charles; London: A. and C. Black, 1902).

24. Newman, "Ancient," 18.

25. J. A. Fitzmyer, *The Genesis Apocryphon of Qumran Cave 1: A Commentary* (Rome: Pontifical Biblical Institute, 1966) 43–45; cf. Newman, "Ancient," 19.

26. Cf. comments of Newman, "Ancient," 15–16; Wickham, "Sons," 139; U. Cassuto, *Biblical and Oriental Studies, Bible* (Jerusalem: Magnes, 1973), 1, 17.

27. This interpretation of Philo has been challenged because he is not always clear. Cf. Newman, "Ancient," 19–20; D. Winston and J. Dillon, *Two Treatises of Philo of Alexandria. A Commentary on De Gigantibus and Quod Deus Sit Immutabilis* (Chico: Scholars, 1983).

28. F. Josephus, *Jewish Antiquities* (Cambridge: Harvard University, 1934), vol. 4. Cf. W. Whiston, trans., *The Works of Flavius Josephus* (London: Henry G. Bohn, 1847), 1, 49.

29. See Newman, "Ancient," 21–22; Poulet, "Moral," 295, for the exact citations in the writings of these Church fathers for their interpretation of the "sons of God."

30. Alexander, "Targumim," 68.

31. Wickham, "Sons," 138–39.

32. J. J. Davis, *Paradise to Prison: Studies in Genesis* (Grand Rapids: Baker, 1975) 114.

33. Newman, "Ancient," 36.

34. W. F. Albright, *The Biblical Period from Abraham to Ezra* (New York: Harper, 1963) 45; E. G. Kraeling, "The Significance and Origin of Gen. 6:1–4," *Journal of Near Eastern Studies* 6 (October 1947) 197; Kline, "Divine," 188 n. 7.

35. B. S. Childs, *Myth and Reality in the Old Testament* (London: SCM, 1960) 51; cf. Davis, *Paradise*, 113.

36. W. H. Green, "The Sons of God and the Daughters of Men," *Presbyterian and Reformed Review* 5 (October 1894) 656; cf. J. Murray, *Principles of Conduct: Aspects of Biblical Ethics* (Grand Rapids: Eerdmans, 1957) 246; Poulet, "Moral," 300. Birney, "Exegetical," 46, admits the "argument is weakened by the fact that the exact term 'sons of God' does not appear in the above passages."

37. A view especially espoused by Kline, "Divine," 187–204; D. J. A. Clines, "The Significance of the 'Sons of God' Episode (Gen. 6:1–4) in the Context of 'Primeval History' (Gen. 1–11)," *Journal for the Study of the Old Testament* 13 (1979) 33–46. For a refutation of this interpretation see Van Gemeren, "Sons," 339–43.

38. Van Gemeren, "Sons," 342.

39. Boice, *Genesis*, 246.

40. For a good discussion of the problem see Cassuto, *Biblical*, 19.

41. Unger, *Biblical*, 50.

42. Baxter, *Studies*, 152.

43. Boice, *Genesis*, 248, agrees.

44. R. Wolff, *General Epistles of James and Jude* (Wheaton: Tyndale House, 1969) 99.

45. W. Brueggemann, *Genesis* (Atlanta: John Knox, 1982) 70, says it belongs to "the common mythological tradition of the ancient Near East"; Childs, *Myth*, 56, calls it a "foreign particle of pagan mythology"; J. Skinner, *A Critical and Exegetical Commentary on Genesis* (2d ed.; Edinburgh: T. and T. Clark, 1930) 140, says it "belongs to the class of aetiological myths"; E. A. Speiser, *Genesis* (Garden City: Doubleday, 1964) 45, describes it as "undisguised mythology"; Westermann, *Genesis 1–11*, 369, calls it "a myth." Cf. Cassuto, *Biblical*, 28, who argues that the intention of the passage is to contradict pagan legends.

46. Childs, *Myth*, 56.

47. Poulet, "Moral," 302, discusses the various proposed roots of *nĕphîlîm*. It has been taken from "fall," "fall upon" (thus violent), "destroyer," "to be tall," "judge," "intercede/pray." Although the etymology is uncertain, that it means "giants" is clear from the only other use of the word in the Old Testament in Num. 13:33.

48. Cassuto, *Biblical*, 27.

49. See Van Gemeren, "Sons," 327–30, for a good defense of the relationship of Gen. 6:1–4 with the flood narrative that follows.

NO

1. This view was supported by many of the Church fathers and by modern commentators such as Keil, Aalders, and Leupold.

2. This view is supported by most modern commentators with a slight alteration. The sons of God are materially distinct as lower-echelon deities rather than as angels (cf. Cassuto, von Rad, Skinner, Speiser, Vawter, Westermann). The identification as angels was supported in antiquity as early as 1 Enoch 6, Philo, and Josephus.

3. This view appears in early Jewish interpretation (such as Targum Onkelos and *Bereshith Rabbah* 26:5) and in the medieval commentators (e.g. Rashi and Nachmanides). It is sporadically supported by modern Jewish commentators, e.g. Jacob.

4. E. G. Kraeling, "The Significance and Origin of Genesis 6:1–4," *Journal of Near Eastern Studies* 6 (1947) 193–208.

5. E. A. Speiser, *Genesis* (New York: Doubleday, 1964) 45–46.

6. U. Cassuto, "The Episode of the Sons of God and the Daughters of Man," *Biblical and Oriental Studies* (Jerusalem: Magnes, 1973) 21–22.

7. B. Vawter, *On Genesis* (New York: Doubleday, 1977) 112.

8. C. Westermann, *Genesis 1–11* (Minneapolis: Augsburg, 1984) 371–72.

9. E.g. Vawter, who sees divine aspirations reflected in the sacred marriage ritual.

10. Cf. Exod. 21:6; 22:8, 9, 28.

11. M. Kline, "Divine Kingship and Genesis 6:1–4," *Westminster Theological Journal* 24 (1962) 187–204.

12. D. J. A. Clines, "The Significance of the 'Sons of God' Episode (Gen. 6:1–4) in the Context of the 'Primeval History' (Gen. 1–11)," *Journal for the Study of the Old Testament* 13 (1979) 33–46.

13. Ibid., 35.

14. Ibid.

15. Cassuto, *Biblical,* 19.

16. R. C. Newman, "The Ancient Exegesis of Genesis 6:2, 4," *Grace Theological Journal* 5 (1984) 13–36.

17. H. Haag, *Theological Dictionary of the Old Testament, 2,* 150–53.

18. C. F. Keil, *Commentary on the Old Testament, 1,* 130–31.

19. Newman, "Ancient," 13–36.

20. Cassuto, *Biblical,* 20.

21. Newman, "Ancient," 31.

22. Keil, *Commentary,* 132–35 n. 1.

23. Newman, "Ancient," 28.

24. Keil, *Commentary,* 134. See particularly 1 Enoch 21; 54:3–6.

25. Ibid., 135.

26. Clines, "Significance," 36.

27. Akkadian text: *šit-tin-šú* DINGIR-*ma šul-lul-ta-šú a-me-lu-tu.*

28. Akkadian text: *šèr* DINGIR.MEŠ *zumuršu.*

29. J. Tigay, *The Evolution of the Gilgamesh Epic* (Philadelphia: University of Pennsylvania, 1983) 153. Texts and translations used in this paper are drawn from Tigay's work.

30. Ibid., 156 n. 67, as supported by his previous pages of evidence.

31. From the so-called Vulture Stela. See T. Jacobsen, "The Concept of Divine Parentage of the Ruler in the Stela of the Vultures," *Journal of Near Eastern Studies* 2 (1943) 119–21.

32. H. Frankfort, *Kingship and the Gods* (Chicago: University Press, 1948) 300–01.

33. UR.SAĜ = *qarràdu.*

34. Tigay, *Evolution,* 153.

35. This follows the Septuagint reading *gigantes.* Keil has disputed this understanding, and it must be admitted that the evidence is hardly overwhelming.

36. Cf. Westermann, *Genesis 1–11,* 378.

37. 1.2.6–30.

38. Akkadian text: *ul ú-maš-šar* ᵈGIŠ.GIN.MAŠ SAL.KAL.TUR *a-na []ma-rat qu-ra-di ḫi-rat e[ṭ-l]i.*

39. Tigay, *Evolution*, 183. Cf. 265 note on 2.16.

40. Gilg. P, 4.32–34; see Tigay, *Evolution*, 182.

41. Akkadian text: *aššat šîmâtim iraḫḫi šú panânumma mûtum warkânu.* Cf. Tigay, *Evolution*, 182.

42. Ibid., 182–84.

43. As Tigay mentions, the ancient evidence for this practice is sparse but not totally absent. Cf. *Evolution*, 182 n.15, where he cites Herodotus 4.168 as well as several rabbinic sources. Certainly earlier evidence would be preferred, but this text is not ambiguous in the Gilgamesh epic.

44. Clines, "Significance," 44 n.18.

45. Westermann surveys six different options, identifying them all as only conjecture; *Genesis 1–11*, 375.

46. Ibid., 375–76.

47. For a new suggestion concerning the *nĕphîlîm* see A. Kilmer, "The Mesopotamian Counterparts to the Biblical *Nĕphîlîm*," in the Francis I. Andersen *Festschrift* (Winona Lake: Eisenbrauns, 1986). Kilmer's suggestion of a correlation between the *nephîlîm* and the *apkallû*, the ancient sages of Mesopotamia, is intriguing (though, as she admits, speculative).

10 *Did Noah's Flood*

Cover the Entire World?

YES: STEVEN A. AUSTIN

Scriptural Evidence

To the question of the geographic extent of Noah's flood the book of Genesis gives the simple yet profound answer: "The waters were upon the face of the whole earth" (8:9 KJV). The Hebrew phrase translated "upon the face of all the earth" (7:3; 8:9) might be interpreted to comprise only the local land surface within the knowledge of the narrator, except for the fact that the phrase is used in Genesis four

NO: DONALD C. BOARDMAN

To understand why there might be controversy over the extent of the Noahic flood it is important to consider the history of the relationship between science and biblical interpretation. When modern science first became a factor in the thinking of educated persons, the Church was the authority in all areas of thought. Thus when questions came up about interpretations of Scripture in light of scientific discoveries, the theologians usually subscribed to explanations that had been ap-

times outside the flood account only in the universal sense. Thus God gave mankind the mandate that we can eat "every herb bearing seed which is upon the face of all the earth" (1:29 KJV), which includes grain grown anywhere on the globe, not just that from a particular region. Similarly in the confusion of languages at the tower of Babel shortly after the flood: "From thence did the LORD scatter them abroad upon the face of all the earth" (11:9; cf. 11:4, 8 KJV). The diverse languages of peoples on every continent demonstrate that God's purpose was accomplished. Are we to suppose that the statement "the waters were upon the face of all the earth" (8:9) means anything less than the entire land surface of the globe?

That Noah's flood was global is inescapable from the Hebrew syntax of Genesis 7:19. The account says that "all the high hills that were under the whole heaven were covered." Because "all . . . hills" might be understood to comprise only those hills within the geographic knowledge of the narrator, the Hebrew writer removes all possible ambiguity

YES

NO

proved by the organized Church. This led to much controversy. For example, Copernicus caused much unrest in the fifteenth century when he proposed that the earth revolved about the sun, a view contrary to that held by the Church.

In many cases simple interpretations prove to be the best. Even today the gospel, which is the heart of the Bible, can be understood in very simple terms. Science cannot explain how God created or why sin can only be blotted out by the sacrifice of Christ on the cross. As time went on, however, scientists and Bible scholars recognized that in many areas the Bible could be more easily understood with the help of science. The consideration of the extent of the flood described in Genesis might be cited as one of these areas.

Whether this deluge was local, covered a limited area in the region of the Tigris-Euphrates rivers, or was universal should not limit our acceptance of the historical accuracy of the Bible. Proponents of each of these views believe that the flood was a real occurrence and was a miracle performed by God to punish sin on the

by attaching the phrase "under the whole heaven." The Hebrew phrase "under the whole heaven" appears six other times in the Old Testament, each being used in the universal sense.[1] The phrase is used to illustrate God's omniscience ("For He looks to the ends of the earth and sees under the whole heavens," Job 28:24 NKJV) and sovereignty ("Whatsoever is under the whole heaven is mine," 41:11 KJV). The God of the Old Testament does not see and own only what resides within the boundary of the nation Israel; he sees the whole earth and owns all of it. Because the same terminology is used to describe Noah's flood, it cannot be geographically restricted but must be universal.[2]

The geologic cause of Noah's flood also argues for the global nature of the catastrophe. The phrase "all fountains of the great deep broken up" (7:11) refers to a general upheaval on the ocean floor. The stereotyped compound noun "great deep" appears four times in the Hebrew Old Testament, with Isaiah 51:10 showing its meaning as a

YES

NO

earth. As Bernard Ramm has said: "The problem is one of interpretation, not inspiration. Those who believe in the local flood believe in the divine inspiration of the Bible; otherwise they would believe in no flood."[1]

Some arguments for a limited flood can be derived from observations made in physical and biological science. Others deal with the meaning of the words used in the biblical narrative and their context. All conclusions should relate the interpretation of the flood account to the general purpose of the biblical record.

Geological Considerations

Although all branches of geology must be considered in studying the flood, perhaps the most important evidences are in the fields of sedimentation and stratigraphy. Sedimentation deals with the origin, transportation, and deposition of rock particles, principally by air and water. Stratigraphy is the study of the layers (usually referred to as strata or beds) laid down by geologic processes. By knowing what kinds of strata are deposited by various media and under differing condi-

large sea or ocean. The Hebrew verb "broken up" is used elsewhere in the Old Testament (Zech. 14:4; Num. 16:31; Judg. 15:19; Mic. 1:4) to describe the geologic process of faulting or cleavage of the earth's crust. Not just one sea-floor spring was cleaved but "all" were broken up, implying a catastrophe not geographically restricted.

The undersea explosion in 1883 of Krakatoa, the Indonesian island volcano, provides insight into the "fountains of the great deep," the potent physical cause of Noah's flood. The eruption of Krakatoa moved material from the sea floor, displacing ocean water and creating a sea wave that inundated coastal areas of Java and Sumatra up to an elevation of 130 feet above sea level. The sea wave penetrated as much as six miles inland from the shore, devastated 295 villages and towns, killed more than 36,000 people, and destroyed 5,000 boats in coastal areas. The steamship Berouw was torn from its mooring in a harbor and deposited in a river valley upright and virtually intact one and a half miles inland from the sea. After traveling at

YES

NO

tions, the geologist can come to a conclusion as to the nature of the environment at the time each stratum in the geologic column was deposited. The velocity of running water determines the size of particles that can be picked up, transported, and deposited. As velocity increases, successively larger material is eroded and transported. With a decrease in velocity the larger particles are deposited first. With changing conditions each bed is unique. In a sequence of strata there are usually some beds so distinctive in texture, material content, thickness, and color that they can be recognized a considerable distance from the place of original observation.

Stratigraphic studies are important in considering the biblical flood, for if the waters covered the whole earth some distinctive layers that can be dated at the time of the flood should be found.

It has sometimes been argued that a flood that lasted for only about one year would not cause enough erosion to make any significant deposits. This might very well be true of a local flood, although even floods of short duration cause a tremendous movement of material

speeds of about 400 miles per hour through the open ocean, the waves were recorded on tide gauges in South Africa (5,000 miles away), Alaska (6,000 miles away), California (8,000 miles away) and the English Channel (11,000 miles away).

The nearest survivors to the Krakatoa sea wave, to our astonishment, were in ships afloat on the deep ocean within thirty miles of the volcano. In proximity to the volcano the deep ocean waves were only a few feet high and very long between crest and trough, being indistinguishable to observers in ships in deep water. The captain's log of HMS Charles Bal describes how sailors saw no perceptible displacement of their vessel from sea level, while the ocean near their location rose over Button Island.[3] The waves were later observed to impact the Java shore with devastating effects.

Krakatoa's major displacement of the ocean floor lasted only a few seconds and produced extraordinary sea waves detected around the world. How much more severe would

YES have been the breakup of "all the fountains of the great

NO both organic and inorganic. Soils scientists, in studying the effect of storms on the erosion of farmlands, have found that 95 percent of all erosion is caused by 5 percent of the rainstorms. A storm that caused the loss of over 225 lives in Rapid City, South Dakota, in 1972 lasted only a few hours, yet some canyons were deepened as much as twenty feet. A flood about sixty years earlier had caused similar erosion. During the interval between these two floods very little erosion had been observed.

Because water flows to lower elevations, as the water of the Noahic flood left the land it uncovered the higher elevations first. In doing this, however, large areas of the continents that are inland basins retained water that had to flow out through channels of limited size. To remove the volume of water required by a universal covering of the earth would result in very large velocities through such channels. Between such outlets to the inland continental areas and the sea there would be great canyons cut. Careful examination of the great canyons

deep" during Noah's flood? Those fountains were broken open at numerous locations—not just one place—on the ocean floor, with the disturbance lasting up to 150 days (compare 7:11 and 8:2-3)—not just seconds.

One finds it impossible to postulate an oceanic energy impulse mechanism for Noah's flood. One can imagine a continent surrounded on four sides by oceans containing many seafloor springs that were ruptured. Waves created by many point sources of energy would have impinged on the continent from all sides with waters continuing to rise over the continent as long as the energetic disturbance of the oceans was maintained. The rise of water over the continent would have caused a corresponding lowering of the level of the oceans until the continent was completely covered. During the high water of the flood, the water over the continent could have had an elevation a few thousand feet higher than the water of the ocean basins, being maintained in deference to the force of gravity by the energy impulse to the ocean floor. The Krakatoa sea wave and hurricane storm surges in coastal areas show on a minia-

YES

NO

of the earth does not indicate such rapid erosion.

To further apply the principles described above it is necessary to determine the time of the flood in relation to geologic and human history. Different writers have speculated on this matter. All seem to come to the conclusion that we do not know when it happened but that it occurred after the retreat of the last Pleistocene glacier. Mitchell says, "The effective end of the last glaciation may be dated about 10,000 B.C., so that it may be that Noah and his contemporaries are to be given an antiquity of this magnitude."[2]

Youngblood places it from 10,000 to 3500 B.C.[3] Custance refers to the Hebrew text as interpreted by Anstey to indicate a probable date of about 4,481 years before the present.[4] Kidner indicates he believes it was "some millennia before the Babylonian floods of around 3000 BC which left their physical traces at different times at Ur, Shuruppak, Kish and elsewhere. But it would be guess-work to be more specific than this."[5]

The Pleistocene is the most recent of geologic ages. The last continental glacier retreated from the mid-

ture scale that water is able to pile up on continental areas. Because the volume of the present oceans is thirty-six times the volume of the continents above sea level, there was ample water to cover not just one continent but every continent.[4]

The direction of drift of the ark and its final landing place requires the flood to have been of immense geographic extent. After floating for 150 days through a forty-day rainstorm and continued upheaval of the ocean floor, the ark came to rest on "the mountains of Ararat" (8:4). Assyrian inscriptions link Ararat to the mountainous kingdom of Urartu, which is the plateau of Armenia in eastern Turkey, the headwaters of the Euphrates River, having an elevation averaging 6,000 feet above sea level. Although the text of Genesis does not specify that the ark rested on Mount Ararat (a 16,900-foot volcano), it requires the ark's landing in that mountainous region.

If the water in the Ararat district that deposited the ark was not surrounded by water in adjacent regions to similar depths but was simply collected rainwater of a local flood

YES

NO

western United States less than 12,000 years ago. The glaciers advanced several times in the northern hemisphere, and as they receded they left distinctive deposits that can be seen in many places in North America and Europe. Examination of the glacial deposits makes it apparent that they have not been eroded by a universal flood. Wayne Ault has given an extensive analysis of the relation between the Noahic flood and Pleistocene glaciation.[6]

There has been much publicity about continental drift in the last thirty years. It is generally accepted by scientists today that all the earth's continents were at some time in the past one great landmass. This could have been any place on the earth. For convenience of study this mass is considered to have been where Africa is today. It would be easy to assume that the flood took place when all the continents were together, making a universal flood more likely. Overwhelming evidence is that the drifting of the continents has been very slow. Even the most active areas move at the rate of a few inches or feet per century.

on the plateau, the water carrying the ark would have run off the plateau under the sole influence of gravity with an average velocity of at least ten feet per second as is typical of the Euphrates River in deep flood. Assuming unsurrounded water on the plateau with flow velocity of ten feet per second off the plateau, the ark could have drifted an incredible distance of almost 25,000 miles (a distance equal to the circumference of the earth) during the 150 days it was afloat.

In such a flood the ark might have been deposited on a beach along the Persian Gulf, but it hardly would be expected to come to rest in the mountains of Armenia. If, however, the water in the Ararat district was supported by deep water surrounding it during a global flood, the landing place of the ark might be expected on the highest landmass. Indeed, if the oceanic energy impulse mechanism for the flood is correct, the ark would have drifted toward the center of a continent.

The receding of the floodwaters is described twice (Gen.

YES

NO

The San Andreas fault in California is one of the great evidences for moving landmasses. The western part of California is moving northwest, and it is believed that this mass of land will in time move entirely away from what we know as North America. In fact Baja, California has already separated from the larger landmass. The Gulf of California is now between the California peninsula and the continent. The San Andreas fault has been investigated extensively. It is readily accessible to a number of research institutions. There is incentive for research because of the large population along its length. Study over more than one hundred years indicates that the movement is from one and one-half to three centimeters each year, or five to ten feet per century.

One of the youngest mountain ranges is the Himalayan. This vast upheaval of rock material was caused when two continental masses (the Asian and the Indo-Pakistani) came together. Here the movement is comparatively rapid as evidenced by the large number of earthquakes in the region. Even here, however, the

8:3a, 5a) by Hebrew phrases that are not properly translated in most English Bibles. The *King James II Version* of
8:3a, 5a is: "And the waters retreated from the earth, going
and retreating, . . . And the waters were going and falling
until the tenth month." The phrase "going and retreating"
involves a Hebrew construction similar to that of the raven's
motion (8:7), indicating that the waters were rushing back
and forth with an action resembling tidal movement as the
overall level of water progressively declined. The "going
and retreating" of the water supports the oceanic energy
impulse model of the flood because, after the explosion of
Krakatoa, tide gauges recorded oscillatory water movements for several days.

During Noah's flood the oscillatory water motion lasted
for seventy-four days after the first 150 days (see 8:3-5)
until the water had receded enough for the tops of mountains to be seen. The notion that the flood was merely of

YES   local or regional extent is incongruous with the Genesis ac-

---

NO   mountains have been almost the same elevation for
many hundreds of thousands of years.

Erosion takes place not only by running water but by
wave action that modifies shorelines. Some rock types
erode very slowly, whereas others (such as clays and
unconsolidated volcanic ash) are easily washed away
by waves. In considering the local nature of the flood
one must examine deposits that were present when the
flood occurred to see how they might be affected by
wave action. Conical hills made of volcanic cinders
have been cited by a number of authors to illustrate the
improbability of a universal flood. Such cones in
Auvergne, France are mentioned by Ramm.[7] There are
many other places where similar cones are found that
predate the flood. In Arizona a number of such cones
near Flagstaff have been made over a long period of
time. If these cones were subjected to wave action or
stream erosion they would be easily destroyed. The fact
that these cinder cones have not been destroyed, or at
least eroded greatly, again indicates that there has
been no universal flood since they were formed.

It thus seems most likely that the continents at the

count of the activity of the water and the duration of flooding.

Geologic Evidence

A catastrophe of the scale and duration of Noah's flood would be expected to leave abundant evidence in the crust of the earth. However, the question of geologic evidence of the flood continues to be debated by geologists according to the view they take on the validity of Scripture and according to the interpretive framework they adopt for conducting geologic science. Most geologists during the last 150 years have questioned the scriptural account of the flood and have adopted a philosophy of uniformitarianism, which excludes consideration of global catastrophes from the mainstream of geologic theory. The apostle Peter warned us that the philosophy that "all things continue as they were from the beginning of creation" (2 Pet. 3:4) would prevail in the last days and would oppose the historicity of Noah's flood. Peter encouraged us to recog-

YES

NO

time of the flood were about the same as they are now, both in extent and in elevation. Geologists should be able to find evidence of a flood that covered the entire earth within the last few thousand years. No distinctive beds, sequence of beds, or erosional features that are the result of running water or wave action have been recognized, and it is reasonable to assume that such are not present.

Biological Considerations

The ark that carried Noah, his family and the animals was a large ship but still had its limits when the number of animals on the earth at that time is considered. Custance[8] has given some indication of the size of the ark. He estimates it to be half the length of the liner Queen Mary (1,018 feet). It is doubtful that even a vessel this size could accommodate two of all the species then in existence. Fossil evidence around the globe shows that there was an abundant animal population in every continent for many millions of years before the Pleistocene Ice Age. In the western hemisphere there is

nize the world-changing effect of Noah's flood and adopt a catastrophist framework for geology (3:5-6).

Among catastrophist geologists who recognize the flood to have been global, two views have prevailed: (1) the diluvium theory, and (2) the flood strata theory. William Buckland and George Cuvier, advocates of the diluvium theory in the early nineteenth century, proposed that a surficial gravel, boulder and silt layer found on at least four continents was evidence of Noah's flood. They pointed to bones of Pleistocene and recent animals (mammoths, rhinoceros, deer, bears, and many smaller mammals) in the diluvium as evidence of the catastrophe and attributed strata below the diluvium to catastrophes before Noah's flood.

Recently, however, the theory has been challenged by the assignment of many of the boulder and gravel deposits to glacial, not hydraulic, deposition. Critics pointed out that loose scoria and volcanic ash in the region of Auvergne, France, which allegedly are thousands of years older than the supposed date of Noah's flood, were not dis-

YES

NO   indication that successive migrations of animals from Asia crossed the area now covered by the Bering Straits each time the glaciers retreated during the Pleistocene. As the next glacial advance occurred these animals were moved south. The next migration from Asia appears to have pushed the previous group of animals still farther south. Thus the animals of southern South America can be distinguished from those farther north.

There is no evidence that these animals of North and South America have been destroyed since the last glacial advance. Some (such as the mastodon and mammoth) have become extinct, but others have continued to the present. Even the mastodon has been present in North America as recently as less than 10,000 years ago, and there is much evidence that ancestors of present-day man used mammoths for food even more recently.

Not only is there the problem of accommodating all species or varieties of animals in the space provided, but also the problem of a few persons caring for these animals for the duration of the flood seems immense.

persed and redeposited by the waters of the flood. Further-more, archaeological investigations of Mesopotamia have failed to reveal a plausible layer that can be assigned to Noah's flood (the "flood stratum" discovered by Leonard Woolley at Ur did not correlate to a similar stratum at Kish).

The second theory, the flood strata theory, is more au-dacious in its challenge to uniformitarian orthodoxy in ge-ology. The theory suggests that many thick successions of sedimentary strata, conventionally interpreted as being slowly deposited during ages of millions of years, were in-stead accumulated rapidly during Noah's flood. Three criti-cal evidences for the flood strata theory are (1) large-scale, soft-sediment deformation features, (2) widespread, cata-strophically deposited sedimentary strata, and (3) wide-spread, elevated erosional surfaces.

Large-scale, soft-sediment deformation features are common in thick successions of strata of the earth. An ex-ample is a faulted succession of 14,000 feet of strata on the east side of the Front Range of the Rocky Mountains near Colorado Springs, Colorado. Along the Ute Pass Fault, which forms the eastern flank of the Front Range, sand

YES

NO

As Custance says: "The size of the animal cargo and the nature of the animals which constituted it must be determined to a great extent by the size of the crew which had to care for them, not merely by the size of the ark."[9]

The Scriptures do not state how long Noah was in-volved in making the ark and assembling the animals to be its cargo. Bringing the many animals from the far corners of the earth requires considerable time. It seems unlikely that other than those animals present in the area of the ark were included.

There are a number of animals that have been con-fined to local areas since before the Pleistocene. If these (the kangaroos of Australia being an example) were to be brought to the ark in Mesopotamia and then re-leased after the flood, it does not seem possible that they would migrate back to their previous locations without populating other parts of the world.[10]

Some animals, both fish and mammals, have as

from the lowest sedimentary strata (the "Sawatch Sandstone," assigned to the "Cambrian System" and conventionally believed to have an age of about 600 million years) was injected while in an unconsolidated or nonlithified state into surrounding rocks forming what geologists call "clastic dikes." The position and orientation of these dikes show that the soft-sediment deformation occurred after the entire thickness of 14,000 feet of strata had been deposited, with the deformation and intrusion of dikes being associated with the slip on the Ute Pass Fault that uplifted the Front Range (the "Laramide Orogeny" assigned to the "Cretaceous" and conventionally believed to have an age of about 70 million years).[5]

Uniformitarian geologists are faced with the difficult problem of explaining how the lowest sedimentary formation in the 14,000 feet of strata could keep from being cemented by mineral-bearing solutions while deeply buried for an enormous period of time (supposedly 500 million years) until it was injected into fractures by the action of

YES

NO   their living environment fresh and salt water. Fish such as the salmon live part of their lives in fresh water, migrate to the salt ocean and then return to fresh water to spawn. Other animals live in estuaries and lagoons near the sea and seem to be at home in either fresh or salt water. Most organic forms, however, are confined to one environment. Ships accumulate barnacles in the ocean. To kill these organisms the ships, when able to do so, will be taken for a period of time into fresh water. It is said that ships going through the Panama Canal will arrange their passage so that they can be in the fresh water portion of the canal long enough to rid the hull of barnacles.

In October of 1985 there was a great deal of interest in a humpback whale that made a wrong turn in its migration from Alaska to Hawaii and ended up in the Sacramento River in California some sixty miles from the ocean. Biologists were concerned, since the animal's eyes and skin were seriously affected by the fresh water. It was believed that the whale could not survive a great length of time in such an unnatural environment.

faulting. Catastrophist geologists can accept this as evidence that 14,000 feet of strata were accumulated rapidly, presumably during the flood, and then were faulted while still in a poorly consolidated state, presumably in a late stage of the flood, to form the Rocky Mountains.

Widespread, catastrophically deposited sedimentary strata also support the flood strata theory. The St. Peter Sandstone and correlating sandstones (conventionally assigned to the "Ordovician System)" form a thin, blanketlike sheet of sand covering twenty-two states in the United States—from Vermont to California and from Tennessee to British Columbia.[6] Internal cross-bedding indicates that the sand was deposited in deep water by current action, but no modern sedimentary environment is known to accumulate sand under water on so extensive a scale. The Shinarump conglomerate of the Chinle Formation (conventionally assigned to the "Triassic System") contains sand, pebbles, and cobbles distributed over an area of 125,000 square miles in parts of five states in the southwestern United States. The sandstone and conglomerate, which averages less than one hundred feet in thickness, required sheet

YES

NO

Thus it can be seen that the saline condition of the water in which animals live is important. It is not known what the mineral content was of the mass of water of the flood, but whatever it was it seems probable that those animals whose tolerance for other than their natural environment is small would probably die. If the flood was of limited extent this would not adversely affect the overall animal population.

Textual Considerations

As translators through the ages have labored over the transfer of words from one language to another, it has been their task to use the best word that their experience has given them to express the meaning of the original language. This has been done worldwide by the Wycliffe Bible Translators, who employ native helpers to try to discover the correct word. It is also necessary that translations of words be consistent with the context—the meaning of the narrative being told. In

flooding of a very broad area on a scale far exceeding any modern flood.

The Morrison Formation of the Rocky Mountain region also is tremendously extensive, occurring from New Mexico to Canada and from Kansas to Utah. It is world-famous for its dinosaur fossils. Morrison Formation dinosaur skeletons are often articulated, requiring that muscles and ligaments of the large animals were present at the time they were rapidly buried. Sedimentary formations indicating catastrophic flood processes are not confined to North America but occur on other continents as well.

Elevated low-relief erosional surfaces occur in various parts of the world, challenging our way of thinking about how landscapes form. According to uniformitarian theory, elevated plains should be incised by erosion and bear a well-developed drainage system after only a few million years of erosion. Elevated low-relief land surfaces, therefore, should be very transitory features in the uniformitarian system. Several geologists have argued that old, ele-

YES

NO

considering the Genesis account of the flood these principles must always be kept in mind.

A number of Bible scholars have addressed themselves to this problem. It will be possible to cite only a few of these to show that the text can very well be interpreted to indicate that the flood was not worldwide.

Mitchell[11] points out that *'ereṣ* (Gen. 6:17; 7:17, 23) is translated "earth," *šāmayim* (6:17; 7:19) is translated "heaven," and *'ădāmâ* (7:23) is rendered "ground." He says, "*'Ereṣ* can mean 'land' (e.g. Gen. 10:10), *šāmayim* can mean 'sky', or the visible part of heaven within the horizon (e.g. 1 Kin. 18:45)." He then reasons that the extent of the area of the word *'ădāmâ* would be determined by the other two words. Thus the *'ereṣ* in that area is that part of the earth under the part of the sky visible to the people of Noah's culture and not necessarily the entire globe.

Custance goes into the matter of the translation of words in considerable detail. He also has studied the use of the word *'ereṣ*. By referring to concordances he points out that the Hebrew word "is translated 'earth' in

vated surfaces of low relief constitute a significant part of many contemporaneous landscapes in various parts of the world.[7] Examples of elevated plains include the enormous Gondwana Surface of southern Africa, various plains in central and western Australia, and various plains of the Colorado plateau in the southwestern United States.

These surfaces are not forming by modern erosional agents, and it is very difficult to imagine a slow erosional process that could form them. If, however, Noah's flood stood over large continental areas it would be expected to cause sheetlike denudation on elevated planar surfaces, especially as the flood retreated. Because the sedimentary deposits under these plains would not have been completely consolidated, erosion by retreating floodwater would have been effective at causing significant topographic changes.

Conclusion

The author of the Genesis account of Noah's flood used terminology and syntax that clearly communicates the fact that the flood was global. The statement that the flood cov-

YES

NO

Genesis 6:4, 5, 6, 11, 12, etc., and is translated 'country' 140 times, 'ground' 96 times. It is also rendered 'field' once and by several other words in a very small number of instances."[12] He says that *'ereṣ* is translated "earth" 677 times and "land" 1,458 times.

It is suggested by Custance[13] that considering the fact that *'ereṣ* is used for "land" more than twice as many times as for "earth," Genesis 6:11–13 might very well be translated as follows: "The land also was corrupt before God, and the land was filled with violence. And God looked upon the land and, behold, it was corrupt; for all flesh had corrupted its way upon the land. And God said unto Noah, 'The end of all flesh is come before me; for the land is filled with violence through them; and, behold, I will destroy them with the land.'"

If this translation for *'ereṣ* had been used in this passage, there might be no controversy as to the extent of the flood.

Ramm[14] has cited a large number of passages of

ered "all high hills under the whole heaven" (7:19) is an affirmation that although the narrator's geographic experience may have been limited, the flood covered mountains everywhere. The physical cause of the flood included cleavage of seafloor springs, a process that was similar (but on a larger scale) to the 1883 explosion of Krakatoa, which produced sea waves recorded around the world.

The landing of the ark on an elevated plateau after being afloat for 150 days requires that deep water with immense geographic extent surrounded the mountains of Ararat for several months. The retreat of the flood, which had oscillatory water motion for the seventy-four days, resembled the Krakatoa sea wave but was of much longer duration. Thus the activity of the floodwaters and their duration of flooding are fully consistent with a universal flood and confirm the author's statements about universal extent, but they are at odds with a local or regional flood.

A catastrophe on the scale and duration of Noah's flood would be expected to leave abundant geologic evidence. Geology has much to learn about how the earth formed

YES

NO

Scripture in which words that seem to indicate universality are actually used to tell of limited actions, space or time: Psalm 22:17 ("I tell all my bones"); John 4:39 (the Samaritan woman said, "He told me all the things that I have done"); Matthew 3:5 (of John's ministry it is said that "Jerusalem was going out to him, and all Judea, and all the district around the Jordan"). In each of these cases it is evident that totality is not indicated. Other passages that indicate a similar meaning include Genesis 41:56–57; 1 Kings 18:10; Deuteronomy 2:25; Acts 2:5; Colossians 1:23.

Final Considerations

In reaching any conclusion regarding the extent of the flood two things must always be considered. First is the purpose of this act of God (to punish sin). The second is how he deals with people on the earth. Throughout Scripture it is evident that God chooses certain

and particularly about the flood because of its lack of contemporary analog. At the present time catastrophist geology is successful at interpreting the significance of large amounts of data, especially mysteries long ignored by uniformitarian theory. Three primary evidences supporting the existence of thick successions of flood strata are (1) large-scale, soft-sediment deformation features, (2) widespread, catastrophically deposited sedimentary strata, and (3) widespread, elevated erosional surfaces.

YES

NO

people or a group of people to carry on his work. He made a covenant with Abraham, and the Old Testament is almost entirely a history of his dealing with the Israelites. There is little evidence from the Scriptures concerning how God was dealing with people in other parts of the earth. It seems logical in the light of these evidences that, in the case of Noahic society, God was dealing with a local society and that his punishment was upon a limited number of persons at that time.

ENDNOTES

YES

1. Deut. 2:25; 4:19; Job 28:24; 37:3; 41:11; Dan. 9:12. The phrase in Deut. 2:25 is qualified and limited to those "who shall hear the report of thee" and should not be considered an exception to the universal sense.

2. Bible scholars recognize the universal language at 7:19. C. F. Keil and F. Delitzsch, *Commentary on the Old Testament* (Grand Rapids: Eerdmans), 1, 146: "This clearly indicates the universality of the flood"; M. F. Unger, *Unger's Commentary on the Old Testament* (Chicago: Moody), 1, 42: "Nothing less than a universal deluge"; G. Archer, *Encyclopedia of Bible Difficulties* (Grand Rapids: Zondervan) 82: "We must conclude that the Flood was indeed universal, or else that the bibli-

cal record was grievously in error"; G. Hasel, "The Biblical View of the Extent of the Flood," *Origins*, 2, 87, 78: "The way it is written in the Hebrew excludes any local or limited concept"; J. Whitcomb and H. Morris, *The Genesis Flood* (Presbyterian and Reformed) 1: "One of the most important Biblical arguments for a universal flood."

3. For published captain's log see S. A. Austin, *Catastrophes in Earth History: a Source Book of Geologic Evidence, Speculation and Theory* (El Cajon: Institute for Creation Research, 1984) 75. For other descriptions of the Krakatoa sea wave see T. Simkin and R. Fiske, *Krakatau 1883: The Volcanic Eruption and Its Effects* (Smithsonian Institution Press, 1983).

4. For a computer model of a dynamic universal flood see M. E. Clark and H. D. Voss, "Computer Simulation of Large-scale Wave Motions Associated with the Genesis Flood," *Creation Research Society Quarterly* 17 (1980) 28–40. In addition to water waves rising over a continent, it is probable that vertical tectonic forces uplifted ocean basins and depressed continents. It was not necessary for the waters of the flood to have covered Mount Everest at its present elevation inasmuch as Everest is one of the earth's most recent tectonic features.

5. J. C. Harms, "Sandstone Dikes in Relation to Laramide Faults and Stress Distribution in the Southern Front Range, Colorado," *Geological Society of America Bulletin* 76 (1965) 981–1001; G. R. Scott and R. A. Wobus, "Reconnaissance Geologic Map of Colorado Springs and Vicinity, Colorado" (U.S. Geological Survey Miscellaneous Field Studies Map MF-482, 1973).

6. H. E. Wheeler, "Post-Sauk and Pre-Absaroka Paleozoic Stratigraphic Patterns in North America," *American Association of Petroleum Geologists Bulletin* 47 (1963) 1497–1526.

7. C. R. Twidale, "On the Survival of Paleoforms," *American Journal of Science* 276 (1976) 77–95; L. C. King, *Morphology of the Earth* (Edinburgh: Oliver and Boyd, 1960).

NO

1. B. Ramm, *The Christian View of Science and Scripture* (Grand Rapids: Eerdmans, 1954) 240.

2. T. C. Mitchell in *New Bible Dictionary* (ed. J. D. Douglas; Grand Rapids: Eerdmans, 1962) 429.

3. R. Youngblood, *How It All Began* (Ventura. Regal/GL, 1980) 136.

4. A. C. Custance, *The Flood: Local or Global?* (Grand Rapids: Zondervan, 1979) 54.

5. D. Kidner, *Genesis* (Downers Grove: InterVarsity, 1967) 95.

6. W. U. Ault in *Zondervan Pictorial Encyclopedia of the Bible* (ed. M. C. Tenney; Grand Rapids: Zondervan, 1975), 2, 551.

7. Ramm, *Christian*, 245.

8. Custance, *Flood*, 37.

9. Ibid., 37.

10. Ault in *Zondervan Pictorial Encyclopedia*, 555.
11. Mitchell in *New Bible Dictionary*, 427.
12. Custance, *Flood*, 15.
13. Ibid., 16.
14. Ramm, *Christian*, 241.

11 *Does Genesis 9 Justify Capital Punishment?*

YES: CARL F. H. HENRY

The classical text around which discussion of capital punishment centrally revolves is Genesis 9:6: "Whoso sheddeth man's blood, by man shall his blood be shed; for in the image of God made he man" (KJV).

The ethical demand, here as elsewhere in Scripture, flows from a theological premise. It is because mankind is created in God's image that human blood is not to be shed (cf. Lev. 17:14; Exod. 20:7 for similar theological substantiations). Biblical passages ground some divine commands

NO: MALCOLM A. REID

Genesis 9 cannot be used to justify capital punishment. Even an incomplete survey of the literature on the subject reveals a fascinating array of contending interpretations. For many theologians and moralists Genesis 9 provides unequivocal support for capital punishment in any society at any time.[1] Others argue that it does not even speak to the issue.[2] While they may grant that other passages of Scripture either require or permit capital punishment, Genesis 9:6, at least, "is too

in Hebrew saving history (e.g. Exod. 23:15; Lev. 23:43: Deut. 5:15), a theological substantiation for which, as Gerhard von Rad notes, no parallel exists in the great legal codes outside of Israel.[1] But the prohibition of murder is grounded in the fact of God's creation of mankind in the divine image.

In contrast to the Babylonian creation myth, there is not in Genesis any suggestion of physical kinship between God and mankind. But, as Edmond Jacob remarks, to do violence to a human being is in some sense also to lay hands on God, whose image every human is.[2] So inviolable is human life, in view of the divine image, that even an unthinking animal that kills a human being was to be destroyed by stoning and its flesh not eaten (Exod. 21:28).

It is true, of course, that all life—animal and vegetative no less than human—is the gift of the Creator. Th. C. Vriezen observes that "animal life *originally* was not given into the power of man" (cf. Gen. 1:29-30; 9:1 ff.).[3] Even when animals are destroyed by wild beasts (Exod. 22:31; Lev. 17:12 ff.; 22:8), God has an eye for the blood of ani-

YES

---

obscure, too broad, and too dubious to be a divinely issued mandate for all human societies to kill their killers."[3]

NO

I will argue for the strong counter-thesis that Genesis 9 is irrelevant to the issue of capital punishment. More particularly I will maintain (1) that reasons may be given to cast doubt on the idea that the primary focus of Genesis 9, and in particular verses 5–6, is capital punishment, and (2) that anyone who does appeal to it (to show that the Scriptures require the practice of capital punishment) faces textual, contextual, hermeneutical, and moral difficulties that, taken together, are insuperable.

The text of Genesis 9:5–6 reads as follows: "For your lifeblood I will surely require a reckoning; of every beast I will require it, and of man; of every man's brother I will require the life of man. Whoever sheds the blood of man, by man shall his blood be shed; for God made man in his own image."

In order to understand the significance of these solemn words it is necessary to see them in the context of

mals. Their slaughter is controlled by the law (Gen. 11:1 ff.; Lev. 17:10, 12 ff.), in attestation of a proper respect for the divine ground of all creaturely life. Vriezen suggests that the cautious linkage of plant life with divine power in the Genesis creation account may be due, among other things, to a veiled protest against the Canaanite myth that all nature immediately discloses the divine life as an immanent supernatural power.

But human beings are prohibited from shedding the blood of fellow humans (Gen. 4; 9:6; Exod. 20:13) because man expressly bears the *imago Dei*. As Robert Davidson comments, in the case of humans it is "not simply the fact that life as God's gift . . . guarantees its sanctity" but the additional "peculiar relationship to God" indicated by the divine image.[4]

The insistence in Genesis 9:6 that mankind—even after the fall, and after the flood, and despite the continuing sinfulness of the human race—has not lost the divine image, at least not in its totality, indicates that the likeness to God **YES** here in view is not simply a matter of man's moral confor-

---

NO the whole story of Noah and the first covenant God established with Noah as the representative of all men and indeed with "every living creature" (cf. Gen. 6:18–19; 9:10–11, 12, 15–17). It is important to recognize that a covenant is an entirely gracious act of God, sovereign in origin and redemptive in purpose. Strict justice would call for allowing the pride and violence of men to work their inevitable self-destruction. But God shows grace to the "blameless" Noah and through him to "all future generations" (6:9; 9:12).

The deepest theological lesson of the flood story is not the truism that the wicked will be destroyed and the righteous saved. It is the deeper, starker truth: "If the righteous man is scarcely saved, where will the impious and the sinner appear?" (1 Pet. 4:18, quoting Prov. 11:31 LXX).[4] Genesis 9:5–6 is contained in a paragraph in which God blesses Noah and his family (verses 1–7); it is preceded by his solemn promise (8:21–22) and followed by his covenant (9:8–17). But surely it is very odd to call such a disturbing passage a "blessing." It is true that in one sense it is a blessing because, in spite of the

mity. Rather, Genesis 9:6 depicts a special relationship to God the Creator of life in which mankind perpetually stands in distinction from the animal and vegetable worlds.

In eight sweeping preliminary chapters we see man who was fashioned in God's image (1:26) disobediently aspiring to transcend creatureliness by plucking the forbidden fruit, collapsing to the power of Satan, and falling prey to death. The offspring of Adam and Eve slays his brother, envious of God's approval of him. Cain seemed to sense that he deserved death and feared that he would be slain by anyone who discovered him (4:14-15). Paul Heinisch holds that although the criminal character of murder must have been clear from the first, God did not impose the death penalty until after the flood.[5]

Yahweh expels Cain from his presence, yet protects him from retaliation in order to emphasize the worth even of the offending murderer's life. So fundamental is the sanctity of human life that thereafter God mandates the death of a murderer. In the face of ongoing violence God puts man- **YES**

NO

fall, God reaffirms his earlier provisions for the welfare of his living creatures.

On the other hand the reality of the fall casts its chilling shadow over them all. Man is still to be "fruitful and multiply, and fill the earth," but that amity between him and other creatures has been destroyed: "The fear and the dread of you shall be on every beast of the earth" (verses 1–2). Formerly he was given every green plant for food (1:29; 2:9, 16); now the animals too are his food, with the stipulation that unbled meat not be eaten (verses 3–4). Men and women retain "the image of God"; they are his representatives on earth. But since they no longer honor the inviolability of this "image" in each other, God must require a reckoning: "Of every man's brother I will require the life of man" (verse 5).

Before setting forth the case against thinking that Genesis 9 supports the present practice of capital punishment, it is necessary to point out that this position does not entail a denial of the following related but different claims: (1) that under the Mosaic covenant and law codes capital punishment was mandated for an array of fifteen or more crimes, most of which did not in-

kind under the protection of his absolute sovereignty while simultaneously burdening humanity itself with the duty of avenging murder.

Genesis 9:6 does not stipulate how or by whom the offender's life is to be taken. There is no express indication of judicial proceedings in the context of governmental authority. The passage "does not attempt to legislate or to stipulate a definite pattern of law and order for society," Davidson remarks. "It seeks solely to enunciate a fundamental religious principle, the sanctity of human life."[6] Genesis states the principle, not the procedure.

The later Mosaic law restricts the right of blood vengeance. Yet Numbers 35:19 ff. and Deuteronomy 12 may nonetheless imply that this was one way of avenging murder. Perhaps, in the immediate aftermath of the flood, the family had as large a role as did the community, since civil government was not yet established in the full sense.

YES

Some commentators contend that God's intervention to

NO

volve the taking of life,[5] and (2) that elsewhere in the Scriptures the practice of capital punishment by civil authorities could, under certain conditions, be required.

The issue before us here is this more limited one: Does Genesis 9 justify capital punishment? In the course of arguing that it does not, the following subsidiary questions will be addressed: Is Genesis 9 irrelevant to the whole question of capital punishment? Are there textual or contextual matters that provide evidence or reasons for interpreting Genesis 9:5–6 as mandating capital punishment? Does Genesis 9:6 imply that governmental authority may take human life but that individuals may not? How is the "image of God" in Genesis 9:6 to be understood, and how is it related to the statements about the shedding of blood stated there? Finally, are those responsible for executing a murderer as guilty of violating Genesis 9:6 as is the murderer himself?

1. Determining whether or in what sense Genesis 9 is relevant to the subject of capital punishment is hardly easy, but it will take us to the heart of the matter. The following considerations make problematic any claims that its relevance is obvious.[6]

protect Cain implies a divine rejection of blood vengeance and that Genesis 9:6 by contrast implies political administration. But it is difficult to derive this from the texts. In any case, it was divine mercy that Cain was punished by lifelong banishment rather than by death, even if its purpose was to establish the dignity of the life even of the vilest murderer. The concept of civil government may be implicit in Genesis 9:6, but it is not expressly indicated.

Some hold that the phrase "at the hand of every man's brother" (Gen. 9:5) implies a judicial responsibility. Otto Eissfeldt calls attention to the solemnity of 9:6, characteristic of legal custom not only in Israel but everywhere else. He thinks the passage may have been spoken at the pronouncement of or implementation of the death sentence.[7]

Cuthbert A. Simpson thinks the poetic form of 9:6 "suggests that the author has here incorporated into his narrative an ancient judicial formula which had become proverbial."[8] The formula, which elders later repeated in the town involved when murder was committed by an uni-

YES

NO

First, while verses 5–6 clearly state that God requires a "reckoning" of both the person and the beast who shed the blood of anyone, it does not include those qualifications that are necessary to distinguish "murder" from "killing." Both man and beast are held responsible even though the capacity to make moral discriminations, or to act intentionally, was not attributed to animals by the Hebrews any more than it is presently by us. But for a "killing" to also be a "murder" it is necessary to presuppose that the perpetrator possesses just such capacities. If the passage is appealed to directly as a justification for capital punishment for human killers of any sort, it must by parity of reasoning also require it for an animal of any sort. Now it may be objected that "there was the principle of animal liability in the law (Exod. 21:28–36)" and that this should help us to see that this is what is intended here.[7]

Two cautions render this a dubious position. The Exodus provisions are included in the Mosaic covenant and code, a covenant that is not between God and every living creature, as is the Noahic, but between God and Israel. Furthermore, a careful reading of the Exodus passage reveals that the "animal liability" claimed is of

dentified person, is reflected in Deuteronomy 21:7-8. Murder endangers the whole community and puts it at peril, even before the crime's consequences overtake the criminal (cf. 21:4-8). Even in the case of murder by an unknown slayer, expiation by vicarious animal sacrifice was considered necessary to avert a divine curse because of the calamity brought upon Israel, particularly in the locale of the crime.

Yet, as J. Barton Payne observes, the concept of personal responsibility with the larger community also underlies the Hebrew view. When the land was defiled by blood, "only the blood of the individual murderer could make atonement for such pollution."[9] Moreover, a murderer could be executed only for his own crime. One could not be put to death for a crime committed by one's kin (Deut. 24:16; 2 Kgs. 14:6).

YES

The sixth commandment of the Decalogue ("Thou shalt

NO

a very limited kind. It speaks of a domesticated animal, the ox, not just any animal. Second, other qualifications important to distinguishing "killing" from "murder" are also ignored. They do not distinguish intentional murder from negligent homicide or both from accidental manslaughter. And no distinction is made between adults who commit such acts and those who do not, either because they are not of age, or they are but are *non compos mentis*.

Again, those who urge us to accept Genesis 9:5–6 as justifying capital punishment generally accept the restriction that it ought not to be carried out on anyone who has not received due process of law and whose guilt has not been proved beyond reasonable doubt—a restriction about which these verses too are silent. Finally, while verse 6 does say that it is "by man" that the blood of the killer is to be shed, it does not reserve this power exclusively to governmental authority, as both the supporters and the detractors of capital punishment would require.[8]

For all of these reasons it is far from clear that Genesis 9:5–6 is even relevant for the purpose of providing scriptural support for the practice of capital punishment. Perhaps the most telling of these reasons is the

not kill," Exod. 20:13), as Payne notes, employs the verb *rāsaḥ*, which designates murder, not the authorized taking of human life (or the commandment would contravert Gen. 9:6; cf. also Exod. 21:12; Num. 35:1). It therefore carries forward the earlier Noahic prohibition—and indeed the morality of creation itself. "The law given at Sinai," William Dyrness remarks, "was not so much a new law as an authoritative formulation of already existing instruction (see Gen. 2:2-3 on the sabbath; 9:5 on murder; 26:9-10 on adultery)."[10]

During the Old Testament theocracy the death penalty was imposed for many more offenses than murder. Walter C. Kaiser, Jr., lists sixteen offenses that required capital punishment.[11] In the theocracy death was prescribed not only for murder but also for deliberately subverting the judicial process as well as for adultery, incest, and other offenses. R. J. Rushdoony and G. Bahnsen hold that these Old Testament legal sanctions are still in force. But that de-

YES

NO

lack of any distinction between the amorality of animal killing and human capacity—indeed, proclivity—to commit the great evil of murder: "For your lifeblood I will surely require a reckoning; of every beast I will require it and of man."

How can this text be said to require capital punishment for murder when it includes animals that all agree are incapable of it? Some other interpretation of this sobering text must be sought. Immediately to fasten upon it as a justification for capital punishment may not only be a good example of a "proof-text" approach to a serious issue; it may also miss an intended theological message.

What may be missed is not the obvious point that "the shedding of blood" is a metaphor for death but that it has theological significance as God's remedy for the original sin of human pride—a pride that manifests itself so horribly in all flesh by shedding each other's blood. It is precisely through this act by which men or animals demonstrate the fallenness of the world that God redeems and restores it. As that most Hebrew of all New Testament books declares: "Under the law almost everything is purified with blood, and without the shed-

bate falls outside the purview of this essay. We are not now living in a divine theocracy. In any case, the Old Testament prohibition of murder is linked not simply to theocratic legislation but even in Noahic times had universal sanction on the basis of the *imago Dei*.

Daniel W. Van Ness notes that the Mosaic commandment against killing did not consider the life of slaves and women as less valuable than that of nobility and free men. By contrast the Akkadian laws of Eshnunna, which required the murderer of a free man to be executed, stipulated that only restitution be made for the murder of a slave, and the Babylonian Code of Hammurapi, which shared these positions, required in addition that the murderer's daughter was to be put to death if a free man killed the daughter of another free man.[12]

YES The Old Testament emphasis on punishment matching the seriousness of the offense is distinctive in numerous

---

NO ding of blood there is no forgiveness of sins" (Heb. 9:22). On this reading "the central significance of blood in the divine plan of redemption is being heralded to the new social order."[9]

It may be objected that the text no more says this directly than that it provides a legal sanction against murder. That is true, for all that the text says directly is (1) that God will demand an accounting from every man or animal that kills another man (verse 5); (2) that anyone who sheds the blood of another can expect to have his own blood shed in turn; and (3) that to kill another is not just to shed his blood but to destroy that which was created in the image of God (verse 6). This interpretation depends upon an understanding of the theological significance of blood in the redemptive purposes of God.

The covenant with Noah originates in the sheer grace of God: He binds himself to his creatures in spite of their sin. But God's justice cannot be flouted or ignored as it is by those who kill that creature whom God has created in his own image. God will require a reckoning, but there is no mention of man requiring it.

2. Are there textual or contextual matters that provide evidence or reasons for interpreting Genesis 9:5–6

ways. The *lex talionis* (law of retribution)—"But if there is a serious injury, you are to take life for life, *eye for eye*, tooth for tooth, hand for hand, foot for foot, burn for burn, wound for wound, bruise for bruise" (Exod. 21:23-25)—stipulated the limits of justice. By contrast, the Code of Hammurapi originally imposed the death penalty in all cases of theft. Yet the Old Testament insists that human life is more valuable by far than property. Even the ancient Germanic tribes in the medieval era thought that murder could be compensated by the imposition of a fine of cattle and sheep. The severity of the Old Testament penalty for murder was, as Geerhardus Vos comments, "proportional to the seriousness of the offense."[13]

The Old Testament provision of six cities of refuge protected the life of the accused until formal judicial procedure could establish guilt or innocence (Deut. 24:16) by providing places of security in the event the temple altar was inac-

YES

NO

as mandating capital punishment? A number of biblical scholars think that there are at least three grammatical points that support this view.[10] The first has to do with the Hebrew form of the verb *yiššāpēk* ("it may or shall be shed"). While it is granted that it does not have to be translated as a command ("his blood must be shed") on grammatical grounds it is nevertheless maintained that "the context makes it plain that the verb *yiššāpēk*, 'he shall shed,' must be a command."[11]

The context adduced is the statement made in verse 5 that God "will demand an accounting for human life" together with the prepositional phrase "by man" (*bā'ādām*) in verse 6. The latter phrase is thought to provide clear textual support for the view that God demands that any manslayer be put to death in this life by the hand of some other person.

Unfortunately, this line of argument begs the question at issue, for it assumes that in verse 6 the verb *yiššāpēk* has prescriptive force. But this is the very point that the appeal to "context" was supposed to settle. However, if the verb is translated predictively, as it is in the RSV and other translations, then it could be understood as a reference to blood revenge. If anyone sheds the blood of his neighbor, then he knows that

cessible. The accused was not allowed to leave the city until the high priest's death. Where the death of the victim was accidental, the unintentional slayer could argue his case before the elders of the city of refuge.

Does Genesis 9:6 teach that the death penalty is a mandatory penalty for murder? J. B. Payne notes that "the Hebrew verb *yishshāfēkh*, 'be shed,' might be taken either as an indicative description, 'It will be shed by man' . . . , or as a jussive requirement, 'Let it be shed by man,' which indicates capital punishment."[14] He points out that the probable sense is the mandatory imposition of the death penalty, since the preceding phrase ("I will require it") indicates "a necessary enforcement (cf. Ezek. 33:16; Deut. 18:9)." G. Charles Aalders comments likewise that the passage states "a divine prescription: God wills the taking of a murderer's life for shedding another human's blood."[15]

YES

Yet the Old Testament itself stipulates lesser penalties ap-

NO

that person's kin will seek to kill him. This interpretation certainly fits well with the larger context of Genesis 3–11. Cain apparently thought his banishment a punishment "greater than he could bear" (4:13), in part at least because he could not face the prospect of constantly trying to protect himself from his brother's avenger.

The final textual point has to do with the Hebrew word that begins the last clause of verse 6: "*for* God made man in his own image." Some commentators who read the preceding clauses prescriptively take *kî* to be introducing a powerful theological reason for this momentous decision by God to put the right of judicial killing into the hands of people. So Keil and Delitzsch: "Murder was to be punished with death because it destroyed the image of God in man."[12]

Aalders' view is more complicated and, for the line of interpretation being offered here, more interesting. He agrees with Keil and Delitzsch (1) that *kî* is to be taken as a causal conjunction and (2) that the first half of verse 6 is not "a bare statement of fact" but rather that "we are dealing here with a divine prescription."[13] But he thinks that there are both "formal" and "material" reasons for rejecting the Keil-Delitzsch view that *kî* joins the two halves of verse 6.[14] As the Hebrew text

propriate to accidental slaying of a human being, in distinction from the penalty appropriate to deliberate murder (Exod. 21:13). Since the external consequences are the same, the difference between premeditated murder and unintentional manslaughter turns on motivation.

But the Old Testament does not teach that capital punishment is always mandatory even when intentional killing is involved. Discretion is necessary in applying the mandate that the murderer is to be punished by a sentence of death; the deliberate murderer need not under all circumstances be put to death. Deuteronomy 9:15 stipulates that the offender is not to be convicted on the testimony of but one witness; required are two eyewitnesses whose testimony agrees. Moreover, although Scripture protects even the life of a burglar during the course of his capture (Exod. 22:3), it states that a person who kills a thief overtaken in the act of theft is not to be penalized (22:2). The classical biblical text on capital punishment does not therefore require imposition of the death penalty for all acts of murder.

Some have argued that if the divine image is the ration-   **YES**

NO

stands, the first part of verse 6 has a form unique in this passage: The word order of the second clause is the exact reverse of the first ("Whoever sheds the blood of man, by man shall his blood be shed").

Given the peculiar structure of this sentence Aalders thinks it is better to take the final clause as referring "to everything that precedes it in this pericope."[15] He further argues that connecting the idea of man being made in the image of God with the blessing of fruitfulness and dominion over the animals with which this paragraph begins and ends (verses 1, 2, 7) fits—in a way that the other reading does not—the conjoining of these same ideas in 1:26–28. On this view, then, the fact that man is created in the image of God is not a reason for applying the death penalty to murderers.

Rather, it has a much broader application: It is the reason why God saved in Noah a remnant of the human race, why he renewed the blessing of fruitfulness and the dominion over the animals. And Aalders adds, as I would not, it is why he here "protects people from the threats of wild animals and other human beings."[16]

ale for imposing death for murder, should not every attack on the human person be considered a violation of the divine image? The substantiatory statement "for in the image of God has God made man" may in fact be referred not only to the immediately preceding statement, "Whoever sheds man's blood, by man shall his blood be shed," but also to the entire preceding pericope. God's special care is thus connected with the renewal of his creation blessing (9:1) after the deluge and includes protection from wild beasts (9:2-4) as well as from murderous humans (9:6). Aalders supports this interpretation. He thinks that, while the preceding verses contain God's word to Noah, the second half of verse 6 was added by the inspired writer to identify the divine motivation for the divine sparing of the human race from total destruction by the deluge.[16]

The issue of whether capital punishment has a divine basis even in New Testament times has become a publicized contemporary ethical issue. Some scholars argue that, even if Genesis 9:6 affirms capital punishment, there is rea-

YES

NO

What he should have said is that it provides a reason why God will require a reckoning of anyone, man or beast, who kills a person. And if, as I have argued above, the verb in the first half of verse 6 is to be understood predictively rather than prescriptively then, as John Gibson has noted, verse 6 "is more a sad admission on God's part that his creatures regard human life as infinitely less precious than he does."[17]

Beyond these grammatical, textual, and contextual considerations Aalders apparently has a moral objection to the view of Keil and Delitzsch. To see the last clause of verse 6 as "motivation for applying the death penalty to murderers" is, he claims, to open "a line of reasoning" that could have "far-reaching" and "untenable consequences." Why? Because "it would imply that every attack on the human person would be a violation of the image of God, and therefore would warrant the death sentence."[18] Unfortunately he does not go on to say why he thinks that the death sentence for every attack on the human person is "untenable." I can only surmise (from what he says elsewhere on the interpretation of verses 5-6) that it has to do with the lack of

son to hold that the death sentence should now be eliminated altogether, or made merely a nominal matter by
universal clemency. It is often said, even in Christian circles, that capital punishment belongs to an inferior Old Testament theology of vengeance and that Jesus' theology of
forgiving love and the New Testament doctrine of grace an-
nul it.

Some seek exemption from its universal applicability on
other grounds, as when Dietrich Bonhoeffer thought a
moral case could be made for the interpersonal killing of
Adolf Hilter on the principle of love for the German people
because of the devastation that Hitler was unleashing upon
humanity. The appeal to compassion as a justification for
the taking of the life of another is now increasingly made by
human beings who seek to relieve the suffering of senile
parents or physically or mentally debilitated mates and
who think such acts should be approved as legally unpun-
ishable.

The general principle that Jesus embodies divine love **YES**

***

NO

relevant moral restrictions with respect to the determination of which sort of killing warrants the death
penalty.[19]

However, if we consider the view taken here—
namely, that verse 5 simply states that God will demand an accounting from those who kill other people
and that verse 6 is God's realistic recognition that fallen
men will seek blood vengeance—then we realize that
the moral scruples referring to judicial killing are beside the point. As Aalders correctly notes, "for the
avenger, the mere fact that blood has been shed is all
that is taken into account."[20] Just so—for it is, I conclude, all that needs to be taken into account in the interpretation of Genesis 9:6.

3. It should be clear from what has been said already what must be the answer to our next question:
"Does Genesis 9:6 imply that governmental authority
may take human life but that individuals may not?"
Since Genesis 6 does not say anything about governmental authority, it cannot say anything about taking
or not taking human life. While Genesis 6 does not say
directly that human life ought not to be taken, it does

has been invoked to justify the morality of sexual permissiveness and the immorality of capital punishment, but the specifics of biblical teaching provide no basis for such doctrinal novelties. Gordon H. Clark emphasizes that capital punishment is "an integral part of Christian ethics" and that "abolition of the death penalty presupposes the falsity of Christian principles."[17] Clark ascribes contemporary efforts to abolish capital punishment to a non-Christian view of man, a secular theory of criminal law, and a low estimate of the value of human life.

Jesus seems to accept the legitimacy of governmental imposition of capital punishment. Not only does he bow to Pilate's verdict, terrible as is its miscarriage of justice, but he emphatically reminds Pilate that civil authority is divinely conferred for responsible implementation (John 19:11). The Christian Church recalls the Roman procurator's unjust fulfillment whenever it repeats the Apostles' Creed ("suffered under Pontius Pilate"). Jesus implies the propriety of capital punishment for murder when he reminds Peter, who presumably sought to slay the high priest's ser-

YES

NO

imply this. For if God demands that everyone is to answer to him for the taking of life precisely because that life, like his own, belongs to God, then it follows that no individual has the right to take the life of another. It follows so long as the premise "we ought not to take what belongs to God" is granted.

4. The second part of the next question—"How is the 'image of God' related to the statements about the shedding of blood in Genesis 6?"—has also been answered. However, nothing yet has been said about the first part—namely, "How is the 'image of God' to be understood?"

Much traditional interpretation of Genesis 1:26–28; 9:6 seems to have been influenced more by anthropological assumptions brought to the text than by the context of the Old Testament itself. The "image of God" has been identified with one or more of the following sorts of powers or qualities: the possession of an immortal soul, a reasoning capacity, free will, self-consciousness, conscience, and the like. It is quite possible to grant, as I do, that we possess such powers

vant Malchus, that "whoever lives by the sword will die by the sword" (Matt. 26:52).

The New Testament connects administration of the death penalty with the authority of civil government. Capital punishment is specified in Romans 13:4 as a right divinely accorded to civil government, and it is approved in Acts 25:11, where Paul, in appealing to Caesar, states that if he is in truth "an offender worthy of death" he would accept a death sentence.

Except in the case of deliberate murder, where the criminal surrenders his own life, the Old Testament conspicuously connects retribution with restitution to the victims of crime. This does not necessarily mean that a penal theory of restitution wholly satisfies the regard for crime as an offense both to God and society, a violated justice in which the larger community is aggrieved. But Christian critics of modern penology point out that not only do overcrowded prisons today tend to worsen the character of prisoners rather than to rehabilitate them but that the plight also of the victims of crime is usually ignored and uncompensated.

The fact that more than 1500 men and women are today **YES**

---

and yet to question whether, individually or collectively, they are what that phrase means in these texts. **NO**

A better way to begin is to ask how the term "image" (*ṣelem*) is used in the Old Testament. The striking linguistic fact is that outside of Genesis 1—9 the Hebrew words translated "image" are almost always used to refer to man-made idols.[21] In light of this it is tempting to think that the writer was deliberately choosing this word as if to say, ironically, "The idolater foolishly believes he can represent God in wood or stone, but the irony is that he himself is already an image of the God who created him." But this does not by itself tell us precisely what it means to "image" God. I take it to mean something like the following.

While on the one hand man is weak and vulnerable like any other creature, on the other hand he has been chosen by God to be his representative or ambassador, to assist God in furthering his purposes within the created order. For mankind to carry out this role he must

on death row in the United States has propelled the discussion of capital punishment into one of the most pressing criminal justice issues of our time. The mass media have publicized not only gruesome features of capital punishment but also instances in which wrong persons may have been condemned to death. Much has been made of the release of Bradford Brown from Lorton Reformatory after he had served almost four years of an eighteen-year-to-life sentence for murder. When police finally located the real criminal, the courts awarded Brown $325,000.

Shocking as Brown's case is, it should be noted that the lack of conclusive evidence accounts for his imprisonment rather than execution and that the legal system incorporates provisions for retrial when new evidence emerges. Deplorable as is the conviction of an innocent, the issue remains whether 1500 murderers should be exempted from capital punishment because one may not be guilty. The Old Testament required high caution in imposing the death penalty. Its gravity was kept in the forefront not only by the requirement of two eyewitnesses but also by the require-

YES

NO

have the ability to communicate with God, understand his will for the world, and respond to it with conscious volition. It is precisely his failure to act responsively and responsibly in this role that the defacing or obscuring, but not the obliterating, of "the image of God" in man consists. The reaffirmation of this calling of human beings to be God's ambassadors within the world in Genesis 9:6 has at least two important consequences.

First, it means this "image," this responsible role people have in the world in obedience to the will of God, has not been lost as a result of the fall. Second, it means that since they still have this exalted role God will require a reckoning of anyone who presumes to take his life.

5. The final question—"Are those responsible for executing a murderer as guilty of violating Genesis 9:6 as is the murderer himself?"—is intended to question the moral rightness of judicial killing. It is not a question about the moral permissibility of any punishment but only of one kind of punishment. Given the interpretation of Genesis 9:6 offered above, this question cannot,

ment that the convening witnesses throw the first stones in the case of execution by stoning (Deut. 17).

Protests against the inhumaneness of hanging and of the electric chair are often mounted independently of attention to the inhumaneness of the gruesome nature of the slaughter of many murder victims. Yet the one does not justify the other. Malfunctioning apparatus has fueled controversy over capital punishment, and more and more states are approving the option of death by injection of lethal drugs.

The argument that legal procedures today are so expensive that only the poor receive death sentences while the rich escape is a distortion, although it has some merit. Judicial leniency has meant that many murderers escape capital punishment irrespective of their financial condition. But insofar as statistics may support the complaint, the situation does not call for elimination of capital punishment but for justices and juries determined to apply the law indiscriminately.

During the past decade American evangelicals have

YES

NO

strictly speaking, be entertained because it presupposes that this verse is to be understood prescriptively. One can "violate" a command but not a prediction.

However, insofar as it does speak of those who kill—including those whose killing is murder—it is appropriate to ask if the practice of judicial killing is as morally unworthy as the murder it is intended to punish. Punishment is by its nature retributive. And any just retribution has properly been thought to require (1) that the crime must be punished and (2) that the punishment must fit the crime. The second is morally and practically more problematic than the first. Whether judicial killing is judged to be a morally right or morally wrong, morally permissible or morally impermissible, punishment that uniquely "fits" the crime of murder will depend upon a person's most basic metaphysical and moral beliefs.

For example, if a person believes, as many Christians do, that God is a perfect moral being, that on the authority of Scripture we know that he requires or permits judicial killing for murder, then judicial killing will be judged to be morally required or permitted. While no

looked with new compassion upon criminals confined to prisons, including those on death row awaiting execution. Prison Fellowship, founded by Charles Colson, has established Justice Fellowship to promote improved prison conditions and justice in criminal proceedings, alongside nationwide and worldwide interest in the spiritual and moral plight of prisoners.[18]

In any case, the prevalent recent penal theory that the purpose of punishment is the rehabilitation of the offender has broken down. Not only does it suffer from the optimistic liberal misconception that environment is the decisive key to character, but it also is embarrassed by the fact that conditions inside modern prisons can be as bad as the slums outside.

YES

NO

argument can be given for it here, I will suggest that Christians should regard judicial killing as Jesus did divorce. "For your hardness of heart Moses allowed you to divorce your wives, but from the beginning it was not so" (Matt. 19:8). For the most terrible hardness of heart—murder—God allowed judicial killing of the murderer, "but from the beginning it was not so." But to have said this is to have gone far beyond anything said in Genesis 9.[22]

ENDNOTES

YES

1. G. von Rad, *Old Testament Theology* (Edinburgh: Oliver and Boyd, 1962), 1, 198.

2. E. Jacob, *Theology of the Old Testament* (London: Hodder and Stoughton, 1958) 169.

3. Th. C. Vriezen, *An Outline of Old Testament Theology* (Oxford: Basil Blackwell, 1958) 192 n. 1.

4. R. Davidson, *Genesis 1-11* (Cambridge: University Press, 1973) 89.

5. P. Heinisch, *Theology of the Old Testament* (Collegeville: Liturgical Press, 1950) 172.

6. Davidson, *Genesis*, 89.

7. O. Eissfeldt, *The Old Testament: An Introduction* (New York: Harper, 1965) 68.

8. *Interpreter's Bible*, 1, 550.

9. J. B. Payne, *The Theology of the Older Testament* (Grand Rapids: Zondervan, 1962) 230.

10. W. Dyrness, *Themes in Old Testament Theology* (Downers Grove: InterVarsity, 1979) 177.

11. W. C. Kaiser, Jr., *Toward Old Testament Ethics* (Grand Rapids: Zondervan, 1983).

12. D. W. Van Ness, *Victims and Criminals* (Downers Grove: InterVarsity, 1985).

13. G. Vos, *Biblical Theology* (Grand Rapids: Eerdmans, 1948) 58.

14. Payne, *Theology*, 317.

15. G. Ch. Aalders, *Genesis* (Grand Rapids: Zondervan, 1981), 2, 184.

16. Ibid., 186 ff.

17. G. H. Clark, "Capital Punishment," in *Baker's Dictionary of Christian Ethics* (ed. C. F. H. Henry; Grand Rapids: Baker, 1973) 84.

18. Cf. D. Van Ness, *A Call to Dialogue on Capital Punishment: A Working Paper* (Washington: Justice Fellowship, 1984).

NO

1. W. C. Kaiser, Jr., *Toward Old Testament Ethics* (Grand Rapids: Zondervan, 1983) 165–68; G. Ch. Aalders, *Genesis* (Grand Rapids: Zondervan, 1981), 1, 184–88; A. Richardson, *Genesis I-XI* (London: SCM, 1953) 109–10; N. L. Geisler, *Ethics: Alternatives and Issues* (Grand Rapids: Zondervan, 1971) 240–48; J. Murray, *Principles of Conduct* (London: Tyndale, 1957) 109–13.

2. J. C. L. Gibson, *Genesis* (Edinburgh: Saint Andrews, 1981), 1, 195; D. Kidner, *Genesis: An Introduction and Commentary* (Downers Grove: InterVarsity, 1967) 101; N. Anderson, *Issues of Life and Death* (Downers Grove: InterVarsity, 1978) 112; L. B. Smedes, *Mere Morality* (Grand Rapids: Eerdmans, 1983) 119–24; E. E. Hobbs and W. C. Hobbs, "Contemporary Capital Punishment: Biblical Difficulties with the Biblically Permissible," *Christian Scholar's Review* 11 (1982) 250–62.

3. Smedes, *Mere*, 121.

4. Gibson, *Genesis*, 1, 193.

5. Cf. Exodus 21, 22; Leviticus 20; Deuteronomy 22. Kaiser, *Toward*, 91–92, 298, provides two lists, one of sixteen crimes and the other of eighteen. Fourteen are common to both lists.

6. Kaiser, *Toward*, 165–66, argues that Gen. 9:5–6 is "the key passage" for the support of the necessity of capital punishment. Gibson, *Genesis*, 1, 195, on the other hand claims that this passage is not to be taken as "a legal sanction against murder or as a justification for capital punishment." Kidner, *Genesis*, 101, too, thinks that "one cannot simply transfer verse 6 to the statute book unless one is prepared to include verses 4 and 5a with it. Capital punishment has to be defended on wider grounds."

7. Kaiser, *Toward*, 167.

8. Geisler, *Ethics*, 240, claims that Gen. 9:6 is "the first reference to capital punishment" in Scripture, though later he says that Cain's fear "that whoever finds me will slay me" (4:14) only makes sense on the supposition "that capital punishment was his own natural expectation" (243). But is it so clear that capital punishment here is distinguished from blood vengeance? Here we are very far from due process of law,

guilt beyond a reasonable doubt, and capital punishment administered by the state.

9. Hobbs and Hobbs, "Contemporary," 257.

10. Kaiser, *Toward,* 166; Aalders, *Genesis,* 1, 184.

11. Kaiser, *Toward,* 166.

12. C. F. Keil and F. Delitzsch, *Commentary on the Old Testament* (Grand Rapids: Eerdmans, 1975), 1, 153.

13. Aalders, *Genesis,* 1, 184; cf. Murray, *Principles,* 110–11.

14. Aalders, *Genesis,* 1, 186–87.

15. Ibid., 187.

16. Ibid.

17. Gibson, *Genesis,* 1, 195.

18. Aalders, *Genesis,* 1, 186.

19. Ibid., 183–87.

20. Ibid., 186.

21. Cf. Num. 33:52; 1 Sam. 6:5, 11; Ps. 73:20; Ezek. 7:20; Dan. 2:31–3:15 (fourteen times).

22. Any reader interested in pursuing this question further could not do better than begin with J. H. Richards' probing essay, "Alan Donagan, Hebrew-Christian Morality, and Capital Punishment," *Journal of Christian Ethics* 8 (1980) 302–29.